Transact-SQL Cookbook

Transact-SQL Cookbook

Aleš Špetič and Jonathan Gennick

O'REILLY®

Beijing · Cambridge · Farnham · Köln · Paris · Sebastopol · Taipei · Tokyo

Transact-SQL Cookbook
by Aleš Špetič and Jonathan Gennick

Copyright © 2002 O'Reilly & Associates, Inc. All rights reserved.
Printed in the United States of America.

Published by O'Reilly & Associates, Inc., 1005 Gravenstein Highway North,
Sebastopol, CA 95472.

O'Reilly & Associates books may be purchased for educational, business, or sales promotional
use. Online editions are also available for most titles (*safari.oreilly.com*). For more information,
contact our corporate/institutional sales department: (800) 998-9938 or *corporate@oreilly.com*.

Editor:	Robert Denn
Production Editor:	Jeffrey Holcomb
Cover Designer:	Ellie Volckhausen
Interior Designer:	David Futato

Printing History:

March 2002:   First Edition.

ISBN: 1-56592-756-7
[C]

To my family: Helena, Peter, Mojca, and Bostjan

—Aleš

To Donna, Jenny, and Jeff

—Jonathan

Table of Contents

Preface

SQL in general, and Transact-SQL in particular, is so deceptively simple that few people take the time to master it. Many of the SQL books currently on the market contribute to this state of affairs by not taking their readers very far beyond the simple `SELECT column_name FROM table_name WHERE conditions` pattern of writing SQL SELECT statements. In this book, we hope to take you far beyond the level of writing simple SQL statements and open your eyes to the full power of SQL and Transact-SQL.

For many years, SQL has been the domain of large corporations using high-end databases such as Oracle, Sybase, Informix, and DB2. Microsoft's entry into the market with Microsoft SQL Server brought Transact-SQL to the workgroup server and desktop level, thereby broadening the market for Transact-SQL programmers. More systems are being programmed in SQL and Transact-SQL, and if you're a Transact-SQL programmer, you'll want to leverage Transact-SQL to its fullest.

Getting the most out of SQL and Transact-SQL requires a particular way of thinking. SQL is a set-oriented language in which you focus on end results, not on the procedures used to accomplish those results. If you're used to thinking procedurally, this shift to set-oriented thinking can be jarring. The SQL solutions to problems that are easily described procedurally are often not obvious. So why bother with the set-oriented SQL solutions? It's true that Transact-SQL provides you with procedural capabilities, but use of those capabilities is no excuse for not utilizing the core SQL language to its fullest. SQL solutions are often magnitudes more efficient than the corresponding procedural solutions.

Why We Wrote This Book

We have many years experience working in SQL environments, and over the years we've developed, or stumbled across, a number of useful SQL design patterns that we apply to problems that we encounter in our day-to-day work. Knowing these patterns gives us an edge and allows us to accomplish things with ease that might otherwise be difficult.

Looking back over our careers, we remember the "magic" of discovering a new and innovative SQL-based solution to a programming problem. There was the sudden flash of light and a rush of adrenalin as a whole new vista of possibilities opened up before us. It's our hope that we can share some of that magic with you. For that matter, we each learned a few pieces of magic from the other while collaborating on this book.

Audience for This Book

We have two target audiences in mind for this book: those who have just recently learned SQL and those who have been using SQL for several years. This is not a learning-SQL type of book. We assume that you have a working knowledge of the basic SQL statements: INSERT, UPDATE, DELETE, and SELECT. We also assume that you are passingly familiar with Transact-SQL's procedural capabilities.

If you have recently learned SQL, then you know the basic statements. Next you need to learn how to "think SQL" to creatively apply SQL to the programming problems you encounter daily. This is difficult to teach; the creative application of SQL is best learned by example. The purpose of this book is to provide nonobvious examples of SQL being used creatively to solve everyday problems. You'll be able to apply our patterns to your own work, and hopefully you'll be inspired to discover creative solutions of your own.

This book isn't just for newcomers to SQL. We think an experienced SQL programmer will discover at least one new technique in this book. We have even learned from each other as coauthors by reading over each other's recipes.

Which Platform and Version?

All the recipes in this book were tested for compatibility with SQL Server 2000. Most of them have also been tested on SQL Server 7. Some recipes use the new ANSI join syntax supported by SQL Server 2000. Those recipes will require some minor modifications for them to work on older SQL Server releases.

While not as commonly encountered as it used to be, Sybase also uses Transact-SQL. Sybase's Transact-SQL is not 100% compatible with Microsoft's Transact-SQL, but we've coded the recipes so that, in the vast majority of cases, they will also work for Sybase.

Structure of This Book

This book is divided into eight chapters. You can read through all eight chapters sequentially, or you can read only those chapters that pertain to problems you are solving at any given time.

The only exception is Chapter 1, which you should read first no matter which other chapter you read next.

- Chapter 1, *Pivot Tables*, introduces the concept and use of a Pivot table. This recipe is in a chapter by itself, because we use the Pivot table pattern in many other recipes throughout the book. This is a must-read chapter.

- Chapter 2, *Sets*, focuses on the core of SQL's functionality: set manipulation. In this chapter, you'll find techniques for performing the set operations you learned in elementary school, such as difference, intersection, and compliment, using SQL. You'll also find techniques for returning the top-n values from a set and for implementing various types of aggregation.

- Chapter 3, *Data Structures*, shows you how to implement lists, stacks, queues, arrays, and matrices using Transact-SQL. Such structures are often considered the domain of other programming languages, but it's sometimes advantageous to implement them at the database level.

- Chapter 4, *Hierarchies in SQL*, shows you several useful techniques for dealing with hierarchical data from SQL. Hierarchical data presents some special challenges because SQL is optimized for relational data. Readers who have been in the industry long enough will recall that relational databases *replaced* hierarchical databases. Nonetheless, hierarchical data exists and we must deal with it.

- Chapter 5, *Temporal Data*, demonstrates the ins and outs of working with time-based, or temporal, data. Temporal data is frequently encountered in the business world, and failure to recognize the subtleties of querying such data is a common source of errors. In this chapter, you'll learn about granularity and about SQL Server's built-in support for temporal data. You'll then find a number of recipes that show SQL being used creatively to solve various time- and date-related problems.

- Chapter 6, *Audit Logging*, deals with the problem of logging changes and implementing audit trails. Learn how to implement an audit-trail mechanism using Transact-SQL, how to generate audit snapshots of a given point in time, and other related techniques.

- Chapter 7, *Importing and Transforming Data*, speaks to the issues involved with getting data into SQL Server from external sources. You'll find recipes for importing data into "live" systems, for validating imported data, and for dealing with master/detail data.

- Chapter 8, *Statistics in SQL*, is a mini-course in statistics. You'll see how to use SQL to calculate means, modes, medians, standard deviations, variances, and standard errors. You'll also learn how to implement moving averages, calculate correlations, and use confidence intervals.

Wherever possible, recipes build on data from previous recipes in the same chapter, so reading through a chapter should be fairly straightforward. If you want to experiment with just one particular recipe, check the beginning of its chapter for a description of the example data used in that chapter, or download the recipe-specific script files that create example data from this book's web page (*http://oreilly.com/catalog/transqlcook*).

Conventions Used in This Book

The following typographical conventions are used in this book:

Italic

> Is used for filenames, directory names, and URLs. It is also used for emphasis and for the first use of a technical term.

`Constant width`

> Is used for examples and to show the contents of files and the output of commands.

`Constant width italic`

> Is used for replaceable elements in examples.

`Constant width bold`

> Indicates code in an example that we want you to pay special attention to.

UPPERCASE

> In syntax descriptions, usually indicates keywords.

lowercase

> In syntax descriptions, usually indicates user-defined items, such as variables.

[ ]

> In syntax descriptions, square brackets enclose optional items.

{ }

> In syntax descriptions, curly brackets enclose a set of items from which you must choose only one.

|

> In syntax descriptions, a vertical bar separates the items enclosed in curly or square brackets, as in {ON | OFF | YES | NO | TRUE | FALSE}.

...

> In code listings, ellipses indicate missing output that is not critical to understanding the example and that has been removed in the interest of not taking up inordinate amounts of space in the book.

> Indicates a tip, suggestion, or general note.

> Indicates a warning or caution.

Sample output in code listings has been adapted to fit the size of the book. Strings that contain a lot of spaces have been shortened, and numeric values that extend over two decimal places have been either rounded or truncated. These changes create more readable output and maximize the amount of information we can pack into a sample listing.

About the Code

The main purpose of this book is to explain concepts and ways of solving problems in Transact-SQL. Some recipes might seem superficial and unnecessary; however, they are important for demonstration purposes.

The code is often fragmented. We strongly encourage you to try to understand its purpose before you use it in production code. There is almost no error-handling included. We wanted to convey each idea as clearly as possible.

We wrote the recipes from a programmer's perspective and do not include a DBA's viewpoint. We don't want anyone to use this book as the sole source of information for their SQL systems. Delivering a proper database system is much more than just programmer's work, which should be clear to anyone in the business. Programmers, designers, and DBAs should work together to design databases properly, program code, and adjust indices and other mechanisms to deliver optimum performance.

This book is an attempt to assist SQL programmers and to bring another experienced view into perspective. Most of the recipes have been tried in practice in real-world systems, and the recipes work. Other recipes have been added to complete the chapters and the topic; this fact does not diminish their importance.

Comments and Questions

Please address comments and questions concerning this book to the publisher:

O'Reilly & Associates, Inc.
1005 Gravenstein Highway North
Sebastopol, CA 95472
(800) 998-9938 (in the United States or Canada)
(707) 829-0515 (international or local)
(707) 829-0104 (fax)

We have a web page for this book, where we list errata, examples, or any additional information. You can access this page at:

http://www.oreilly.com/catalog/transqlcook

To comment or ask technical questions about this book, send email to:

bookquestions@oreilly.com

For more information about our books, conferences, Resource Centers, and the O'Reilly Network, see our web site at:

http://www.oreilly.com

Acknowledgments

We would like to thank O'Reilly, our favorite publisher, for their trust in us and their investment in our project. Particularly, many thanks to Gigi Estabrook, our first editor, who had the courage and vision to start this project and bring us together. Robert Denn picked it up, when Gigi decided to pursue other challenges in her life. He gave us space and time to develop our ideas and brought this project to a successful end.

Invaluable comments from Wayne Snyder, Kevin Kline, and Baya Pavliashvili, our tech reviewers, improved this text. They found mistakes that we had missed even after we had read each chapter several times. They also provided several good suggestions for clarifying the text.

From Aleš

I hope that this book will complement the existing opuses of outstanding authors like Joe Celko, David Rozenshtein, Anatoly Abramovich, Eugine Birger, Iztik Ben-Gan, Richard Snodgrass, and others. I spent many nights studying their work, and I learned almost everything I know from their books. As I'm writing these lines, I'm aware that for every night I spent discovering their secrets, they must have spent 10 nights putting their knowledge into a consistent and readable form. It is an honor to be able to give something back to the SQL community.

This book could never have happened without Jonathan. In the beginning, I was looking for somebody who could correct my English and reshape the text into a readable form. However, after reading the first few pages from him, I knew I had hit the jackpot. Jonathan is an outstanding SQL expert. What seemed, in the beginning, a fairly straightforward read-and-reshape-into-proper-English task became the full-sized burden of creating a new book. We constantly exchanged ideas and new recipes. I am proud to have him as a coauthor and even prouder to gain a new friend. In his first email he sent me, he had a line in the signature, which I'll probably remember for the rest of my life: "Brighten the Corner Where You Are." Well, he did. And it tells everything about him.

I would also like to mention a few people who touched my professional life and influenced me significantly one way or another: Tomaz Gaspersic, Primoz Krajnik, Marko Hrcek, Anton Imre, Robert Reinhardt, Professor Sasa Divjak, and Professor Kurt Leube. They were, and still are, my dearest colleagues, friends, and mentors.

I could never have completed this book without my family and, of course, without Helena. She was always there for me. When we went on vacations and I dragged along a suitcase full of books, cables, and a notebook computer, she calmly read her novel. She didn't say a word. Many times when the sun was shining outside and I was staring at the computer, she often came to me: "You have to have a walk!!!!" When she was vacuuming and made me lift my feet to clean under the table, to prevent suffocation from dust pollution, she just gave me a kiss. She didn't say a word. Then in the evenings when sitting in our living room, she always said she believed that everything would be fine. I didn't. She did. She was right. And she was always there.

As I reflect on this project, I'm taken aback by the amount of work involved. Consider this: over 500,000 characters, each retyped at least twice, 2 years of writing, uncountable hours and nights spent over it. This works out to about 1,300 characters typed each day. The smallest revision number (the number of times a chapter has been revisited, reread, and changed) is 8, and the largest, 14. Conservatively speaking, we had to reread an average chapter 10 times before we were happy with it. This sums to 5 million characters read. A huge burden to go through—2 years of dedicated work by two experts—and yet, in computer terms, only 500 KB read 10 times over. Having finished such a project, and after doing the previous calculations, I find it fascinating how easily we, in the database industry, talk about megabytes, gigabytes, and terabytes. And yet, in the end, it feels good to do such an exercise once in a while. It makes one humble; it made us better.

From Jonathan

I'd like to start off by thanking Aleš for bringing me into his project to write this Transact-SQL Cookbook. Aleš is an excellent programmer, and I learned a lot from him while collaborating on this book. Most of the recipes in this book are in fact his, though I did manage to contribute a few of my own.

I also wish to thank my neighbor and good friend Bill Worth for loaning me his copy of *How to Lie With Statistics* so that I could refresh my memory as to the difference between modes, medians, and means.

Finally, as always is the case with my books, I owe a great debt to my family for putting up with my long hours researching, writing, and experimenting. My wife Donna especially deserves my thanks not only for being more supportive of my writing career than I can possibly deserve, but for her consistent support during the many career vicissitudes that I've experienced during my lifetime.

There's an interesting anecdote I'd like to share from back when this book first got started. Aleš is from Slovenia, and I'm from Michigan. When I was first contacted about this book, it so happened that I was vacationing in the small town of Baraga in Michigan's Upper Peninsula. The town is named after Bishop Frederic Baraga, a well-known Slovenian priest who traveled and ministered widely along the Lake Superior shoreline in the mid-1800s. Because he often made winter journeys of up to 60 miles on foot, Father Baraga became widely known as the "Snowshoe Priest."

In addition to his work as a missionary, Father Baraga became fluent in the local language and wrote the first *English-Ojibwa Dictionary and Grammar*; a work that is still in use today. With that, he invented written language for the Ojibwa and preserved their language forever. He also wrote a book about the history and life of native tribes in which he describes the story of a native girl who saved the life of Englishman John Smith. 150 years later she became a movie star. Her name was Pocahontas.

 Learn more about Father Baraga and his influence on Michigan's north country by visiting *http://www.exploringthenorth.com/bishopb/ shrine.html.*

As if the coincidence of my being in Baraga, Michigan at the beginning of this project wasn't enough, I actually moved to Michigan's Upper Peninsula during the course of this book. Settling in Munising, I found myself a mere 24 miles from the town of Traunik (*http://www.traunik.com*), home to a thriving Slovenian community for many years during the early and mid-1900s. Having Aleš as a coauthor, Traunik as a neighbor, and living under the shadow of Father Baraga makes me feel strongly connected to this tiny country of Slovenia, which perhaps someday I'll even be lucky enough to visit.

CHAPTER 1

Pivot Tables

1.1 Using a Pivot Table

Problem

Support for a sequence of elements is often needed to solve various SQL problems. For example, given a range of dates, you may wish to generate one row for each date in the range. Or, you may wish to translate a series of values returned in separate rows into a series of values in separate columns of the same row. To implement such functionality, you can use a permanent table that stores a series of sequential numbers. Such a table is referred to as a Pivot table.

Many of the recipes in our book use a Pivot table, and, in all cases, the table's name is Pivot. This recipe shows you how to create that table.

Solution

First, create the Pivot table. Next, create a table named Foo that will help you populate the Pivot table:

```
CREATE TABLE Pivot (
   i INT,
   PRIMARY KEY(i)
)

CREATE TABLE Foo(
   i CHAR(1)
)
```

The Foo table is a simple support table into which you should insert the following 10 rows:

```
INSERT INTO Foo VALUES('0')
INSERT INTO Foo VALUES('1')
INSERT INTO Foo VALUES('2')
INSERT INTO Foo VALUES('3')
```

```
INSERT INTO Foo VALUES('4')
INSERT INTO Foo VALUES('5')
INSERT INTO Foo VALUES('6')
INSERT INTO Foo VALUES('7')
INSERT INTO Foo VALUES('8')
INSERT INTO Foo VALUES('9')
```

Using the 10 rows in the Foo table, you can easily populate the Pivot table with 1,000 rows. To get 1,000 rows from 10 rows, join Foo to itself three times to create a Cartesian product:

```
INSERT INTO Pivot
   SELECT f1.i+f2.i+f3.i
   FROM Foo f1, Foo F2, Foo f3
```

If you list the rows of Pivot table, you'll see that it has the desired number of elements and that they will be numbered from 0 through 999.

 You can generate more rows by increasing the number of joins. Join Foo four times, and you'll end up with 10,000 rows (10 * 10 * 10 * 10).

Discussion

As you'll see in recipes that follow in this book, the Pivot table is often used to add a sequencing property to a query. Some form of Pivot table is found in many SQL-based systems, though it is often hidden from the user and used primarily within pre-defined queries and procedures.

You've seen how the number of table joins (of the Foo table) controls the number of rows that our INSERT statement generates for the Pivot table. The values from 0 through 999 are generated by concatenating strings. The digit values in Foo are character strings. Thus, when the plus (+) operator is used to concatenate them, we get results such as the following:

```
'0' + '0' + '0' = '000'
'0' + '0' + '1' = '001'
...
```

These results are inserted into the INTEGER column in the destination Pivot table. When you use an INSERT statement to insert strings into an INTEGER column, the database implicitly converts those strings into integers. The Cartesian product of the Foo instances ensures that all possible combinations are generated, and, therefore, that all possible values from 0 through 999 are generated.

It is worthwhile pointing out that this example uses rows from 0 to 999 and no negative numbers. You could easily generate negative numbers, if required, by repeating the INSERT statement with the "–" sign in front of the concatenated string and being a bit careful about the 0 row. There's no such thing as a –0, so you wouldn't want to insert the '000' row when generating negative Pivot numbers. If you did so, you'd end up with two 0 rows in your Pivot table. In our case, two 0 rows are not possible, because we define a primary key for our Pivot table.

The Pivot table is probably the most useful table in the SQL world. Once you get used to it, it is almost impossible to create a serious SQL application without it. As a demonstration, let us use the Pivot table to generate an ASCII chart quickly from the code 32 through 126:

```
SELECT i Ascii_Code, CHAR(i) Ascii_Char FROM Pivot
WHERE i BETWEEN 32 AND 126

Ascii_Code  Ascii_Char
----------- ----------
32
33              !
34              "
35              #
36              $
37              %
38              &
39              '
40              (
41              )
42              *
43              +
44              ,
45              -
46              .
47              /
48              0
49              1
50              2
51              3
...
```

What's great about the use of the Pivot table in this particular instance is that you generated rows of output without having an equal number of rows of input. Without the Pivot table, this is a difficult, if not impossible, task. Simply by specifying a range and then selecting Pivot rows based on that range, we were able to generate data that doesn't exist in any database table.

 You must have enough Pivot table rows to accommodate the range that you specify. Had we used BETWEEN 32 AND 2000, our query would have failed, because our Pivot table has only 1,000 rows, not the 2,001 that would be required by such a large range.

As another example of the Pivot table's usefulness, we can use it easily to generate a calendar for the next seven days:

```
SELECT
   CONVERT(CHAR(10),DATEADD(d,i,CURRENT_TIMESTAMP), 121) date,
   DATENAME(dw,DATEADD(d,i,CURRENT_TIMESTAMP)) day FROM Pivot
WHERE i BETWEEN 0 AND 6

date       day
---------- -----------------------------
2001-11-05 Monday
2001-11-06 Tuesday
2001-11-07 Wednesday
2001-11-08 Thursday
2001-11-09 Friday
2001-11-10 Saturday
2001-11-11 Sunday
```

These two queries are just quick teasers, listed here to show you how a Pivot table can be used in SQL. As you'll see in other recipes, the Pivot table is often an indispensable tool for quick and efficient problem solving.

CHAPTER 2

Sets

SQL, as a language, was developed around the concept of a set. You may remember studying sets in elementary school, or perhaps you studied set algebra in high school or college. While SQL statements such as SELECT, UPDATE, and DELETE can be used to work on one row of data at a time, the statements were designed to operate on sets of data, and you gain the best advantage when using them that way. In spite of all this, we commonly see programs that use SQL to manipulate data one row at a time rather than take advantage of the SQL's powerful set-processing capabilities. We hope that, with this chapter, we can open your eyes to the power of set manipulation.

When you write SQL statements, try not to think in terms of procedures such as selecting a record, updating it, and then selecting another. Instead, think in terms of operating on a set of records all at once. If you're used to procedural thinking, set thinking can take some getting used to. To help you along, this chapter presents some recipes that demonstrate the power of a set-oriented approach to programming with SQL.

The recipes in this chapter are organized to demonstrate different types of operations that can be performed on sets. You'll see how to find common elements, summarize the data in a set, and find the element in a set that represents an extreme. The operations don't necessarily conform to the mathematical definition of set operations. Rather, we extend those definitions and use algebraic terminology to solve real-world problems. In the real world, some deviations from tight mathematical definitions are necessary. For example, it's often necessary to order the elements in a set, an operation that is not possible with mathematically defined sets.

2.1   Introduction

Before diving into the recipes, we would like to step briefly through some basic set concepts and define the terminology used in this chapter. Although we are sure you are familiar with the mathematical concepts of sets, intersections, and unions, we would like to put each of these set-algebra terms into the context of a real-world example.

Components

There are three types of components to be aware of when working with sets. First is the set itself. A set is a collection of elements, and, for our purposes, an element is a row in a database table or a row returned by a query. Lastly, we have the universe, which is a term we use to refer to the set of all possible elements for a given set.

Sets

A *set* is a collection of elements. By definition, the elements must not be duplicated, and they are not ordered. Here, the mathematical definition of a set differs from its practical use in SQL. In the real world, it's often useful to sort the elements of a set into a specified order. Doing so allows you to find extremes such as the top five, or bottom five, records. Figure 2-1 shows an example of two sets. We'll be referring to these examples as we discuss various aspects of set terminology.

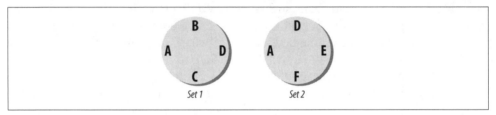

Figure 2-1. Two sets

For our purposes, we will consider a set to be a collection of rows from a table identified by one common element. Consider, for example, the following table of order items. This table is a collection of sets, where each set is identified by a unique order-identification number.

```
CREATE TABLE OrderItems(
    OrderId INTEGER,
    ItemId INTEGER,
    ProductId CHAR(10),
    Qty INTEGER,
    PRIMARY KEY(OrderId,ItemId)
)
```

Each set in this case represents an order and will have a number of elements that are not duplicated. The elements will be rows defining the products and the quantity of those products being ordered. The common element is the OrderId column.

Using SQL, it is easy to list all elements from a set. You simply issue a SELECT statement with a WHERE clause that identifies the specific set of interest. The following query returns all line-item records in the set identified by order #112:

```
SELECT * FROM OrderItems WHERE OrderId=112
```

Sets and Primary Keys

How does the primary key relate to the common element that defines a set? The answer is that they really don't need to be related at all. Any column, or combination of columns, in your table can be thought of as defining a set. It's really a matter of thinking about the data in a way that is useful to you. In the OrderItems table, the OrderId column is the common column that defines the set of all line items for an order. That's certainly a useful view of the data, but there are other ways to look at the data as well. The ProductId column, for example, defines the set of line items for a particular product. In real life, the sets you think about most are likely to correspond to your foreign-key columns.

While more than one column can be used to define a set, it's highly unlikely for that list of columns to contain the table's primary key. If that were the case, each "set" would consist of only one record. If your sets only contain one record, you should probably reconsider your table structure or your interpretation of the sets in your table. Otherwise, you might run into trouble trying to apply the recipes shown in this chapter.

In this chapter, we will work with sets that are always in one table. Many authors try to demonstrate set operations using two different tables. This approach has two problems. First, while advantageous from a demonstration perspective, you will seldom find a database with two tables that both have the same structure. Second, there are many hidden possibilities for writing queries that come to light when you think of different sets as different slices of the same table. By focusing our recipes on a single table, we hope to open your mind to these possibilities.

Elements

An *element* is a member of a set. In Figure 2-1, each individual letter is an element. For our purposes, when working with SQL, an element is a row of a table. In SQL, it is often useful not to think of elements as unified entities. In the pure mathematical sense of the term, it's not possible to divide an element of a set into two or more components. In SQL, however, you can divide an element into components. A table is usually composed of many different columns, and you'll often write queries that operate on only a subset of those columns.

For example, let's say that you want to find the set of all orders that contain an explosive, regardless of the quantity. Your elements are the rows in the OrderItems table. You'll need to use the ProductId column to identify explosives, and you'll need to return the OrderId column to identify the orders, but you have no use for the other columns in the table. Here's the query:

```
SELECT OrderId
FROM OrderItems o
GROUP BY OrderId
```

```
HAVING EXISTS(
    SELECT *
    FROM OrderItems o1
    WHERE o1.ProductId='Explosive' AND o.OrderId=o1.OrderId)
```

This query actually uses one of the set operations that you'll read about in this chapter. The operation is known as the *contains* operation, and it corresponds to the SQL keyword EXISTS.

Universes

A *universe* is the set of all possible elements that can be part of a given set. Consider Sets 1 and 2 from Figure 2-1. Each set is composed of letters of the alphabet. If we decided that only letters could be set elements, the universe for the two sets would be the set of all letters as shown in Figure 2-2.

Figure 2-2. A possible universe for Sets 1 and 2

For a more real-life example of a set universe, assume that a school offers 40 possible courses to its students. Each student selects a small number of those 40 courses to take during a given semester. The courses are the elements. The courses that a given student is taking constitute a set. Different students are taking different combinations and numbers of courses. The sets are not all the same, nor are they all the same size, yet they all contain elements from the same universe. Each student must choose from among the same 40 possibilities.

In the student/course example just given, all elements of all sets come from the same universe. It's also possible for some sets in a table to have different universes than others. For example, assume that a table contains a list of finished case studies that students have presented. Further assume that the universe of possible case studies is different for each course. If you consider a set to be defined by a course and a student, the universe of elements that applies depends on the course that the student took. Each course will have a different universe.

Set Operations

Set operations allow you to take two sets and return some sort of meaningful result. The exact result depends on the operation being performed. For example, you can take two sets and return only those elements that appear in both sets. This operation is known as the intersection. Other operations include: contains, union, complement, and difference.

Contains

The *contains* operation tells you whether a specific element can be found within a set. Figure 2-3 shows that Set 1 (from Figure 2-1) contains the letter "D."

Figure 2-3. Set 1 contains a "D"

Contains is one of the very basic set-algebra operations and can be implemented directly in SQL by combining a SELECT statement with an EXISTS clause. For example, in the following query, EXISTS is used for each student in the Student-Master table to see if that student is also in the set of students who have taken the course numbered ACCN101:

```
SELECT * FROM StudentMaster sm
WHERE EXISTS (SELECT * FROM Students s
              WHERE sm.StudentName = s.StudentName
                AND s.CourseId = 'ACCN101')
```

The use of EXISTS is so common that you might not even think much about the underlying set operation that it represents.

Intersection

An *intersection* is an operation where two or more sets are compared for common elements. For example, Figure 2-4 shows the intersection between sets 1 and 2.

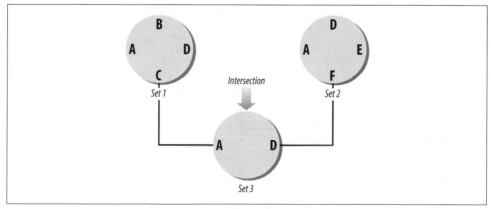

Figure 2-4. Set 3 is the intersection of Sets 1 and 2

A typical question answered by an intersection is which students have taken ACCN101 who have also taken MGMT120. The SQL-92 standards specify the use of the keyword INTERSECT to implement the intersection operation. Thus, you should be able to write:

```
SELECT DISTINCT StudentName
FROM Students
WHERE CourseId='ACCN101'
INTERSECT
SELECT DISTINCT StudentName
FROM Students
WHERE CourseId='MGMT120'
```

Unfortunately, SQL Server does not implement the INTERSECT keyword. The intersection recipes in this chapter show some techniques for working around this limitation. In addition, this chapter shows you how to perform a partial intersection. A partial intersection allows you to find elements that belong to a specific number of sets, but not necessarily to all sets.

Union

A *union* is a way to combine two or more sets into one larger set, as shown in Figure 2-5. The resulting set contains all elements from both sets.

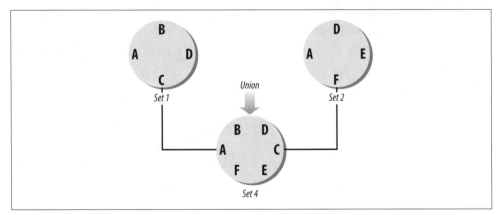

Figure 2-5. Set 4 is the union of Sets 1 and 2

SQL (as a language) is well-equipped to work with unions and implements the union operation using the UNION keyword. This allows you to take the rows returned by two SELECT statements and blend them together into one result set. For example, the following query returns a list of students who have taken either ACCN101 or MGMT120:

```
SELECT * FROM Students
WHERE CourseId = 'ACCN101'
UNION
SELECT * FROM Students
WHERE CourseId = 'MGMT120'
```

In SQL, the UNION operation removes all duplicate rows from the result. With respect to this example, if a student has taken both courses, he will still only be listed once. If you want to preserve the duplicated rows, you can use UNION ALL in place of UNION.

When you execute a SELECT statement using the UNION operator, the server must execute each query separately. In many cases, unions can be achieved more efficiently without the UNION operator. One typical example is when you define a WHERE clause as a range that combines two or more set identifications. Another such case is when you are calculating aggregated information over several sets.

Complement

A *complement* is the set of all elements in a universe that are missing from a set. Figure 2-6 shows Set 1 and its complement with respect to the universe shown earlier in Figure 2-2.

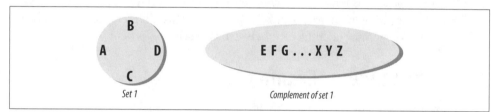

Figure 2-6. A set and its complement

The complement operation is closely related to the universe of the set, and a union of both a complement and the original set gives you the universe for that set. As you'll later see in one of the recipes, an example of such an operation is to search a student's records and generate a list of missing term papers.

Do not be misled by the simplicity of this concept. Working with complements requires the definition of a universe. It is often possible to define a universe with a range; for example, you can define a particular container to have 100 possible slots. In such a case, it is fairly easy to operate with complements. However, if your problem requires that you specifically define every possible element for a set, the complexity of the complement operation will increase. In that case, you'll have to define a universe in a different table and join that table to your query.

Difference

The *difference* between two sets is the set of elements in one set that is not present in the other. Figure 2-7 illustrates the difference between Set 1 and Set 2.

Set difference is a common problem when programming with sets, and it's useful when you want to find discrepancies between two or more sets. You can subtract one set from another, one set from all others, or many sets from one specific set.

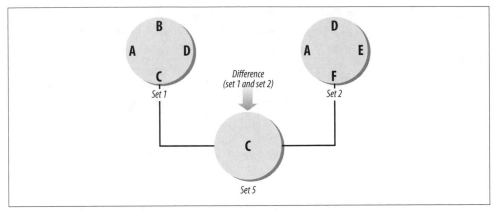

Figure 2-7. The difference between two sets

The SQL-92 standard specifies that the EXCEPT keyword be used to implement the set-difference operation. Unfortunately, as with INTERSECTION, the EXCEPT keyword hasn't been implemented yet in SQL Server. In this chapter, we'll show you a different way to generate the difference between two sets.

2.2   The Students Example

All the examples in this chapter make use of a set of tables in a system that tracks students, courses, and grades. You are a database administrator at the local university, which keeps students' records in a relational database. The university requires that each student prepare several term papers for each course that they take. A professor grades each paper that is submitted, and the Score is stored in a table.

The table in which term paper Scores are recorded is named Students. Each row contains a course ID, the student's name (used as a unique identifier for students), and the Score earned for a term paper. Each term paper can have a maximum Score of 25, so you do not have to normalize the Score to a unique base. Term papers are identified by a sequential integer that starts over at 1 for each new course that a student takes. Here is the table structure:

```
CREATE TABLE Students (
    CourseId CHAR(20),
    StudentName CHAR(40),
    Score DECIMAL(4,2),
    TermPaper INTEGER
)
```

If you execute the *ch01.ImplementingSetDifference.objects.sql* script, all the tables needed for the recipes in this chapter will be created and populated with data. The data in the Students table will then look like this:

```
CourseId              StudentName        Score   TermPaper
--------------------  ----------------   ------  -----------
ACCN101               Andrew             15.60   4
ACCN101               Andrew             10.40   2
ACCN101               Andrew             11.00   3
ACCN101               Bert               13.40   1
ACCN101               Bert               11.20   2
ACCN101               Bert               13.00   3
ACCN101               Cindy              12.10   1
ACCN101               Cindy              16.20   2
MGMT120               Andrew             20.20   1
MGMT120               Andrew             21.70   2
MGMT120               Andrew             23.10   3
MGMT120               Cindy              12.10   1
MGMT120               Cindy              14.40   2
MGMT120               Cindy              16.00   3
```

Each student needs to write three term papers for each of two courses. Currently, Andrew has submitted three papers for the accounting and management class, Cindy has submitted two for accounting and three for management, and Bert has submitted three for accounting and none for the management class.

Other tables related to this example that you may see used in the recipes include: StudentMaster, CourseMaster, and CreditRules. The StudentMaster table tells you which courses a student has registered to take. The CourseMaster table tells you the number of term papers required for each course. The CreditRules table is used in only one recipe and serves to link together the term papers necessary to achieve a specific grade in a course. The structure of these tables will be explained later in the chapter.

2.3   Implementing Set Difference

Problem

You want to compute the difference between two sets. For example, you want to find all the courses Andrew has taken that Cindy has not yet taken. As a variation on this problem, you also want to subtract one set from the combination of all other sets. In other words, Cindy wants to find out how her friends are doing by listing all term papers that they have completed that she has not.

Solution

There are two problems in this recipe. The first is a simple subtraction of one set from another. The second is a subtraction of one set from the union of all other sets. The solution to both is really one and the same because the union of more than one set is simply a larger set.

Subtracting one set from another

Consider the problem of finding out which term papers Andrew has completed that Cindy has not completed. There are two sets involved: the set of papers that Andrew has completed and the set of papers that Cindy has completed. The following query returns the difference between these two sets:

```
SELECT s.CourseId, s.TermPaper
FROM Students s
WHERE s.StudentName='Andrew' AND
    NOT EXISTS(
        SELECT * FROM Students s1
        WHERE s1.CourseId=s.CourseId AND
            s1.TermPaper=s.TermPaper AND
            s1.StudentName='Cindy')
```

The results returned by this query will look like this:

```
CourseId   TermPaper
---------  -----------
ACCN101    4
ACCN101    3
```

Subtracting one set from all others

A slight variation on this problem is to subtract one specific set from the union of all other sets. This leads to the second part of our problem—that of finding which term papers Cindy's friends have taken, but not Cindy. The following query will do this:

```
SELECT s.StudentName, s.CourseId, s.TermPaper
FROM Students s
WHERE s.StudentName<>'Cindy' AND
    NOT EXISTS(
        SELECT * FROM Students s1
        WHERE s.CourseId=s1.CourseId AND
            s.TermPaper=s1.TermPaper AND
            s1.StudentName='Cindy')
```

This query returns the following result:

```
StudentName    CourseId   TermPaper
-------------  ---------  -----------
Andrew         ACCN101    4
Andrew         ACCN101    3
Bert           ACCN101    3
```

Now we know that of all the people in school, only Andrew and Bert have turned in term papers that Cindy hasn't written yet.

Discussion

Finding the difference between two sets requires the use of subqueries and is usually an expensive task in terms of CPU and memory consumption. The key to solving such a problem lies in defining the sets involved. For example, the set of term papers

Cindy has taken is one set that appears in both problems posed in this recipe. Once you've defined your sets, you can use a SELECT statement with a NOT EXISTS predicate to return the difference between those sets.

Subtracting one set from another

The first SELECT statement subtracts the set of term papers written by Cindy from the set written by Andrew. The outer SELECT statement returns all term papers written by Andrew. The NOT EXISTS predicate modifies the results of that query so that they exclude all term papers taken by Cindy; the SELECT statement within the predicate defines Cindy's set of term papers. The result returned by the query as a whole is the list of term papers written by Andrew, but not yet by Cindy.

Subtracting one set from all others

The second SELECT statement subtracts the set of term papers written by Cindy from each of the other sets. The skeleton of the solution is the same as for the prior problem. The only difference is that the set defined by the outer SELECT statement includes term papers for all students but Cindy.

The result returned by the second SELECT statement is a list of all term papers turned in by other students, but not yet by Cindy. Because several students can work on the same term paper, the student name is included in the results to give them meaning. Cindy wants to know *who* has submitted papers that she hasn't.

Subtracting other sets from one

The second query actually leads to a solution for yet a third possibility for computing set differences—that of subtracting many sets from one. Say that you want a list of papers written by Andrew, but which have not yet been written by any other student. You could generate that using the following query:

```
SELECT s.CourseId, s.TermPaper
FROM Students s
WHERE s.StudentName='Andrew' AND
    NOT EXISTS(
        SELECT * FROM Students s1
        WHERE s1.CourseId=s.CourseId AND
            s1.TermPaper=s.TermPaper AND
            s1.StudentName<>'Andrew')
```

In this case, the outer SELECT statement returns the list of term papers written by Andrew. That's the starting point. The subquery then defines the list of term papers taken by other students. The two lists are subtracted, and the result is a list of term papers that only Andrew has submitted.

2.4   Comparing Two Sets for Equality

Problem

You want to compare two sets of rows for equality. For example, you took a snapshot of the Students table in October and another in November. Now, you want to compare those two copies.

The snapshot for October:

CourseId	StudentName	Score	TermPaper
ACCN101	Andrew	11.00	3

And for November:

CourseId	StudentName	Score	TermPaper
ACCN101	Andrew	11.00	3
ACCN101	Andrew	11.00	3
ACCN101	Bert	13.40	1

Solution

One solution is to consider the two tables as two different sets. You can then adapt the "Implementing Set Difference" recipe to this problem by using it to report rows in one table that are not also contained in the other. The following query will do this for two tables named StudentsOct and StudentsNov:

```
SELECT so.*, COUNT(*) DupeCount, 'StudentsOct' TableName
FROM StudentsOct so
GROUP BY so.CourseId, so.StudentName, so.Score, so.TermPaper
HAVING NOT EXISTS (
      SELECT sn.*, COUNT(*)
      FROM StudentsNov sn
      GROUP BY sn.CourseId, sn.StudentName, sn.Score, sn.TermPaper
      HAVING sn.CourseId=so.CourseId AND
         sn.TermPaper=so.TermPaper AND
         sn.StudentName=so.StudentName AND
         COUNT(*) = COUNT(ALL so.CourseId))
UNION
SELECT sn.*, COUNT(*) DupeCount, 'StudentsNov' TableName
FROM StudentsNov sn
GROUP BY sn.CourseId, sn.StudentName, sn.Score, sn.TermPaper
HAVING NOT EXISTS (
      SELECT so.*, COUNT(*)
      FROM StudentsOct so
      GROUP BY so.CourseId, so.StudentName, so.Score, so.TermPaper
      HAVING so.CourseId=sn.CourseId AND
         so.TermPaper=sn.TermPaper AND
         so.StudentName=sn.StudentName AND
         COUNT(*) = COUNT(ALL sn.CourseId))
```

Discussion

This is a somewhat complex query. However, it's really the union of two very similar SELECT statements. Once you understand the first, you'll understand the second. The first SELECT statement in the UNION returns a list of rows in StudentsOct that do not also exist in StudentsNov. The second SELECT statement does the reverse—it returns a list of rows from StudentsNov that are not also in StudentsOct. Both of these SELECT statements represent difference operations. If the two tables are equal, neither SELECT will return any rows.

Let's focus on the first part of the SELECT statement:

```
SELECT so.*, COUNT(*) dupeCount, 'StudentsOct' tableName
FROM StudentsOct so
GROUP BY so.CourseId, so.StudentName, so.Score, so.TermPaper
```

This SELECT statement retrieves all columns from the StudentsOct table, groups the data by those columns, and uses the aggregate function COUNT to return the number of rows in each group. For example:

```
CourseId      StudentName Score TermPaper  DupeCount   TableName
------------  ----------- ------ ---------- ----------- -----------
ACCN101       Andrew      11.00 3          1           StudentsOct
...
```

It's important that the GROUP BY clause lists each column in the StudentsOct table. In this example, we added an extra TableName column so that we can easily see to which table any extra rows belong. The purpose of the grouping operation is to deal with duplicate rows. If the StudentsOct table has two identical rows, then the StudentsNov table must also have two identical rows that match. The only way to check for this is to group the data by all columns in the table, count up the number of occurrences in each group, and then compare those counts across the two tables.

The HAVING clause functions as a WHERE clause, but at the group level. For each group of one table, the HAVING clause checks to be sure that there is a corresponding group of records in the other. All columns must match, and the row count for the groups must match as well.

The two queries in the union are symmetrical. Together, they compute the table differences from two different directions. The following possible table data illustrates why this is necessary:

```
SELECT * FROM StudentsOct
CourseId              StudentName    Score TermPaper
-------------------- ------------- ------ -----------
ACCN101              Andrew        11.00 3

(1 row(s) affected)

SELECT * FROM StudentsNov
```

```
CourseId              StudentName      Score  TermPaper
--------------------  ---------------  -----  -----------
ACCN101               Andrew           11.00  3
ACCN101               Andrew           11.00  3
ACCN101               Bert             13.40  1
(3 row(s) affected)
```

Notice that the StudentsNov table contains all the rows from the StudentsOct table and then some. The first union query, which reports all rows found in StudentsOct but not in StudentsNov, will return a row for Andrew because Andrew has one row in the first table that occurs twice in the second table. That row will be detected because the counts are different. However, the first union query will not detect the row for Bert in the second table at all. That's because the subquery only checks the second table for rows that exist in the first table. The second union query, however, turns that around and will detect that the row for Bert in the StudentsNov table has no counterpart in the StudentsOct table. For example:

```
SELECT sn.*, COUNT(*) DupeCount, 'StudentsNov' TableName
FROM StudentsNov sn
GROUP BY sn.CourseId, sn.StudentName, sn.Score, sn.TermPaper
HAVING NOT EXISTS (
      SELECT so.*, COUNT(*)
      FROM StudentsOct so
      GROUP BY so.CourseId, so.StudentName, so.Score, so.TermPaper
      HAVING so.CourseId=sn.CourseId AND
        so.TermPaper=sn.TermPaper AND
        so.StudentName=sn.StudentName AND
        COUNT(*) = COUNT(ALL sn.CourseId))
```

```
CourseId   StudentName  Score  TermPaper   DupeCount   TableName
---------  -----------  -----  ----------- ----------- -----------
ACCN101    Andrew       11.00  3           2           StudentsNov
ACCN101    Bert         13.40  1           1           StudentsNov
```

If neither query generates any results, then neither table has any rows that are not also held by the other, so the two tables must be equal.

2.5   Implementing Partial Intersection

Problem

You have a set of sets. You want to find the elements that represent intersections between those sets, and then you want to count the number of sets to which each of those elements belongs. The intersections can be partial. In other words, it is not necessary for an element to be present in all sets. However, you do want to specify a threshold, in terms of the number of sets, so the query results will exlude an element that falls below it. As an example of this type of problem, you want to list all term papers and show how many students have submitted each one of them.

Solution

The solution to this problem is fairly trivial. You have to count the number of term papers that occurs in the table, so you can use a GROUP BY query as shown in the following example:

```
SELECT CourseId, TermPaper, COUNT(*) NumStudents
FROM Students
GROUP BY TermPaper, CourseId
ORDER BY  COUNT(*) DESC
```

This query will return the submission count for each term paper. If you want to impose a threshold—say that you only care about term papers that have been turned in by at least two students—you can add a HAVING clause as follows:

```
SELECT CourseId, TermPaper, COUNT(*) NumStudents
FROM Students
GROUP BY TermPaper, CourseId
HAVING COUNT(*) >= 2
ORDER BY COUNT(*) DESC
```

Run against the sample data provided with this chapter, this query will produce the following result:

CourseId	TermPaper	NumStudents
ACCN101	2	3
ACCN101	1	2
ACCN101	3	2
MGMT120	1	2
MGMT120	2	2
MGMT120	3	2

Discussion

The GROUP BY query takes the rows from the Students table and sorts them into groups based on term papers. Term papers are uniquely identified by a combination of course ID and term paper number. The COUNT(*) in the SELECT list causes the rows in each group to be counted. The result is the number of times each paper has been submitted.

Strictly speaking, if a count is less than 2, then it doesn't represent an intersection at all. Either nobody has written the term paper yet or only one person has written it. If you need a mathematically correct intersection, specify a minimum count of 2 in the HAVING clause. That way you will only see term papers that fall into at least two sets. The following query, for example, returns the intersection between the set of term papers written by Andrew and the set written by Cindy:

```
SELECT CourseId, TermPaper
FROM Students
WHERE StudentName IN ('Andrew','Cindy')
GROUP BY TermPaper, CourseId
HAVING COUNT(*) >= 2
ORDER BY  COUNT(*) DESC
```

The way that this works is that the WHERE clause restricts the query to only those papers written by either Andrew or Cindy. The GROUP BY then sorts and counts by paper. A count of 2 indicates that both Andrew and Cindy must have submitted a paper. The HAVING clause further restricts the query's results to only those term papers.

 All of the queries shown in this recipe are predicated on the assumption that a student cannot submit the same term paper twice or, at least, that such a double submission will not be recorded twice in the Students table.

2.6   Implementing Full Intersection

Problem

You have a set of sets, and you want to find the full intersection between them. Continuing with the students example, you want to list the term papers that have been handed in by all students.

Solution

One solution is to count the students, count the number of times each term paper has been submitted, and return only those term papers where the two counts are equal. For example:

```
SELECT CourseId, TermPaper
FROM Students
GROUP BY TermPaper, CourseId
HAVING COUNT(*)=(SELECT COUNT(DISTINCT StudentName) FROM Students)
```

When run against the sample data for this chapter, this query will return the following result:

```
CourseId              TermPaper
--------------------  -----------
ACCN101               2
```

Discussion

The query might look a bit strange at first. However, it follows the logic introduced in the previous recipe. The sets in the problem are groups of term papers identified by student and course IDs. In other words, we are dealing with the different sets of term papers turned in by each student. Contrary to what your initial instincts might be, we do not group the term papers into sets by students; rather, we group them into sets by paper. The GROUP BY CourseId, TermPaper clause does this for us.

The idea is that for each term paper, we use COUNT(*) in the HAVING clause to count the number of submissions. Then we compare this number to the total count of students in the table. If there are as many students in the table as there are term papers of one kind, all students have handed in the term paper and can be included in the query's result set.

Please note the DISTINCT clause in the second SELECT. It's a common mistake to forget that. That would be a mistake because then the inner SELECT would count all rows in the table instead of counting the number of distinct students.

2.7 Classifying Subsets

Problem

You want to classify aggregated results from subsets into classes of common properties. For example, you want to give each student a grade for each course they are taking. Grades are based on the average Score calculated from term papers in each course. The query has to implement the following grading rules shown in Table 2-1.

Table 2-1. Average scores required for a given grade

Grade	Average score
A	22
B	19
C	16
D	13
E	10

Solution

You have to calculate an average term paper Score per student and then classify that average according to the grading rules laid down in Table 2-1. The following query does this:

```
SELECT CourseId, StudentName, AVG(Score) Score,(
    CASE WHEN AVG(Score)>=22 THEN 'A'
        WHEN AVG(Score)>=19 THEN 'B'
        WHEN AVG(Score)>=16 THEN 'C'
        WHEN AVG(Score)>=13 THEN 'D'
        WHEN AVG(Score)>=10 THEN 'E'
        ELSE 'F' END) Grade
FROM Students s
GROUP BY CourseId, StudentName
```

This query will return the following results:

```
CourseId   StudentName   Score grade
---------  ------------  ----- -----
ACCN101    Andrew        12.33   E
MGMT120    Andrew        21.66   B
ACCN101    Bert          12.53   E
ACCN101    Cindy         14.15   D
MGMT120    Cindy         14.16   D
```

Discussion

The solution uses the CASE function to classify the results. It groups term papers together into sets based on student and course. It then calculates an average Score for the term papers present in a particular set. Then, in the CASE statement, the calculated average is compared to the grading rules, and appropriate grades are returned.

You'll notice that the AVG function occurs several times in the query. Don't worry about that. The function has to be repeated for syntactical purposes—columns not listed in the GROUP BY clause must be enclosed by an aggregate function. Rest assured, however, that the database engine will calculate the average just once for each group.

It is important to keep the grading rules in the proper order in the CASE statement used for this solution. Because the greater-than-or-equal-to operator (>=) is used, the first WHEN clause must correspond to the highest interval from Table 2-1. The second WHEN clause must correspond to the second highest interval, and so on.

If you don't want to list your grading rules in order, or if you do not have contiguous ranges, then you can modify your WHEN clauses to specify both the upper and lower limit for each range. For example, the following WHEN clause could be used to compute a D grade:

```
WHEN AVG(Score)>=13 AND AVG(Score)<16 THEN 'D'
```

As you can see, the solution described in this recipe needs to make only one pass through the table to obtain the result. An alternative solution would be to combine the result set from several queries using the UNION operator. The following union query, for example, is equivalent to the nonunion query shown earlier:

```
SELECT CourseId, StudentName, AVG(Score) Score, 'A' grade
FROM Students s
GROUP BY CourseId, StudentName
HAVING AVG(Score)<=25 and AVG(Score)>=22
UNION
SELECT CourseId, StudentName, AVG(Score) Score, 'B' grade
FROM Students s
GROUP BY CourseId, StudentName
HAVING AVG(Score)<22 and AVG(Score)>=19
UNION
SELECT CourseId, StudentName, AVG(Score) Score, 'C' grade
FROM Students s
GROUP BY CourseId, StudentName
HAVING AVG(Score)<19 and AVG(Score)>=16
UNION
SELECT CourseId, StudentName, AVG(Score) Score, 'D' grade
FROM Students s
GROUP BY CourseId, StudentName
HAVING AVG(Score)<16 and AVG(Score)>=13
UNION
SELECT CourseId, StudentName, AVG(Score) Score, 'E' grade
FROM Students s
GROUP BY CourseId, StudentName
HAVING AVG(Score)<13 and AVG(Score)>=10
UNION
SELECT CourseId, StudentName, AVG(Score) Score, 'F' grade
FROM Students s
GROUP BY CourseId, StudentName
HAVING AVG(Score)<10
```

As you can see, the union query is long and ugly. Even if there were no other issues with this query, artistic reasons might prevent you from wanting to use it. However, there are more than artistic reasons for not using a union query such as the one shown here. The UNION query represents the execution of several SELECT statements, each of which requires a complete pass through the Students table. Consequently, it will be much less efficient than the alternative query that uses a CASE statement and that only requires one pass through the table.

2.8   Summarizing Classes of Sets

Problem

You want to calculate the number of times subsets fall into different classes, and you want to measure the sizes of those classes when classification is performed on non-aggregated data. As an example of this type of problem, let's say you want to count the number of A papers, B papers, and so forth for each student.

Solution

An alternative way of stating the problem is to say that you need to count the number of times each student is given each grade. The following query does this:

```
SELECT s.StudentName,(
    CASE WHEN s.Score>=22 THEN 'A'
        WHEN s.Score>=19 THEN 'B'
        WHEN s.Score>=16 THEN 'C'
        WHEN s.Score>=13 THEN 'D'
        WHEN s.Score>=10 THEN 'E'
        ELSE 'F' END) Grade,
    COUNT(*) NoOfPapers
FROM Students s
GROUP BY s.StudentName,
    CASE WHEN s.Score>=22 THEN 'A'
        WHEN s.Score>=19 THEN 'B'
        WHEN s.Score>=16 THEN 'C'
        WHEN s.Score>=13 THEN 'D'
        WHEN s.Score>=10 THEN 'E'
        ELSE 'F' END
ORDER BY s.StudentName
```

The results returned by this query will resemble these:

```
StudentName Grade NoOfPapers
----------- ----- ----------
Andrew      A     1
Andrew      B     2
Andrew      D     1
Andrew      E     2
Bert        D     2
Bert        E     1
Cindy       C     2
Cindy       D     1
Cindy       E     2
```

Discussion

The code demonstrates an interesting feature of SQL that is not used very often—the use of a CASE statement within a GROUP BY clause. This not often seen, though it is a fairly powerful construct. The first CASE statement, the one in the main part of the query, assigns a grade to each term paper. Instead of aggregating the results by student and paper, the results are then aggregated by student and grade. By counting the number of records in each group, we find out how many A grades a student has, how many B grades, and so forth. The following example illustrates this grouping and counting process:

```
StudentName Grade NoOfPapers
----------- ----- -----------
Andrew      B
Andrew      B
COUNT(*)             2

Bert        D
Bert        D
COUNT(*)             2
```

If you wanted to, you could extend the query so that it also calculated the percentage that each grade represented out of the total number of term papers taken. The following SELECT list shows the extra column that you would need to add to do this:

```
SELECT s.StudentName,(
    CASE WHEN s.Score>=22 THEN 'A'
        WHEN s.Score>=19 THEN 'B'
        WHEN s.Score>=16 THEN 'C'
        WHEN s.Score>=13 THEN 'D'
        WHEN s.Score>=10 THEN 'E'
        ELSE 'F' END) Grade,
    COUNT(*) NoOfPapers,
    100*count(*)/(
    SELECT count(*) FROM Students s1
        WHERE s1.StudentName=s.StudentName) Per
...
```

This modified query will return the following results:

```
StudentName Grade NoOfPapers  Per
----------- ----- ----------- -----------
Andrew      A     1           16
Andrew      B     2           33
Andrew      D     1           16
Andrew      E     2           33
Bert        D     2           66
Bert        E     1           33
Cindy       C     2           40
Cindy       D     1           20
Cindy       E     2           40
```

2.9 Aggregating Aggregates

Problem

You want to select some data, aggregate it, and then aggregate it again. Here's an example of this type of problem: the administration at the university is preparing an internal report for the dean, who wants to compare grading habits of professors. One of the measures the dean wants to look at is the spread between the average term paper Score for each student in a given course. The spread is the difference between the best and the worst student Score per course. Your job is to find the best and the worst average Score in each course and calculate the difference.

Solution

Use a nested SELECT statement in the FROM clause of your query to generate the first aggregation. Then write your enclosing SQL statement so that it takes those aggregated results and aggregates them again. For example:

```
SELECT CourseId, MAX(l.s) Best ,MIN(l.s) Worst,
    MAX(l.s)-MIN(l.s) Spread
FROM (
    SELECT CourseId, AVG(Score) AS s
    FROM Students
    GROUP BY CourseId, StudentName) AS l
GROUP BY CourseId
```

The query will return the following result:

```
CourseId   Best    Worst   Spread
---------  ------  ------  ---------
ACCN101    14.15   12.33   1.81
MGMT120    21.66   14.16   7.50
```

Discussion

SQL does not allow you to directly enclose one aggregate function within another. In other words, a query written in the following manner would not execute:

```
SELECT CourseId, MAX(AVG(stock)), MIN(AVG(stock))
FROM Students
GROUP BY CourseId, studentsName
```

However, you can work around this by using a result from one query as the source for a second query. This trick can be used as a general solution for problems where you have to aggregate already aggregated data. In the case of the solution shown in this recipe, the innermost query takes all the term paper Scores for each student in each course and returns the average of those Scores. The intermediate results look like this:

```
CourseId              s
--------------------  ---------
ACCN101               12.333333
MGMT120               21.666666
ACCN101               12.533333
ACCN101               14.150000
MGMT120               14.166666
```

The intermediate results are summarized by course and student. The outermost query then summarizes those results, but this time at the course level. This allows the use of the MAX function to compute the highest average student Score in a course, while the MIN function is used to compute the lowest average student Score in a course.

Please note that the query shown in this solution is expensive, because it requires two scans of the table—one for the inner query and one for the outer query. In addition, the ability to nest a SELECT statement in the FROM clause is a recent addition to the SQL standard. Older versions of SQL Server may not support it.

2.10   Summarizing Aggregated Classes

Problem

You want to calculate the number of times subsets fall into different classes, and you want to measure the sizes of those classes when classification is performed on already aggregated data. For example, say you want to count the number of course grades per student. A course grade is calculated by averaging the Score of all papers for a given course and then classifying that average according to Table 2-1. This is similar to the earlier recipe titled "Summarizing Classes of Sets," but this time we must aggregate the data twice.

Solution

The following SQL query combines elements of the previous two recipes to produce the desired result:

```
SELECT s.StudentName,(
    CASE WHEN s.Score>=22 THEN 'A'
        WHEN s.Score>=19 THEN 'B'
        WHEN s.Score>=16 THEN 'C'
        WHEN s.Score>=13 THEN 'D'
        WHEN s.Score>=10 THEN 'E'
        ELSE 'F' END) Grade,
    COUNT(*) NoOfCourses
FROM (
    SELECT CourseId, StudentName, AVG(Score) AS Score
    FROM Students
    GROUP BY CourseId, StudentName) AS s
```

```
GROUP BY s.StudentName,
    CASE WHEN s.Score>=22 THEN 'A'
        WHEN s.Score>=19 THEN 'B'
        WHEN s.Score>=16 THEN 'C'
        WHEN s.Score>=13 THEN 'D'
        WHEN s.Score>=10 THEN 'E'
        ELSE 'F' END
ORDER BY s.StudentName
```

The results from executing this query will look as follows:

```
StudentName Grade NoOfCourses
----------- ----- -----------
Andrew        B    1
Andrew        E    1
Bert          E    1
Cindy         D    2
```

Discussion

At first glance, this query appears a bit complex and intimidating. To understand it, it's best to look at the query as a two-step process. The inline SELECT in the FROM clause calculates an average Score for each course and student combination. This average Score is computed from the individual Scores of all the term papers.

The results from the inline SELECT are fed into the outer query that translates the average Scores into letter grades and then counts up the number of times each grade occurs. The CASE statement in the SELECT list does the classification. The case statement in the GROUP BY clause aggregates the results by grade, allowing the count to be computed.

2.11   Including Nonaggregated Columns

Problem

You want to write a GROUP BY query that returns summarized data, and you want to also include nonaggregated columns in the result. These nonaggregated columns do not appear in the GROUP BY clause. With respect to the students example, let's say that each course is graded according to the best term paper that each student has submitted for that course. For administrative reasons, you must find out which term paper has the best Score for each student/course combination.

Solution

The following query shows each student's highest term paper Score in each class that they took. An inline query is also used to return the specific term paper number that corresponds to that Score.

```
SELECT StudentName,CourseId,
    (SELECT  MAX(TermPaper)
       FROM Students
      WHERE Score=MAX(s.Score)and
          StudentName=s.StudentName and
          CourseId=s.CourseId) TermPaper,
    MAX(s.Score) Score
FROM Students s
GROUP BY CourseId, StudentName
```

The output from this query will be as follows:

```
StudentName  CourseId  TermPaper  Score
-----------  --------- ---------- ------
Andrew       ACCN101   4          15.60
Andrew       MGMT120   3          23.10
Bert         ACCN101   1          13.40
Cindy        ACCN101   2          16.20
Cindy        MGMT120   3          16.00
```

Discussion

This recipe highlights an interesting problem that has been often debated by SQL programmers. The problem is that when an extreme has been identified using an aggregation such as MAX, SQL insists that the SELECT list contain only the result of the aggregation and the columns from the GROUP BY clause. In real life, many programmers have wished for the ability to include nonaggregated columns as well. They not only want to know the maximum term paper Score for a course, but they want to know the number of that term paper. In other words, they want to write a SQL statement such as this:

```
SELECT StudentName, CourseId, TermPaper, MAX(Score)
FROM Students s
GROUP BY CourseId, StudentName
```

This kind of query is invalid. The problem is that it can be executed only if the TermPaper column is added to the GROUP BY clause. We potentially face the same problem when writing our query, but we've avoided it by writing an inline SELECT statement to retrieve the term paper number corresponding to the high Score.

The outer query groups the table into sets based on student names and course identification. Then it finds the best Score for each student in course. That's easily understood. The inner query is where things get interesting. It retrieves the number of a term paper where the Score matches the high Score for the course by the student in question. The query is a correlated subquery, meaning that it's executed once for each course and student combination. It's possible for a student to have two term papers in a course with the same Score. To ensure that only one value is returned, the inner query uses the MAX function on the TermPaper column. Anytime two term papers tie for the highest Score, the term paper listed in the results will be the one with the highest number. This is a rather arbitrary choice, but it's the best you can do under the circumstances.

2.12   Finding the Top N Values in a Set

Problem

You want to find the first N elements of an ordered set. In most cases, this means that you want to find the top N records. Assume that the grading rules of the school require professors to use only the best two Scores from the term papers each student submitted. You need to write a query that returns that information. You don't want all Scores for each student, only the top two.

Solution

The most straightforward solution to this problem is to use the TOP keyword. TOP is a MS SQL Server extension to SQL that allows you to limit a query so that it returns only the first N records. The following query returns the top two Scores for each student in each course:

```
SELECT  s1.StudentName, s1.CourseId, s1.TermPaper, MAX(s1.Score) Score
FROM Students s1
GROUP BY s1.CourseId, s1.StudentName, s1.TermPaper
HAVING MAX(s1.Score) IN
    (SELECT TOP 2 s2.Score
        FROM Students s2
        WHERE s1.CourseId=s2.CourseId AND
            s1.StudentName=s2.StudentName
     ORDER BY s2.Score DESC)
ORDER BY s1.StudentName, s1.CourseId, s1.Score DESC
```

An alternative solution is a bit less Transact-SQL-specific and a bit less intuitive. It is, however, more general, and it conforms with the SQL standard:

```
SELECT  s1.StudentName,s1.CourseId, s1.TermPaper, MAX(s1.Score) Score
FROM Students s1 INNER JOIN Students s2
    ON s1.CourseId=s2.CourseId AND
        s1.StudentName=s2.StudentName
GROUP BY s1.CourseId, s1.StudentName, s1.TermPaper
HAVING SUM(CASE WHEN s1.Score <= s2.Score THEN 1 END) <= 2
ORDER BY s1.StudentName, s1.CourseId, s1.Score DESC
```

Both queries list the two highest-scoring term papers for each student in each course and order the results in descending order by Score. The results will resemble the following output:

```
StudentName   CourseId   TermPaper   Score
-----------   --------   ---------   ------
Andrew        ACCN101    4           15.60
Andrew        ACCN101    3           11.00
Andrew        MGMT120    3           23.10
Andrew        MGMT120    2           21.70
Bert          ACCN101    1           13.40
Bert          ACCN101    3           13.00
```

Cindy	ACCN101	2	16.20
Cindy	ACCN101	1	12.10
Cindy	MGMT120	3	16.00
Cindy	MGMT120	2	14.40

Discussion

Two solutions to the problem of finding the top N rows are presented in this recipe. The first solution uses the TOP keyword, which is a SQL extension implemented by MS SQL Server. The second solution uses a self-join instead of the TOP keyword and is useful to know if you ever need to work in a database environment where TOP is not supported.

Using TOP

The first query uses TOP—an extension to SQL provided by MS SQL Server. The key thing to notice is that the SELECT TOP statement is used in the HAVING clause. While the outer query prepares a list of rows, the HAVING clause makes sure that only rows that match the two Scores for each student in each course are returned in the final result.

The way that TOP works is that SELECT TOP N causes the database server to return only the first N rows returned by the query. It's very important when using TOP to also specify an ORDER BY clause. Since we want the top two Scores, we used ORDER BY s2.Score DESC in the subquery. If you don't specify an ORDER BY clause, you'll still get two rows returned, but they will be a random set of two rows. In this sense, the use of the word TOP is a bit misleading.

 If you're not familiar with TOP, you may want to consult the MS SQL Server documentation for a complete description of this extension.

The core of the query is in the HAVING clause. It checks if the Score of the current group is in the list of the top two Scores for the group:

```
HAVING MAX(s1.Score) IN
    (SELECT TOP 2 s2.Score
        FROM Students s2
      WHERE s1.CourseId=s2.CourseId AND
          s1.StudentName=s2.StudentName
    ORDER BY s2.Score DESC)
```

Note that the MAX function does not have any real effect since the GROUP BY clause separates the data into single rows anyway. There is only one item per group, so MAX returns the Score for that one item. Even though we aren't summarizing the Score, the MAX function is necessary to comply with the rules of SQL. We used MAX(s1.Score) in the select list, so we must use MAX(s1.Score) here as well. The same results could be obtained by not aggregating the Score column and instead adding it to the GROUP BY clause. However, performance would suffer somewhat—the optimizer works better with fewer columns for grouping.

The subquery lists all Scores for the current course and the student, and it ranks them in descending order (using the ORDER BY clause). This ensures that the first two records returned reflect the top two Scores for the student in the course. ORDER BY is necessary here, specifically because TOP is being used.

> Always remember to use ORDER BY in conjunction with TOP.

Using a self-join

The second solution in this recipe uses a self-join to find the two best papers for each student in each course. In the FROM clause we join the Students table to itself. The two copies are given aliases of s1 and s2, respectively. The WHERE clause restricts the join such that we get the Cartesian product (all combinations) of all term papers for each student/course group.

By applying the GROUP BY clause, we form groups identified by a course—a student and a term paper from the first table combined with all possible combinations of those same term papers from the second table. Since we join the tables by course ID and student name, the corresponding columns have equal values and can be treated as one column. In other words, s1.StudentName will always be the same as s2.StudentName. The same is true for s1.CourseId and s2.CourseId.

This is not the case with the term paper column. By using a self-join, we produced a Cartesian product of all possible pairs of term papers for a given student in a given course. This might sound a bit confusing, so consider the following example that shows the Cartesian product of term papers for the student named Andrew in the course named ACCN101:

StudentName	CourseId	s1.TermPaper	s1.Score	s2.TermPaper	s2.Score
Andrew	ACCN101	4	15.60	4	15.60
Andrew	ACCN101	4	15.60	2	10.40
Andrew	ACCN101	4	15.60	3	11.00
Andrew	ACCN101	2	10.40	4	15.60
Andrew	ACCN101	2	10.40	2	10.40
Andrew	ACCN101	2	10.40	3	11.00
Andrew	ACCN101	3	11.00	4	15.60
Andrew	ACCN101	3	11.00	2	10.40
Andrew	ACCN101	3	11.00	3	11.00

After the joining and grouping has taken place, the HAVING clause uses the CASE statement to identify all cases where the Score from the first table (s1) is less than or equal to the Score from the second table (s2). For each row in the group, the CASE statement returns 1 if the condition is met and NULL otherwise. The SUM function then sums the result within a group. The result is that, for each term paper, we know now how many other papers by the same student for the same course have a less-than-or-equal-to Score. Finally, the HAVING clause causes the query to return only those groups that have just one or two less-than-or-equal-to Scores.

To illustrate this, let's work through an example in detail. Here are the first three rows from the previous example for the student named Andrew:

```
Andrew      ACCN101   4          15.60      4          15.60
Andrew      ACCN101   4          15.60      2          10.40
Andrew      ACCN101   4          15.60      3          11.00
```

Apply the CASE statement to the first group, and you'll see that it returns 4 for the first row, NULL for the second row, and NULL for the third row. The sum of those three values (1+NULL+NULL) is 1, which is smaller than 2 as required by the HAVING condition. Therefore, the group is reported in the result. Since the grouping is by student name, course ID, and term paper number, an aggregate function must be used to report the term paper Score. Our query uses the MAX function, but any function could have been used because there is only one term paper in a group.

Similar reasoning applies to the second group of three rows. In that group, the CASE statement returns a 1 for all three rows. The SUM of those values (1+1+1) is 3. Since 3 is not <=2, as the HAVING clause requires, the group is excluded from the result. The third group of three rows for Andrew does meet the specified condition, and, in the final result, you can see that Andrew's best Scores came from his first and third term papers.

 Since TOP is not being used, the ORDER BY clause in the second query only serves to make the output more readable. If order is not important, you'll get better performance by leaving off the ORDER BY clause.

2.13   Reporting the Size of a Set's Complement

Problem

You want to report the number of missing values for a set. As an example, assume that each student must submit four term papers for each course. Not all students have submitted all required papers, and you want to generate a report showing the number that each student has yet to submit for each course.

Solution

```
SELECT  s.StudentName, s.CourseId, 4-COUNT(TermPaper) Missing
FROM Students s
GROUP BY s.StudentName, s.CourseId
ORDER BY s.StudentName
```

Using the sample data provided for this chapter, the query in this solution should return the following result:

```
StudentName  CourseId  Missing
-----------  --------  -----------
Andrew       ACCN101   1
Andrew       MGMT120   1
Bert         ACCN101   1
Cindy        ACCN101   2
Cindy        MGMT120   1
```

Discussion

This query is very straightforward. It's an aggregate query that summarizes results by course and student combination. The aggregate function COUNT(TermPaper) is used to count the number of papers a student submits for a course. That result is then subtracted from the required number—four in this case—and the result is the number of missing term papers.

2.14 Finding the Complement of a Set

Problem

You want to find the complement of a set. Given the students example being used in this chapter, you want to list the missing term papers for each student.

Solution

To list rows that are missing, you have to know the available set of values. For this solution, therefore, it's necessary to create a support table that we can then use to generate the universe of possible term paper values for each student in each course.

Step 1: Create the Pivot table

Since we are dealing with term paper numbers, we need a Pivot table with one numeric column. We'll use the standard Pivot table for that, as explained in the "Using a Pivot Table" recipe in Chapter 1.

It's worth mentioning here that this Pivot table is still useful even if the number of term papers required by each course is different. The key is for the number of rows in the Pivot table to match the largest number of term papers required by any course.

Step 2: Run the query

With the Pivot table in place, the following query will return the list of missing term papers:

```
SELECT  s.StudentName, s.CourseId, f.i TermPaper
FROM Students s, Pivot f
WHERE f.i BETWEEN 1 AND 4
GROUP BY s.StudentName, s.CourseId, f.i
HAVING NOT EXISTS(
    SELECT * FROM Students
    WHERE CourseId=s.CourseId AND
        StudentName=s.StudentName AND
        TermPaper=f.i)
ORDER BY s.StudentName
```

The results returned by this query should resemble the following:

```
StudentName  CourseId  TermPaper
------------ --------- -----------
Andrew       ACCN101   1
Andrew       MGMT120   4
Bert         ACCN101   4
Cindy        ACCN101   3
Cindy        ACCN101   4
Cindy        MGMT120   4
```

Discussion

The queries in this recipe use a Pivot table in addition to the tables that contain the actual data. We need the Pivot table, because we need to know which term paper numbers are possible and we need to generate rows for term papers that don't exist. If a term paper hasn't been handed in, it won't have a corresponding row in the Students table. The Pivot table allows us to generate a row for that missing paper, which will be included in the query's result.

The queries join the Students table to the Pivot table and groups the result by the course ID, student name, and pivot number columns. The WHERE clause in the main query restricts the join to only as many pivot records as correspond to the number of required term papers for each course.

The HAVING statement then checks to see which pivot values do not exist in the list of term papers for each particular group. If a term paper does not exist, the expression in the HAVING clause returns TRUE and the paper pivot number is reported to identify the missing term paper.

It is important to note that data in Pivot tables is not limited to integers. You can create a Pivot table with any kind of data. For example, you could build a Pivot table that contained a list of parts needed to build a product. Then you could write a query to return missing parts for all unfinished products in an assembly plant. However, when using datatypes other than integers, you cannot fill the Pivot table with a large series of values and then limit those values in the WHERE clause. When you create a Pivot table with noninteger data, you need to specify the exact list of all possible values.

2.15　Finding the Complement of a Missing Set

Problem

The query in the previous recipe has one significant drawback: it does not report missing term papers for students who have not yet completed at least one term paper. That's because the driving table is the Students table. If a student hasn't handed in at least one term paper for a course, then there won't be any records in the Students table for that student/course combination. How then, do you report missing term papers for such students?

Solution

The key to reporting missing term papers for students who have not yet turned in any term papers is to find a reliable way to identify those students. There are two possibilities:

- Define an empty row in the Students table to identify each student.
- Create a master table that contains one row for each student.

From a database-design perspective, the second solution is probably the best, because you end up with a typical many-to-one relationship between two tables. The first solution is something of a kludge, because it uses the Students table as both a master table and as a detail table.

Solution 1: Define empty rows in the Students table

Our first solution calls for empty records to be inserted into the Students table for each student/course combination. For example, the following record would be inserted to show that David was enrolled in the ACCN101 course:

```
INSERT INTO Students(CourseId, StudentName, Score, TermPaper)
    VALUES('ACCN101','David',0,0)
```

Notice that the Score and term paper number have both been set to 0. With these records in place, the query presented in the previous recipe can be used to display the list of missing term papers. This list will now include cases where a student has missed all term papers in a given course. The zero-records that we've inserted won't show in the final result because our query excludes the Pivot table row for zero.

Solution 2: Create a student master table

A cleaner option than creating special zero-records in the Students table is to create a completely separate student master table. This table would then track each students's enrollment in the various courses offered by the university. The following shows one possible implementation:

```
CREATE TABLE StudentMaster(
    CourseId CHAR(20),
    StudentName CHAR(40)
)
INSERT INTO StudentMaster VALUES('ACCN101','Andrew')
INSERT INTO StudentMaster VALUES('MGMT120','Andrew')
INSERT INTO StudentMaster VALUES('ACCN101','Bert')
INSERT INTO StudentMaster VALUES('ACCN101','Cindy')
INSERT INTO StudentMaster VALUES('MGMT120','Cindy')
INSERT INTO StudentMaster VALUES('ACCN101','David')
```

With the StudentMaster table in place and populated as shown, you can generate a report of missing term papers using the following query:

```
SELECT   s.StudentName, s.CourseId, f.i TermPaper
FROM StudentMaster s, Pivot f
WHERE f.i BETWEEN 1 AND 4
GROUP BY s.StudentName, s.CourseId, f.i
HAVING NOT EXISTS(
    SELECT * FROM Students
    WHERE CourseId=s.CourseId AND
        StudentName=s.StudentName AND
        TermPaper=f.i)
ORDER BY s.StudentName
```

The report lists the missing term papers for each student:

```
StudentName   CourseId              TermPaper
-------------  --------------------  -----------
Andrew         ACCN101              1
Andrew         MGMT120              4
Bert           ACCN101              4
Cindy          ACCN101              3
Cindy          ACCN101              4
Cindy          MGMT120              4
David          ACCN101              1
David          ACCN101              2
David          ACCN101              3
David          ACCN101              4
```

Discussion

If you think about it, both solutions in this recipe require the creation of a master table for students and courses. In the first solution, that master table is layered onto the existing Students table, while, in the second solution, the master table is a completely separate table named StudentMaster.

The query shown for Solution 2 uses the StudentMaster table as the basis for preparing a list of groups that need to be considered. Each group represents one student and course combination. The master table is joined to the Pivot table, and the result is a complete list of all required term papers for all student/course combinations. The HAVING clause checks the Students table to see what papers have been submitted and reduces the result of the main query to only the term papers.

2.16 Finding Complements of Sets with Different Universes

Problem

You want to write a query that returns the complement of several sets, but each of those sets has a different universe. For example, consider that different courses each require a different number of term papers. You want to list the papers that are missing for each student in each course. Unlike the queries in the previous recipes, this query must correctly handle the different term paper requirements (the universe) of each course.

Solution

You first need a master table to record the number of term papers required for each course:

```
CREATE TABLE CourseMaster(
    CourseId CHAR(20),
    numTermPapers INTEGER
)
```

After creating the CourseMaster table, you need to populate it with data. The following two INSERTs specify that the ACCN101 course requires four term papers and that the MGMT120 course requires three term papers:

```
INSERT INTO CourseMaster VALUES('ACCN101',4)
INSERT INTO CourseMaster VALUES('MGMT120',3)
```

With the CourseMaster table created and populated, you can use the following query to report on term papers that have not yet been submitted:

```
SELECT   s.StudentName, s.CourseId, f.i TermPaper
FROM Students s, Pivot f, CourseMaster c
WHERE f.i BETWEEN 1 AND c.numTermPapers
    AND c.CourseId=s.CourseId
GROUP BY s.StudentName, s.CourseId, f.i
HAVING NOT EXISTS(
    SELECT * FROM Students
    WHERE CourseId=s.CourseId AND
        StudentName=s.StudentName AND
        TermPaper=f.i)
ORDER BY s.StudentName
```

The result is a list of term papers that each student still needs to submit to pass a given course:

```
StudentName  CourseId  TermPaper
------------ --------- ----------
Andrew       ACCN101   1
Bert         ACCN101   4
Cindy        ACCN101   3
Cindy        ACCN101   4
```

Discussion

This query is almost identical to the query presented in the earlier recipe titled "Finding the Complement of a Set." The major difference is how term paper requirements are specified. In the previous recipe, the number of term papers for each course was the same, and that value was represented by a constant:

```
WHERE f.i BETWEEN 1 AND 4
```

For this recipe, each course has a different requirement. That requirement has to be recorded somewhere, and that's where the CourseMaster table comes into play. The first part of the query is then modified as follows:

```
SELECT  s.StudentName, s.CourseId, f.i TermPaper
FROM Students s, Pivot f, CourseMaster c
WHERE f.i BETWEEN 1 AND c.numTermPapers
  AND c.CourseId = s.CourseId
...
```

The CourseMaster table is joined to the Students table based on the CourseId column, thus giving us access to the numTermPapers column. That column contains the course-specific requirement for the number of term papers and replaces the constant used in the earlier version of the query.

2.17 Comparing a Set with Its Universe

Problem

You want to find out if a set contains all the elements of its universe. Then you want to report it as either a full or partial match. For example, assume that you want to generate a list showing which students have fulfilled all requirements with respect to the term papers they are required to turn in and which students have completed only a partial number of their term paper requirements.

Solution

Use the CourseMaster table defined in the previous recipe to determine the universe of required papers for each student and course, and then compare that to the actual papers submitted. Here's one approach to doing this:

```
SELECT s.StudentName, s.CourseId,
    CASE WHEN COUNT(*)=MAX(c.numTermPapers)
        THEN 'All submitted'
        ELSE CONVERT(VARCHAR(8),MAX(c.numTermPapers)-COUNT(*))+' missing'
    END status
FROM Students s JOIN CourseMaster c
    ON s.CourseId=c.CourseId
GROUP BY s.StudentName, s.CourseId
ORDER BY s.StudentName, s.CourseId
```

This query will return results similar to the following:

```
StudentName  CourseId  status
-----------  --------  ----------------
Andrew       ACCN101   1 missing
Andrew       MGMT120   All submitted
Bert         ACCN101   1 missing
Cindy        ACCN101   2 missing
Cindy        MGMT120   All submitted
```

Discussion

The query joins the Students table and the CourseMaster table to find the required number of term papers for each course. The join is done using the CourseId column to retrieve the appropriate numTermPapers value. The results are then grouped so that there is one row for each student and course combination.

The core of the query is the CASE statement. In the set of rows for each course and student, each row represents a term paper. To find the number of term papers the student has handed in, we just need to count the rows. Then the CASE statement compares that count with the required number of papers for the course. The result from the case statement will be a message indicating whether or not all requirements have been fulfilled.

The MAX function in this query is here only for syntactic purposes. The number of term papers is dependent on the CourseId value, so there will only be one number for a given group. MAX is only necessary because numTermPapers is not a GROUP BY column. You could add numTermPapers to the column list in the GROUP BY clause—allowing you to dispense with MAX—but the extra GROUP BY column will hurt the efficiency of the query.

2.18   Dynamic Classification System

Problem

Define a query-processing framework that will classify sets according to rules that you can define and change dynamically. The number of rules is unlimited. As an example, let's say that a special credit system has been introduced at our university as part of a new cross-disciplinary program introduced by a new dean. Students do not get credit points directly for courses they have finished, but instead get credit for different combinations of term papers. A given term paper combination does not need to represent one course and, indeed, is most likely to represent several courses. There are different categories of credits, and the categories are marked by type codes such as A, B, and C. To finish the program, a student must earn at least one credit point in each category. Table 2-2 shows the requirement matrix that controls whether or not credit can be granted in a given category.

Table 2-2. Category credit requirement matrix

Course	Paper 1	Paper 2	Paper 3
ACCN101	A,C2	A,C2	A,B
MGMT120	C1	C1	C1,B

To earn an A credit point, a student must complete the first, second, and third term paper in the ACCN101 course. There are two ways to earn a C credit point. One is to submit the first, second, and third term papers for MGMT120. The other way to earn a C credit point is to submit the first and second term papers for ACCN101.

Solution

This problem can not be solved directly by just applying one query. You first need to create an additional table where you store the rules. Then you can write a query that looks at both the rules and at the actual term papers that students have submitted. That query can apply the rules to the actual results and determine the proper credits to grant in each category.

Step 1: Creating the rules table

The following table can be used to store the rules for our example scenario:

```
CREATE TABLE CreditRules(
    RuleId INTEGER,
    TermId INTEGER,
    CourseId CHAR(20),
    TermPaper INTEGER
)
```

After creating the table, you need to populate it with the credit rules. As you might have observed, the rules can be directly transformed into the following Boolean logic expressions:

```
Rule1: Acc1 AND Acc2 AND Acc3
Rule2: Acc3 AND Mgm3
Rule3: (Mgm1 AND Mgm2 AND Mgm3) OR (Acc1 AND Acc2)
```

The following data shows the representation in the CreditRules table of the rules described in Table 2-2. Each rule is identified by a unique RuleId number. Within each rule, each term is identified by a TermId number.

```
RuleId  TermId  CourseId   TermPaper
-------　-------　---------　-----------
1       1       ACCN101    1
1       1       ACCN101    2
1       1       ACCN101    3
2       1       ACCN101    3
2       1       MGMT120    3
```

3	1	MGMT120	1
3	1	MGMT120	2
3	1	MGMT120	3
3	2	ACCN101	1
3	2	ACCN101	2

One of the rules in Table 2-2 says that to get an A credit, you must submit term papers 1 through 3 from the ACCN 101 course. You can see that rule reflected in the data as rule 1. Notice that there is nothing in the Credit Rules table to link a rule to a specific credit category. The logic to do that resides in the query that you will read about next.

Before proceeding, it's important to understand the use of the terms rule and term in this recipe. *Rules* are composed of terms. A *term* is a set of conditions that, when met, indicates that the rule has been satisfied. Each rule in our scenario corresponds to a specific credit category. Only rule 3 has more than one term. Rule 3 states that there are two different ways to get a C credit. Term 1 says that you can get a C credit by submitting the first three term papers for MGMT120. Term 2 says that you can get a C credit by submitting the first two term papers for ACCT101. Think of the terms as being combined with OR together. Satisfy any term and you've satisfied the rule. Think of the elements of a term as being combined with AND together. To satisfy a term, you must satisfy all the elements.

Step 2: Running the query

Once the CreditRules table has been created and the rules have been defined, you can use the following query to compute each student's entitled credits:

```
SELECT DISTINCT s.StudentName,
    (CASE WHEN c.RuleId=1 THEN 'A'
       WHEN c.RuleId=2 THEN 'B'
       WHEN c.RuleId=3 THEN 'C' END) credit
FROM Students s JOIN CreditRules c
    ON s.CourseId=c.CourseId AND s.TermPaper=c.TermPaper
GROUP BY c.RuleId, c.TermId, s.StudentName
HAVING COUNT(*)=(SELECT COUNT(*)
            FROM CreditRules AS c1
            WHERE c.RuleId=c1.RuleId AND c.TermId=c1.TermId)
ORDER BY StudentName
```

The results from executing this query will resemble the following:

```
StudentName   credit
------------  -------
Andrew          B
Andrew          C
Bert            A
Bert            C
Cindy           C
```

Discussion

As you can see, this solution is dependent on the CreditRules table to store the rules. One advantage of storing the rules in a table like this is that you can easily change the rules without changing the query that assigns the credits. While it would be relatively trivial to embed the rules directly into a query, changes to the rules would then require changes to the query. If the query were embedded within an application, then a change to the query would necessitate recompiling and retesting that application. By using a table-driven approach, you gain the flexibility of changing the rules on the fly without having to do any extra recompiling and retesting.

You'll find a table-driven approach, such as that shown here, to be an efficient solution that can be applied to large record sets. You can deal with a large number of term papers, a large number of rules, or both. It's also a fairly easy task to write an application to allow users to manage the rules themselves, thus saving you work in the long run.

The query

Let's begin our analysis of the query by looking at the basic SELECT statement:

```
SELECT DISTINCT StudentName,
   (CASE WHEN c.RuleId=1 THEN 'A'
      WHEN c.RuleId=2 THEN 'B'
      WHEN c.RuleId=3 THEN 'C' END) credit
FROM Students s, CreditRules c
   ON s.CourseId=c.CourseId AND s.TermPaper=c.TermPaper
```

The Students and the CreditRules table are joined to generate a temporary result set where rows from the Students table are linked with all possible rule terms that could be applied to those records.

The DISTINCT clause is used because it's possible that a student may qualify for a credit in more than one way. Table 2-2, for example, shows two ways to qualify for a C credit. We don't care if a student qualifies for a credit more than once. It's enough to know that the student qualifies at all, so DISTINCT is used to prevent duplicate credits from being reported.

The CASE statement is included in the query to link each rule to a specific credit. You can easily see that the satisfaction of rule 1 results in an A credit. The CASE statement not only makes the results more readable, it insulates the program using this query from needing to know which rule numbers correspond to which credit categories. You could later add a rule number 4 that also corresponds to an A credit, and the program executing the query would not know the difference.

Now, let's look at the GROUP BY part of the statement:

```
GROUP BY c.RuleId, c.TermId, s.StudentName
```

This grouping combines the possible matches from one rule, one term, and one student together. If the group represents a full match, having all term requirements present in the student's record, the student can receive the corresponding credit point.

The HAVING clause in the query is where the check is made to see if all the terms of a rule have been met. Compliance with a rule is indicated when all rows for one of the rule's terms are matched by a Students table record for a given student. To determine if all terms have been met, count the terms and compare that value to the number of matches for a given student. Here is where the HAVING clause comes to our aid. The following HAVING clause does this comparison for us:

```
HAVING COUNT(*)=(SELECT COUNT(*)
          FROM CreditRules AS c1
          WHERE c.RuleId=c1.RuleId AND c.TermId=c1.TermId)
```

The expression in the HAVING clause is evaluated for each group—in other words, for each rule, term, and student combination. The subquery retrieves the total number of terms defined in the rule, and the result is compared against the number of rows in the group. Each row in the group represents a match; if the counts are the same, the conditions of the term are satisfied. The student, therefore, should get the corresponding credit.

CHAPTER 3

Data Structures

Data structures are often considered the domain of other programming languages, and not of SQL. In this chapter, we show that data structures can also be very useful for modeling problems and implementing algorithms in SQL. To solve a real-world problem, it is often helpful to have a number of abstract data models available. If you can adapt the problem to be solved to an abstract model, the implementation of a solution is usually much easier.

Abstract data structures help you solve problems that otherwise seem complex. In this chapter, we show you how to perform operations on linear structures such as lists, stacks, and queues in SQL. We also show several recipes for working with multidimensional data structures, such as matrices and arrays. Please note that by "multidimensional," we are not referring to OLAP data structures, but to arrays and matrices as programmatic data structures.

3.1   Types of Data Structures

In this chapter, we plan to discuss the following three major types of data structures:

- Lists
- Stacks and queues
- Arrays and matrices

Lists, stacks, and queues are all linear data structures; the term *linear* referring to the fact that, conceptually, you're dealing with a set of elements arranged in the form of a line. The use of SQL is well-suited to such structures because they map easily onto the relational table paradigm. Arrays and matrices, on the other hand, are multi-dimensional data structures. You can use SQL to work with arrays and matrices, but it's better-suited for linear structures.

Lists

Lists are the most common linear data structure in computing. In contrast to other programming languages, lists are the easiest type of data structure to implement in SQL. A list is a sequence of elements with a known order. A list is unlimited in size and can shrink or grow on demand. Elements can be added to a list, removed from a list, and you can query to see whether a given element is in a list.

As you can see, the properties of a list are very similar to the properties of a SQL table, with the exception that a list has an order to it. That is why lists are so easy to implement. SQL tables are also unlimited in size, can be queried, and allow for entries to be added (inserted) and removed (deleted).

In this chapter we use a SQL table with an index to define a list:

```
CREATE TABLE List (
    Id INTEGER,
    ...
)
```

A list in SQL is, therefore, a table with at least two attributes. One attribute is an index identifying the order of each element in the list. Any other attributes are data-carrying attributes, meaning that they hold the actual data in the list.

When you implement a list in SQL, it's very helpful if your list index is arithmetically increasing. By arithmetically, we mean that your list index should increase by 1 as new elements are appended to the list. We are going to assume in this chapter's recipes that our lists have arithmetically increasing indices.

All basic list operations are directly implementable in SQL. INSERT is used to add a new element to a list, DELETE is used to remove an element from a list, and SELECT is used to query for elements by value or by index. These operations are so straightforward that we won't show recipes for them in this chapter.

Lists are of particular interest in SQL, since they allow for pattern matching and for cumulative aggregation queries. The most important pattern-matching queries are for finding regions, runs, and sequences. Having said that, let's take a look at what those terms mean.

Cumulative aggregation queries

A *cumulative aggregation query* is similar to a running aggregate query, with only one difference. A *running aggregate* is the type produced by the GROUP BY clause in conjunction with an aggregate function, and it generates one aggregate value for each group of elements. Cumulative aggregates, on the other hand, include all elements from the beginning of the list. For example, you might produce a report showing sales in January, sales in January and February, sales in January through March, and so forth. While running aggregates are used mainly in statistics, cumulative aggregates are used mainly in combinatorial problems.

Regions

A *region* is a continuous pattern in a list in which all values of the elements are the same. A typical usage of such a pattern is when you look for empty slots in a list. Let's say that you have a list where elements can be either empty or full slots. If you are looking for five sequential empty slots, you are actually looking for a region of that size. The most typical example is when you build a warehouse application and you have a triple-size container. To store it, you need to find an empty slot that could fit three containers of regular size. Therefore, you are looking for a region of size three.

Runs

A *run* is a continuous pattern in which values are increasing monotonically. Each value is larger than the previous one. For example, say that you have a list of consecutively taken measurements for a volcano. In a given period of time, you may find that the temperature of the volcano were consistently rising. The measurements in that period of time, each representing a higher temperature than the one previous, would be considered a run.

Sequences

A *sequence* is a run in which values form an arithmetic progression with a difference of 1. Each value is exactly one increment larger than the previous value. With respect to the volcano example that we used to describe a run, a series of temperature measurements in which each measurement was exactly 1 degree higher than the previous would represent a sequence.

Stacks and Queues

When building a software system, there is often a requirement to serialize data that is being processed. In such cases, the following special linear structures are particularly useful:

- Stack
- Queue
- Priority queue

Stacks

A *stack* is a special kind of list in which all addition and removal of elements takes place on one side. A stack is a *last in, first out* (LIFO) structure. The LIFO concept is one that accountants and computer programmers are equally likely to understand. Each element that is added to a stack is put on top of all the others. Only the topmost item is accessible at any given time, and items in a stack are removed from the top down.

The position of an element in the stack is maintained with its index. The top of the stack is the element with the highest index. To find the highest index, a simple query is needed:

```
SELECT MAX(Id) FROM Stack
```

Typical operations on a stack are the following:

PUSH
> To add a new element onto a stack

POP
> To remove the top element from the stack

TOP
> To find the topmost element

Queues

A *queue* is a list to which items are added at the top and from which items are removed at the bottom. Thus, a queue implements a *first in, first out* (FIFO) mechanism. In all other aspects, a queue is exactly the same as a stack. Queues are probably the most used data structure of all because they provide a robust serialization mechanism.

Typical operations on queues are the following:

TOP
> To find the top element

ENQUEUE
> To add a new element to the queue

DEQUEUE
> To remove an element from the queue

In a multiclient application, you can use a queue as a temporary repository for data. For example, several users might collect data through forms on their computers and store the data for each form in a queue. On the server side, you might have one or more interface applications that DEQUEUE and process the sets of data ENQUEUED by the client applications. Serialization is achieved because all client applications place their data into the queue, and all server-side applications pull that data out in the same order in which it was placed into the queue.

Priority queues

A *priority queue* is a special kind of a queue in which the top element—the element that is next in line to be DEQUEUED—is not the oldest one. A priority queue uses a priority property to find the top candidate, thus implementing a *first in, priority out* (FIPO) structure. No matter what the input order, items are DEQUEUED in priority order. The easiest mechanism for implementing a priority queue is to order the elements in the queue by the value of one of their properties. For example, given a queue of scheduling data, you might prioritize based on time, with the most imminent events taking priority over those that are farther out into the future. As you'll see, it is very easy in SQL to implement priority queues once you have the basic mechanisms for stacks and queues in place.

Arrays and Matrices

As opposed to linear data structures, multidimensional data structures are not very natural to SQL. In this chapter, we discuss two types of multidimensional data structure:

- Arrays
- Matrices

It is possible to implement such structures in SQL, but their manipulation soon becomes inefficient, and it is probably worthwhile considering an external implementation where feasible. If you need to perform an operation on arrays or matrices and if you are using MS SQL 2000, consider the TABLE datatype. It provides a convenient way to work with arrays; however, it is limited only to stored procedures and can be used only as temporary storage.

Arrays

An *array* is a multidimensional data structure that, rather than having just one value, can have many values associated with it. An array can have one or more dimensions. A one-dimensional array allows you to store a list of values. A two-dimensional array allows you to store a grid of values, essentially a list of lists. A three-dimensional array allows you to store a cube of values, and so forth. SQL programmers typically must make some compromises when working with arrays to achieve reasonable performance. The most widely used implementation of an array is to have one column in a table store the index of dimension in an array and have other columns store values for the element in question. In other words, each row in an array table stores the coordinates of one array element together with its values.

One of the biggest dangers when working with arrays is to break an array's structure. Therefore, you have to build some mechanism into your implementation to ensure that your array structures remain consistent. Otherwise, operations with arrays are fairly simple. The addition of a new element is as simple as an INSERT with new coordinates. Likewise, the removal of an element is as simple as executing a DELETE.

Matrices

A *matrix* is a special case of array. Matrices have only two dimensions, must be finite, and their indices must arithmetically increase (no gaps). We show operations on matrices to demonstrate that SQL can be used for algebraic operations. However, it is unlikely that you will have much use for matrices in business applications. In the recipes, we show you how to perform arithmetic operations on matrices, how to transpose matrices, how to print matrices, and more.

When working with matrices, SQL can be useful if you store a large number of small matrices in one table. An advantage over other languages is that SQL can easily perform an operation on many elements of a matrix. Other programming languages require you to use a FOR loop or some other kind of looping mechanism to step through all elements of a matrix to perform the operation.

3.2   Working Example

Because of the nature of the material in this chapter, we haven't been able to apply one common example across all the recipes. We have a linear-structure example that we use in our recipes on lists, stacks, and queues. We extend that example to cover arrays. However, when it comes to matrices, we decided to use a simple, textbook-style example for clarity.

Linear Structures

You are building a quality-control system for a biotech company. One of the production lines produces a special liquid for laboratory research. A specific characteristic you need to measure is the liquid's purity, which is indicated by a *purity index*. The normal level of purity is represented by a purity index of 100. Everything over 100 is assumed to be abnormal and requires some action to bring the product back into spec.

The liquid comes off the production line in containers. The table that stores quality control data contains the ID of each container along with the measured purity of the liquid within the container. The following CREATE TABLE statement shows the structure of this table. The ContainerId column contains the container ID numbers, and the Purity column contains the purity index values.

```
CREATE TABLE ProductionLine (
    ContainerId INTEGER,
    Purity INTEGER
)
```

Currently, the table contains purity information on 12 different containers:

```
ContainerId Purity
----------- -----------
1            100
2            100
3            101
4            102
5            103
6            100
7            103
8            108
9            109
10           100
11           100
12           100
```

Your job, our job actually, is to develop some tools to help in evaluating the quality of the product and the functioning of the production machines.

Arrays

To demonstrate the use of arrays, we'll extend our production-line example. If you need to control several production lines, you can represent their purity data as an array. For example:

```
CREATE TABLE ProductionFacility(
    Line INTEGER,
    ContainerId INTEGER,
    Purity INTEGER
)
```

At first glance, this table might not look like an array, but it is. Each row represents one purity-level reading, which is stored in the Purity column. The Line and ContainerId columns are the indices to the array. Given a line number and a container ID number, you can easily retrieve the associated purity value.

Our facility has four production lines, and our ProductionFacility table is currently populated with the following data:

```
Line        ContainerId Purity
----------- ----------- -----------
0           1           100
0           2           100
0           3           100
1           1           102
1           2           103
1           3           100
2           1           103
2           2           108
2           3           109
3           1           100
3           2           100
3           3           100
```

The sequence of rows in this output is not important. And, while we've chosen to identify production lines by number, the production lines could easily be identified by a name or by some other identifier. However, the ContainerId values for each line must not only be numeric; they must be sequential for us to make use of the linear structure and related algorithms that we demonstrate in this chapter's recipes.

Matrices

When you write a program to work with matrices, it's usually best to store your matrices in a table just as you would store arrays. Use one row for each matrix element, and include the element's coordinates as part of that row. For demonstration purposes, we are going to use the following Matrices table:

```
CREATE TABLE Matrices (
    Matrix VARCHAR(20),
    X INTEGER,
    Y INTEGER,
    Value INTEGER
)
```

Each row in the Matrices table represents one matrix element. The columns are used as follows:

Name

Associates a row with a specific matrix. Our table can hold multiple matrices, and each is given a unique name.

X

Holds the X coordinate of the element in question.

Y

Holds the Y coordinate of the element in question.

Value

Holds the value of the element in question.

We fill our sample table with the following:

- Two 2×2 matrices, named A and B
- One vector, named S
- One 3×3 matrix, named D

Following is the output from a SELECT query against the Matrices table, showing the raw data that we are going to operate on in our recipes:

```
SELECT * FROM Matrices:
```

Name	X	Y	Value
A	1	1	6
A	1	2	3
A	2	1	4
A	2	2	7
B	1	1	6
B	1	2	3
B	2	1	5
B	2	2	2
S	1	1	5
S	2	1	6
D	1	1	3
D	1	2	4
D	1	3	5
D	2	1	5
D	2	2	6
D	2	3	7
D	3	1	8
D	3	2	9
D	3	3	0

3.3   Finding Regions

Problem

Find a region in a list. In our example, you must find all containers in the production line that have a purity index of 100. These represent normal production output. Furthermore, you want only cases where at least two containers in succession have a purity of 100. An odd container with a purity of 100 in the midst of a number of containers with bad purity levels is not to be reported as normal production output.

Solution

Look at the problem as a region finding problem and use the following code:

```
SELECT DISTINCT p1.ContainerID
FROM ProductionLine p1, ProductionLine p2
WHERE
    p1.Purity=100 AND p2.Purity=100 AND
    abs(p1.ContainerId-p2.ContainerId)=1

ContainerID
-----------
1
2
10
11
12
```

Discussion

Obviously, if it weren't for the requirement to have at least two containers in a row with normal purity before reporting a container as normal, the result could be obtained by finding all containers with a purity level of 100:

```
SELECT * FROM ProductionLine
WHERE Purity=100
```

To return the correct result, we have to use a technique to find regions in the list. To find neighboring rows with the same value, we need two copies of the same table. We name them p1 and p2:

```
SELECT p1.ContainerID
FROM ProductionLine p1, ProductionLine p2
```

Then, we filter out all rows that do not match the criterion of having one neighbor of the same value. The trick here to finding neighbors is calculating the distance between the p1.ContainerId and p2.ContainerId. If the distance is 1, the two elements are neighbors. If they have the same value, they should be included in the result:

```
SELECT p1.ContainerID
FROM ProductionLine p1, ProductionLine p2
WHERE
    abs(p1.ContainerId-p2.ContainerId)=1
```

We then add another condition to the WHERE clause to restrict the results further to only those cases where the two neighboring containers have a purity of 100:

```
SELECT p1.ContainerID
FROM ProductionLine p1, ProductionLine p2
WHERE
    p1.Purity=100 AND p2.Purity=100 AND
    abs(p1.ContainerId-p2.ContainerId)=1
```

Finally, in the SELECT clause, we use DISTINCT to eliminate repeated references to the same container:

```
SELECT DISTINCT p1.ContainerID
FROM ProductionLine p1, ProductionLine p2
WHERE
    p1.Purity=100 AND p2.Purity=100 AND
    abs(p1.ContainerId-p2.ContainerId)=1
```

You can try to run the query without the DISTINCT clause, and, as you'll see using our sample data, it will return container ID 11 twice. This is because the 11th row has two neighbors with a purity of 100 (10 and 12) and, thus, is reported twice.

3.4   Reporting Region Boundaries

Problem

As in the previous recipe, you want to find regions in the data. However, now you want to report only the boundaries of the regions and not all members of the region. Reporting only region boundaries is useful when a data set is large and/or when the sizes of any regions are expected to be large.

Solution

To find region boundaries in our ProductionLine data, use the following query:

```
SELECT p1.ContainerId RegBeg, p2.ContainerId RegEnd
FROM ProductionLine p1, ProductionLine p2
WHERE (p1.ContainerId < p2.ContainerId) AND
    NOT EXISTS(SELECT * FROM ProductionLine p3
        WHERE (p3.Purity!=100 AND
        p3.ContainerId BETWEEN p1.ContainerId AND p2.ContainerId)
        OR (p3.ContainerId=p1.ContainerId-1 AND p3.Purity=100)
        OR (p3.ContainerId=p2.ContainerId+1 AND p3.Purity=100))

RegBeg      RegEnd
----------- -----------
1           2
10          12
```

Discussion

The solution presented here is based on the idea first published by Rozenshtein, Abramovich, and Birger (*Optimizing Transact-SQL*, Fremont, SQL Forum Press: 1995) and is still considered a classic.

Just as before, we need two tables to find neighboring rows. We name them p1 and p2 and produce a join between them. We then write a "less than" condition in the main query's WHERE clause to make sure that any p1 row represents an element with an index lower than the corresponding p2 row:

```
WHERE (p1.ContainerId < p2.ContainerId) AND
```

Then we write a subquery named p3, which makes use of a third instance of the ProductionLine table. For every candidate pair from the outermost query, we verify that there are no rows between candidates with a purity other than 100:

```
NOT EXISTS(SELECT * FROM ProductionLine p3
       WHERE (p3.Purity!=100 AND
       p3.ContainerId BETWEEN p1.ContainerId AND p2.ContainerId)
```

If there is even one row returned by this subquery, that means the region is broken (i.e., it is not a continuous region of purity=100), and the candidate pair should be discarded. However, this isn't quite enough to get us to our desired result, because the subquery does not eliminate smaller regions that are wholly contained within larger regions. For example, in the region between 10 and 12, we would also find regions 10–11 and 11–12. The solution is in two additional conditions at the end of the subquery that check on the lower and higher boundaries for possible neighbors that comply with the region requirement:

```
(p3.ContainerId=p1.ContainerId-1 AND p3.Purity=100) OR
(p3.ContainerId=p2.ContainerId+1 AND p3.Purity=100)
```

This final set of conditions ensures that only regions that cannot be extended anymore, those that are the largest, are reported.

3.5 Limiting Region Size

Problem

You want to find regions of a certain size. In our example, let's say that you want to find all those regions in which there are exactly two containers of 100 purity. Such regions can be packed automatically for shipment; others must be sorted manually.

Solution

Because we used increasing ContainerId numbers, we can limit the size of a region in the WHERE clause of our query by limiting the distance between indices using the formula SIZE-1. Since we are looking for the regions of size 2, we use 2–1 or 1:

```
SELECT p1.ContainerId RegBeg, p2.ContainerId RegEnd
FROM ProductionLine p1, ProductionLine p2
WHERE (p1.ContainerId < p2.ContainerId) AND
    p2.ContainerId-p1.ContainerId=1 AND
    NOT EXISTS(SELECT * FROM ProductionLine p3
        WHERE (p3.Purity!=100 AND
        p3.ContainerId BETWEEN p1.ContainerId AND p2.ContainerId))
```

```
RegBeg      RegEnd
----------- -----------
1           2
10          11
11          12
```

Discussion

This query is commonly used in various combinatorial problems. It is similar to the query in the previous recipe, but with two important differences. First, it limits the size of the region to a fixed size. Since the table has arithmetically increasing ContainerId values, this can be achieved by a restriction on the difference between two indices.

```
p2.ContainerId-p1.ContainerId=1
```

The second difference is that you do not need to search for the largest possible regions, so the last two conditions in the WHERE clause of the previous recipe's subquery can be omitted from this query.

It is very easy to extend this recipe to find all regions that are larger or smaller than a certain size. For example, to find all regions of two or more containers, use the following WHERE clause restriction:

```
...
p2.ContrainerId - p1.ContainerId >=1
...
```

In the same way, you could limit the query to all regions having five or fewer rows:

```
...
p2.ContrainerId - p1.ContainerId <=4
...
```

These last two modifications would return all candidate regions, even those smaller regions that are inside larger regions. Depending on the results you want, if you use one of these modifications, you may wish to add back those two WHERE conditions from the previous recipe that limited the regions returned to only those that are not contained within another larger region.

3.6 Ranking Regions by Size

Problem

You want to list all regions in the table, and you want to list them according to their size. With respect to our example, you wish to list all regions of two or more containers with a purity of 100, and you wish to sort that list by the number of containers in each region.

Solution

Use the following query to produce the desired list:

```
SELECT
    p1.ContainerId RegBeg, p2.ContainerId RegEnd,
    p2.ContainerId-p1.ContainerId+1 RegionSize
FROM ProductionLine p1, ProductionLine p2
WHERE (p1.ContainerId < p2.ContainerId) AND
    NOT EXISTS(SELECT * FROM ProductionLine p3
        WHERE (p3.Purity!=100 AND
        p3.ContainerId BETWEEN p1.ContainerId AND p2.ContainerId)
        OR (p3.ContainerId=p1.ContainerId-1 AND p3.Purity=100)
        OR (p3.ContainerId=p2.ContainerId+1 AND p3.Purity=100))
ORDER BY p2.ContainerId-p1.ContainerId DESC
```

RegBeg	RegEnd	RegionSize
10	12	3
1	2	2

Discussion

As you can see, this query is similar to the one that is used to find regions. The added feature is the ORDER BY clause, which sorts the regions according to their size. It relies on the fact that the table uses an arithmetically increasing index through which the size of a region can be calculated based on the difference between the two indices making up the region's borders.

Rather than just report the beginning and ending index for each region, this query uses the same calculation in the SELECT list as in the ORDER BY clause to report the size of each region in terms of the number of containers.

The query comes in handy when you have to prepare data for a best-fitting algorithm, and you wish to use the database to presort the data.

You can expand on the solution shown in this recipe, if you like, to show the smallest available region that is still larger than a given size. To do this, add a WHERE clause expression to limit the size of the regions that are sorted. For example:

```
SELECT TOP 1
    p1.ContainerId RegBeg, p2.ContainerId RegEnd,
    p2.ContainerId-p1.ContainerId+1 RegionSize
FROM ProductionLine p1, ProductionLine p2
WHERE
    (p1.ContainerId < p2.ContainerId) AND
    (p2.ContainerId-p1.ContainerId)>=2 AND
    NOT EXISTS(SELECT * FROM ProductionLine p3
        WHERE (p3.Purity!=100 AND
        p3.ContainerId BETWEEN p1.ContainerId AND p2.ContainerId)
        OR (p3.ContainerId=p1.ContainerId-1 AND p3.Purity=100)
        OR (p3.ContainerId=p2.ContainerId+1 AND p3.Purity=100))
ORDER BY p2.ContainerId-p1.ContainerId ASC
```

This query returns the smallest possible region that still fits into the limit. In this case, only the first region that fits the limitations is returned.

3.7   Working with Sequences

Problem

You want to find any arithmetically increasing sequence in the data. In our example, you want to find any sequences in which the purity level is arithmetically increasing (100, 101, 102, etc.). Any such sequences that are three or more containers long indicate that a production line is overheating.

Solution

Find sequences in the ProductionLine data using the following query:

```
SELECT
    p1.ContainerId SeqBeg, p2.ContainerId SeqEnd,
    p2.ContainerId-p1.ContainerId+1 SequenceSize
FROM ProductionLine p1, ProductionLine p2
WHERE
    (p1.ContainerId < p2.ContainerId) AND
    NOT EXISTS(SELECT * FROM ProductionLine p3
        WHERE (p3.Purity-p3.ContainerId!=p1.Purity-p1.ContainerId AND
        p3.ContainerId BETWEEN p1.ContainerId AND p2.ContainerId)
        OR (p3.ContainerId=p1.ContainerId-1 AND
            p3.Purity-p3.ContainerId=p1.Purity-p1.ContainerId)
        OR (p3.ContainerId=p2.ContainerId+1 AND
            p3.Purity-p3.ContainerId=p1.Purity-p1.ContainerId))
```

SeqBeg	SeqEnd	SequenceSize
2	5	4
8	9	2

Discussion

This query uses a framework similar to that used to find regions. The difference is that the subquery contains a WHERE clause condition to identify sequences. To explain exactly how that works, let's begin by looking at the raw data:

ContainerId	Purity	Diff
1	100	99
2	100	98
3	101	98
4	102	98
5	103	98
6	100	94
7	103	96
8	108	100
9	109	100
10	100	90
11	100	89
12	100	88

Notice that the purity levels of containers 2–5 represent an arithmetically increasing sequence. Notice also that the container IDs represent an arithmetically increasing sequence. We can use the fact that both sequences are monotonic to our advantage. It means that, within any given sequence, the difference between the ContainerId and Purity will be a constant. For example:

```
100 - 2 = 98
101 - 3 = 98
...
```

We put knowledge of this pattern to use in the subquery, which uses the following WHERE condition to find any candidates that break the sequence:

```
p3.Purity-p3.ContainerId!=p1.Purity-p1.ContainerId
```

If any row in a candidate sequence (p3) has the same difference as the first row of the sequence (p1), it is a member of the sequence. If not, the candidate pair (p1, p2) should be discarded.

The rest of the framework is exactly the same as for finding regions, and you can easily extend it for sequences in the same ways that you can when finding regions. For example, to find only sequences larger than three rows, add the following WHERE condition:

```
p2.ContainerId-p1.ContainerId>=2 AND
```

For example:

```
SELECT
    p1.ContainerId SeqBeg, p2.ContainerId SeqEnd,
    p2.ContainerId-p1.ContainerId+1 SequenceSize
FROM ProductionLine p1, ProductionLine p2
WHERE
    (p1.ContainerId < p2.ContainerId) AND
    p2.ContainerId-p1.ContainerId>=2 AND
    NOT EXISTS(SELECT * FROM ProductionLine p3
        WHERE (p3.Purity-p3.ContainerId!=p1.Purity-p1.ContainerId AND
        p3.ContainerId BETWEEN p1.ContainerId AND p2.ContainerId)
        OR (p3.ContainerId=p1.ContainerId-1 AND
            p3.Purity-p3.ContainerId=p1.Purity-p1.ContainerId)
        OR (p3.ContainerId=p2.ContainerId+1 AND
            p3.Purity-p3.ContainerId=p1.Purity-p1.ContainerId))
```

SeqBeg	SeqEnd	SequenceSize
2	5	4

With this framework, you can use algorithms for regions and apply them to sequences with minimal changes to the code. Usually, you just have to add an additional condition such as the one we added in this recipe.

3.8   Working with Runs

Problem

You want to find runs in your table. In our example, you want to find any increasing (arithmetically and nonarithmetically) sequences of purity values.

Solutions

Use the following query:

```
SELECT
    p1.ContainerId SeqBeg, p2.ContainerId SeqEnd
FROM ProductionLine p1, ProductionLine p2
WHERE
    (p1.ContainerId < p2.ContainerId) AND
    NOT EXISTS(SELECT * FROM ProductionLine p3, ProductionLine p4
        WHERE (
        p3.Purity<=p4.Purity AND
        p4.ContainerId=p3.ContainerId-1 AND
        p3.ContainerId BETWEEN p1.ContainerId+1 AND p2.ContainerId)
        OR (p3.ContainerId=p1.ContainerId-1 AND p3.Purity<p1.Purity)
        OR (p3.ContainerId=p2.ContainerId+1 AND p3.Purity>p2.Purity))
```

SeqBeg	SeqEnd
2	5
6	9

Discussion

This query uses a framework similar to that which you've seen many times before in this chapter. Unlike a sequence, a run is a continuously increasing, though not necessarily monotonically increasing, series of values. Unlike the previous recipe in which we were looking for monotonically increasing sequences, we do not have a constant difference between ContainerId and Purity values. Consequently, we need a fourth table, p4 in this instance, to check for rows in the middle of a candidate interval that do not comply with the run requirement. This p4 table comes into play in the subquery, where we join it to p3.

For every element between p1 and p2, p3 and its predecessor are compared to see if their values are increasing:

```
p3.Purity<=p4.Purity AND
p4.ContainerId=p3.ContainerId-1 AND
p3.ContainerId BETWEEN p1.ContainerId+1 AND p2.ContainerId
```

The BETWEEN clause limits the scope to rows between the borders (p1 and p2) of the candidate run in question. The p1 border is increased by 1, which covers all pairs within the scope. Note that there is always one less pair than the number of rows.

In a manner similar to other queries for regions and sequences, the last two conditions in the subquery's WHERE clause ensure that the borders of the candidate run cannot be extended:

```
(p3.ContainerId=p1.ContainerId-1 AND p3.Purity<p1.Purity) OR
(p3.ContainerId=p2.ContainerId+1 AND p3.Purity>p2.Purity)
```

If a row can be returned to satisfy these conditions, then the run can be extended and should be rejected in favor of the larger run.

The common framework that this solution shares with earlier recipes allows you to take techniques presented earlier for regions and sequences and apply them to runs.

3.9   Cumulative Aggregates in Lists

Problem

You need to report cumulative totals and averages. With respect to our example, assume that the Purity value is, instead, a measure of weight, say kilograms. For packaging purposes, you want to see at which container the total weight of a production line's output rises above 1,000. Likewise, you are interested to see how each additional container affects the average weight in a shipment.

Solution

Use the following query to calculate both a cumulative total and a running average weight in one pass:

```
SELECT
    p1.ContainerId, SUM(p2.Purity) Total, AVG(p2.Purity) Average
FROM ProductionLine p1, ProductionLine p2
WHERE
    p1.ContainerId >= p2.ContainerId
GROUP BY p1.ContainerId
```

ContainerId	Total	Average
1	100	100
2	200	100
3	301	100
4	403	100
5	506	101
6	606	101
7	709	101
8	817	102
9	926	102
10	1026	102
11	1126	102
12	1226	102

Discussion

The code uses an old SQL trick for ordering. You take two instances of the ProductionLine table, named p1 and p2, and you cross-join them. Then you group the results by p1.ContainerId, and you limit the second table's (p2's) rows so that they have ContainerId values smaller than the p1 row to which they are joined. This forces the server to produce an intermediate result set that looks as follows:

p1_Id	p1_Purity	p2_Id	p2_Purity
1	100	1	100
2	100	1	100
2	100	2	100
3	101	1	100
3	101	2	100
3	101	3	101
4	102	1	100
4	102	2	100
4	102	3	101
4	102	4	102
5	103	1	100
...			

Each group, identified by p1.ContainerId, includes all rows from p2 with lower or equivalent ContainerId values. The AVG and SUM functions are then applied to the p2_Purity column. The two functions work on p2 rows in each group and, thus, calculate cumulative results.

3.10   Implementing a Stack

Problem

You need to implement a stack data structure in SQL. With respect to our example, you need to build an interface to a processing machine that adds and removes containers to and from the production line. The production line should be handled as a stack. Therefore, you must implement the POP, PUSH, and TOP functions.

Solution

Use the ProductionLine table as a stack. The following sections show how to implement the various stack functions using SQL. Notice our use of the ContainerId column to keep stack elements in their proper order. Each new element pushed onto the stack gets a higher ContainerId value than the previous element. The top of the stack is defined as the row with the highest ContainerId value.

TOP function in SQL

Implementing the TOP function is very easy. You just use the SELECT statement to retrieve the most recently added row in the stack, which, by definition, will be the row with the highest ContainerId value.

```
SELECT TOP 1 * FROM ProductionLine ORDER BY ContainerId DESC
```

If you want to embed the query into a procedure and expand it, use the following framework:

```
CREATE PROCEDURE TopProduction
AS
SELECT TOP 1 * FROM ProductionLine ORDER BY ContainerId DESC
```

POP function in SQL

The POP function is implemented here as a procedure to give you a framework that you can build on. The first statement is our TOP function, which retrieves the topmost element in the stack. The second select prints that element. The delete statement then removes the element from the stack.

```
CREATE PROCEDURE Pop
AS
DECLARE @id INTEGER

SELECT TOP 1 @id=ContainerId FROM ProductionLine
    ORDER BY ContainerId DESC
SELECT * FROM ProductionLine WHERE @id=ContainerId
DELETE FROM ProductionLine WHERE @id=ContainerId
```

PUSH function in SQL

The PUSH function adds a new element to the stack. The first SELECT retrieves the top Id. Then the new element is inserted. The last SELECT in the procedure prints the new top element so that you can verify that it was added correctly.

```
CREATE PROCEDURE Push @Purity INTEGER
AS
DECLARE @id INTEGER

SELECT TOP 1 @id=ContainerId FROM ProductionLine
    ORDER BY ContainerId DESC
INSERT INTO ProductionLine(ContainerId,Purity) VALUES(@id+1, @Purity)
SELECT * FROM ProductionLine WHERE ContainerId=@id+1
```

Discussion

SQL is very convenient for the implementation of linear data structures. In this recipe, we work with an often encountered problem, in which serialization is required, but for which there is no need for a full-sized transactional system.

The code shown in our solution is a simplified version of a real-world system. If you want to use the concept in a live system, make sure that you make the procedures transactional. In addition, if more than one user is using the POP and PUSH functions, use some increment mechanism other than the plain MAX function used in our solution. For example, you can use SQL server's native solutions, such as Microsoft's IDENITY or UNIQUEIDENTIFIER datatypes to ensure uniqueness of id values. Be careful: such solutions can be costly and are not always applicable.

In order to test the functions, try the sequence in the following example:

```
PUSH 120


ContainerId Purity
----------- -----------
13          120


PUSH 130


ContainerId Purity
----------- -----------
14          130


POP
```

```
ContainerId Purity
----------- -----------
14          130


POP

ContainerId Purity
----------- -----------
13          120
```

As you can see, the functions work as expected, and they add or remove the elements on the stack.

Our sample functions simply display data retrieved from the stack, but you could easily store the return values in variables for further manipulation.

Following this pattern, you can implement stack mechanisms using any SQL table, as long as there is a column such as ContainerId that you can use to establish an ordering of the stack elements.

3.11   Implementing Queues

Problem

You need to implement a queue with standard operations, such as TOP, ENQUEUE, and DEQUEUE. With respect to our example, you wish to implement the same sort of functionality as in the previous recipe, but this time you wish to treat the production line as a queue, not as a stack.

Solution

Use the ProductionLine table as a queue. The following sections then show you how to implement the standard queuing functions.

TOP function in SQL

```
SELECT TOP 1 *  FROM ProductionLine ORDER BY ContainerId ASC
```

DEQUEUE function in SQL

```
CREATE PROCEDURE dequeue
AS
DECLARE @id INTEGER

SELECT TOP 1 @id=ContainerId FROM ProductionLine ORDER BY ContainerId ASC
SELECT * FROM ProductionLine WHERE @id=ContainerId
DELETE FROM ProductionLine WHERE @id=ContainerId
```

ENQUEUE function in SQL

```
CREATE PROCEDURE enqueue @Purity INTEGER
AS
DECLARE @id INTEGER

SELECT TOP 1 @id=ContainerId FROM ProductionLine ORDER BY ContainerId DESC
INSERT INTO ProductionLine(ContainerId,Purity) VALUES(@id+1, @Purity)
SELECT * FROM ProductionLine WHERE ContainerId=@id+1
```

Discussion

As you can see, the queue mechanisms are very similar to the stack mechanisms. In fact, the only difference is in the TOP function. When working with queues, the TOP function always looks for the oldest element in the table, not for the most recently added element. We accomplished this by ordering ASC rather than DESC.

To create the DEQUEUE function, we took the POP function that we used for our stack solution and changed the TOP statement (the first SELECT) so that the function became a DEQUEUE function. The PUSH and ENQUEUE functions actually use the same code, because the process for adding an element to a queue is the same as for adding an element to a stack.

Please note that since we are adding elements to the top and removing them from the bottom, the ContainerId value is always increasing. If, when implementing a queue, you think you might possibly run out of index values, you'll need to code some sort of reset mechanism to wrap the index back around to the beginning once its upper limit is reached.

3.12   Implementing Priority Queues

Problem

You need to implement priority-based queues. In our example, the higher the purity index, the higher the priority. For these queues, you want to implement standard operations such as TOP, ENQUEUE, or DEQUEUE.

Solution

As with stacks and regular queues, we can implement the priority queue in the ProductionLine table.

TOP function in SQL

```
SELECT TOP 1 *  FROM ProductionLine ORDER BY Purity DESC
```

DEQUEUE function in SQL

```
CREATE PROCEDURE dequeue
AS
DECLARE @id INTEGER

SELECT TOP 1 @id=ContainerId FROM ProductionLine ORDER BY Purity DESC
SELECT * FROM ProductionLine WHERE @id=ContainerId
DELETE FROM ProductionLine WHERE @id=ContainerId
```

ENQUEUE function in SQL

```
CREATE PROCEDURE enqueue @Purity INTEGER
AS
DECLARE @id INTEGER

SELECT TOP 1 @id=ContainerId FROM ProductionLine ORDER BY ContainerId DESC
INSERT INTO ProductionLine(ContainerId,Purity) VALUES(@id+1, @Purity)
SELECT * FROM ProductionLine WHERE ContainerId=@id+1
```

Discussion

Priority queues use a framework almost identical to that used for stacks and regular queues. The difference, again, is only in how the TOP function is implemented. When you adjust TOP to look at the queue in terms of priority, in our case at the Purity column, all the other pieces fall into place. The ENQUEUE function is the same as for regular queues. Except for the use of a priority-based TOP function, the DEQUEUE function is also the same as that for regular queues.

 When you use a table as a priority queue, the ENQUEUE function can no longer ensure a monotonically increasing index (as is the case with stacks and queues). That's because the DEQUEUE function takes elements out of the queue based on their priority and not their index. For example, if you have 10 elements identified with index values 1 through 10 and the fifth element is removed because it has the highest priority, there will be a gap in the index. But when you add a new element, the ENQUEUE function will not fill that gap, but rather add the new element with an index value of 11. It's easy to overlook this behavior, which can cause some confusion, so keep it in mind as you work with priority queues.

3.13   Comparing Two Rows in an Array

Problem

You want to check to see whether two rows in an array are equal. In our example, you want to check if two production lines in the ProductionFacility table are equal.

Solution

To check rows in the table for equality, use the following code. The result will be a list of rows in the array that are equivalent:

```
SELECT p1.Line p1_Line, 'is equal to', p2.Line p2_Line
FROM ProductionFacility p1, ProductionFacility p2
WHERE p1.Purity=p2.Purity AND p1.ContainerId=p2.ContainerId AND
    p1.Line<p2.Line
GROUP BY p1.Line, p2.Line
HAVING
    COUNT(*)=(SELECT COUNT(*) FROM ProductionFacility p3 WHERE p3.Line=p1.Line)
    AND
    COUNT(*)=(SELECT COUNT(*) FROM ProductionFacility p4 WHERE p4.Line=p2.Line)

p1_Line                 p2_Line
----------- ----------- -----------
0           is equal to 3
```

Discussion

This query ends up being quite expensive, using four table instances; as a result, it is a good demonstration of how SQL is not very efficient in working with arrays. However, expensive as it is, it does allow you to get results using only one query.

The FROM clause creates a cross-join between the two instances of the Production-Facility. We name the two instances p1 and p2 for easier reference. We define in the SELECT statement that the result will report one line for each pair of rows that are equal. Since the cross-join produces many rows, we use the GROUP BY statement to limit the result to just one row of output per row in the array.

The WHERE clause specifies three conditions:

- Purity levels must be equal.
- Container IDs must be equal.
- Production-line numbers from p1 must be less than those from p2.

If you work with multidimensional arrays, simply add additional comparison clauses to the WHERE clause to compare parameters for equality. To compare for full equality between two rows, you must have one comparison expression for each dimension in your array. In our example, the two comparison clauses involve the ContainerId and Line columns. The comparison expression involving the Purity columns is what we use to determine whether two array elements are equal. So a match on ContainerId and Line defines two elements that need to be compared, and the test of equality involves the Purity column.

The intermediate results at this point, without the GROUP BY clause, are as follows:

```
SELECT p1.ContainerId, p1.Purity, p1.Line, p2.Line
FROM ProductionFacility p1, ProductionFacility p2
WHERE p1.Purity=p2.Purity AND p1.ContainerId=p2.ContainerId AND
    p1.Line<p2.Line
```

```
ContainerId Purity     Line        Line
----------- ---------- ----------- -----------
3           100        0           1
1           100        0           3
2           100        0           3
3           100        0           3
3           100        1           3
```

Add in the GROUP BY clause and we get:

```
SELECT COUNT(*) ContainerCount, p1.Line, p2.Line
FROM ProductionFacility p1, ProductionFacility p2
WHERE p1.Purity=p2.Purity AND p1.ContainerId=p2.ContainerId AND
    p1.Line<p2.Line
GROUP BY p1.Line, p2.Line
```

```
ContainerCount Line        Line
-------------- ----------- -----------
1              0           1
3              0           3
1              1           3
```

The HAVING clause is the expensive one. It compares the number of matched pairs from the WHERE clause to the number of columns in both rows. The first subquery checks for the number of rows in p1, and the second, for the number of rows in p2. The HAVING clause makes sure that only lines of equal size are reported in the final result. In our example, each production line has produced three containers. Looking at the intermediate results shown here, you can see that the only two production lines with a container count of three are lines 0 and 3. The HAVING clause ensures that those are reported as the final output from the query.

3.14   Printing Matrices and Arrays

Problem

You want to print a matrix and an array.

Solution

Use the following pivoting technique, which, in this case, prints matrix D:

```
SELECT  X,
    MAX(CASE Y WHEN 1 THEN Value END) y1,
    MAX(CASE Y WHEN 2 THEN Value END) y2,
    MAX(CASE Y WHEN 3 THEN Value END) y3
```

```
FROM Matrices
WHERE Matrix='D'
GROUP BY X
ORDER BY X

X            y1           y2           y3
----------- ----------- ----------- -----------
1            3            4            5
2            5            6            7
3            8            9            0
```

Discussion

See the discussion on the use of Pivot tables in Chapter 1. Note particularly that the number of CASE expressions must match the Y dimension of the matrix. In this case, we know the matrix we want to print has three columns, so we wrote three CASE expressions.

Let's say that you want to print an array in a report-like fashion with each dimension in a separate column. In our example, you wish to print a report of purity levels for all containers in all production lines, and you wish each production line to be represented by its own column.

Use the same pivoting technique as used earlier in the recipe for printing matrices:

```
SELECT  ContainerId,
    MAX(CASE Line WHEN 0 THEN Purity END) Line0,
    MAX(CASE Line WHEN 1 THEN Purity END) Line1,
    MAX(CASE Line WHEN 2 THEN Purity END) Line2,
    MAX(CASE Line WHEN 3 THEN Purity END) Line3
FROM ProductionFacility
GROUP BY ContainerId
ORDER BY ContainerId

ContainerId Line0        Line1        Line2        Line3
----------- ----------- ----------- ----------- -----------
1            100          102          103          100
2            100          103          108          100
3            100          100          109          100
```

3.15   Transposing a Matrix

Problem

You want to transpose a matrix. To transpose a matrix, swap all X and Y values. For example, an element located at X=1, Y=2 will be swapped with the element located at X=2, Y=1.

Solution

Follow the pattern used for the following query, which transposes matrix D:

```
SELECT Y AS X, X AS Y, Value
FROM Matrices
WHERE Matrix='D'
```

```
X             Y             Value
-----------   -----------   -----------
1             1             3
2             2             4
3             3             5
1             1             5
2             2             6
3             3             7
1             1             8
2             2             9
3             3             0
```

Discussion

Transposition is probably one of the easiest operations on matrices. The only thing you have to do is to report X as Y and Y as X, and that transposes the matrix. If you wish to store your transposition—this recipe only prints the transposed version—you can write an INSERT . . . SELECT . . . FROM statement:

```
INSERT INTO Matrices
SELECT 'Dt',Y, X, Value
FROM Matrices
WHERE Matrix='D'
```

This statement transposes matrix D and stores the results in a new matrix named Dt.

3.16   Calculating a Matrix Trace

Problem

You want to calculate the trace of a matrix. The *trace* of a matrix is the summation of values along the matrix's main diagonal.

Solution

Use the following query to calculate the trace of a matrix. In this case, we calculate the trace of the matrix D.

```
SELECT SUM(Value) Trace
FROM Matrices
WHERE Matrix='D' and X=Y
```

The result:

```
Trace
-----------
9
```

Discussion

When the X and Y coordinates of an element are the same, the element is on the main diagonal. The WHERE clause in this query restricts the results to only those elements. We need to add those elements together, which we do using the SUM function, and we have the trace of the matrix.

3.17   Comparing Two Matrices for Size

Problem

You want to compare two matrices to see whether they are equal in size. By equal in size, we mean that their highest X and Y dimensions are the same.

Solution

To compare matrices A and B for size, use the following query:

```
SELECT m1.Matrix, 'is of equal size as', m2.Matrix
FROM Matrices m1, Matrices m2
WHERE m1.X=m2.X AND m1.Y=m2.Y AND m1.Matrix='A' AND m2.Matrix='B'
GROUP BY m1.Matrix, m2.Matrix
HAVING
    COUNT(*)=(SELECT COUNT(*) FROM Matrices WHERE Matrix='A')
    AND COUNT(*)=(SELECT COUNT(*) FROM Matrices WHERE Matrix='B')

Matrix                                  Matrix
------------------- ------------------- --------------------
A                   is of equal size as B
```

Discussion

Some matrix operations require that the matrices involved are the same size. Use the query in this recipe to verify that such is the case.

First, we create two instances of the Matrices table (m1 and m2) and restrict each to one of the matrices that we are interested in. In our case, m1 represents matrix A, while m2 represents matrix B. If the matrices are equal, this will give us two rows for each combination of X and Y index values.

Next, in the WHERE clause, we match the coordinates of the two matrices. The GROUP BY clause is used so that query reports only one row of output. The results are grouped by the two matrix names. The HAVING clause then tests to ensure that the total number of rows summarized matches the total number of elements in A and B. If the totals all match, the two matrices are the same size.

3.18   Adding and Subtracting Matrices

Problem

You want to add or subtract matrices in the table.

Solution

To add matrices A and B, use:

```
SELECT DISTINCT m1.X, m2.Y, m1.Value+m2.Value Value
FROM Matrices m1, Matrices m2
WHERE m1.Matrix='A' AND m2.Matrix='B'
   AND m1.X=m2.X AND m1.Y=m2.Y
```

X	Y	Value
1	1	12
1	2	6
2	1	9
2	2	9

To subtract matrix B from matrix A, use this query, but replace the plus sign with a minus sign. The results of A–B are:

x	y	Value
1	1	0
1	2	0
2	1	-1
2	2	5

Discussion

This code follows the definitions of matrix addition and subtraction from algebra. To add two matrices, they must be of the same dimension (i.e., they must be equal), and then you just add elements on the same coordinates. Subtraction works the same way, except that you subtract element values rather than add.

The trick to this recipe's solution is in matching the elements on the same coordinates from the two matrices. We assume that the matrices are already of the same dimension; in other words, we assume they are equal. Then, we create two instances of the Matrices table (m1 and m2). We restrict m1 in the WHERE clause so that it represents matrix A, and we restrict m2 so that it represents matrix B. The elements of each matrix are now matched, and the plus or minus operator in the SELECT clause calculates the sum or difference.

3.19   Multiplying Matrices

Problem

You want to implement matrix multiplication in SQL.

Solution

There are three ways that you can multiply a matrix:

- By a scalar value
- By a vector of values
- By another matrix

When multiplying by a vector, the length of the vector must correspond to the maximum X index. When you multiply two matrices, the matrices must be equal.

Multiplying a matrix by a scalar value

To multiply matrix A by scalar 5, just multiply all rows of that matrix by 5:

```
SELECT DISTINCT X, Y ,Value*5 Value
FROM Matrices
WHERE Matrix='A'
```

```
X           Y           Value
----------- ----------- -----------
1           1           30
1           2           15
2           1           20
2           2           35
```

Multiplying a matrix with a vector

To multiply matrix A by scalar S, use the following query:

```
SELECT m1.X, SUM(m1.Value*v.Value) VALUE
FROM Matrices m1, Matrices v
WHERE m1.Matrix='A' AND v.Matrix='S' AND m1.Y=v.X
GROUP BY m1.X
```

```
X           Value
----------- -----------
1           48
2           62
```

Multiplying two matrices

To multiply matrix A by matrix B, use the following code:

```
SELECT m1.X, m2.Y, SUM(m1.Value*m2.Value) Value
FROM Matrices m1, Matrices m2
WHERE m1.Matrix='A' AND m2.Matrix='B' AND m1.Y=m2.X
GROUP BY m1.X, m2.Y
```

```
X           Y           Value
----------- ----------- -----------
1           1           51
2           1           59
1           2           24
2           2           26
```

Discussion

The biggest danger while working with matrices is in the confusion of indices. The SQL statements in this recipe can be used only if matrices or vectors are represented exactly as in our example. In any case, it is probably a good idea to check the indices carefully in the query.

Another issue to be concerned about is that you must ensure that you are multiplying data with the appropriate dimensions. When multiplying two matrices, their dimensions must match. When multiplying a matrix by a vector, the dimension of the vector must match the X dimension of the matrix. While it's possible to extend these queries to check for dimensional equality, this significantly increases the cost. If you can, it's best to build such checking mechanisms somewhere else.

Multiplying by a scalar

The easiest of multiplications uses SQL features to extract all elements of a matrix easily and just multiply them with a scalar. The SELECT list of such a query simply uses multiplication, in our case Value*5, to return the specified results.

Multiplying by a vector

Multiplication of a matrix by a vector is a bit more difficult. In our example, if we write down the matrix A and the vector S together, we will get the following:

```
Matrix A:   6   3
            4   7

Vector S:   5   6
```

Algebraic rules state that the first vector element multiplies values in the first matrix column, the second vector element multiplies values in the second matrix column, and so forth. This gives us the following matrix of values:

```
6x5   3x6
4x5   7x6
```

The final step is to sum all the values in each row of this matrix, so the result is a vector:

```
6x5 + 3x6 = 30 + 18 = 48
4x5 + 7x6 = 20 + 42 = 62
```

As you can see, the result of multiplying a matrix by a vector is another vector. In our case, the result vector is as follows:

```
48    62
```

Multiplying by a matrix

The query to multiply two matrices together uses the same principle as the query for multiplying a matrix by a vector. The query cross-matches the elements according to their position, performs multiplications, and sums the results of those multiplications so that the result is a vector. In our example, the following two matrices are multiplied together:

```
Matrix A        Matrix B
  6   3           6   3
  4   7           5   2
```

When we say that in matrix multiplication you "cross-match" elements, we mean that that X,Y values from one matrix are multiplied by the corresponding Y,X values from the other. For example, element 1,2 from matrix A must be multiplied by element 2,1 from matrix B. In our example, this cross-matching yields the following multiplications:

```
6*6     3*5
4*6     7*5
6*3     3*2
4*3     7*2
```

The results must then be summed into a vector:

```
6*6 + 3*5 = 36 + 15 = 51
4*6 + 7*5 = 24 + 35 = 59
6*3 + 3*2 = 18 +  6 = 24
4*3 + 7*2 = 12 + 14 = 26
```

Squaring a matrix

The matrix multiplication query can easily be modified to square a matrix. To square a matrix is to multiply it by itself. The only thing that has to be changed is that both m1 and m2 must be restricted to the same matrix. In the following example, m1 and m2 both represent matrix A:

```
SELECT m1.X, m2.Y, SUM(m1.Value*m2.Value) Value
FROM Matrices m1, Matrices m2
WHERE m1.Matrix='A' AND m2.Matrix='A' AND m1.Y=m2.X
GROUP BY m1.X, m2.Y
```

The results are then the square of A:

```
X           Y           Value
----------- ----------- -----------
1           1           48
2           1           52
1           2           39
2           2           61
```

CHAPTER 4
Hierarchies in SQL

Hierarchical structures have a sort of nondeterministic nature in that the exact structure is determined only when you populate the hierarchy with data. This makes them appealing for various sorts of applications. An employment hierarchy is a classical example of such a structure. A company will have employees. Supervisors will be assigned to lead groups of employees. Those supervisors, in turn, will report to managers. Low-level managers will report to higher-level managers. Eventually, you get to the top where you often find a chief executive officer (CEO). If you sketch it out, the typical company organization chart will look like an upside down tree, with some branches in the tree being wider and narrower than others. Hierarchical structures are widely used in procedural languages, such as C, but are rather underutilized in SQL, because they conflict with the inherent table-shaped data layout of relational databases.

Almost any type of complex application can make use of a hierarchical model to some degree or another. The recipes in this chapter show you how to manipulate hierarchical data using Transact-SQL. This chapter will discuss three major topics:

- Specialized hierarchies
- General hierarchies
- Efficiency extensions

Some vendors, Oracle Corporation being among the most notable, have extended their SQL syntax with additional functionality to support querying hierarchical data. Unfortunately, neither Sybase nor Microsoft have chosen to implement such extensions in Transact-SQL. Although the Transact-SQL language hasn't been designed to support dynamic structures such as trees, programmers have come up with some reasonably efficient design patterns that address the common operations that you need to perform on hierarchical data. As an added bonus, the lack of vendor-specific functionality tends to make these solutions more easily portable across database platforms.

4.1   Types of Hierarchies

There are two types of hierarchies that we recognize in this chapter: specialized hierarchies and general hierarchies. In a *specialized hierarchy*, you are limited in the maximum depth of the hierarchy. As you'll see in the recipes, SQL is quite unique since you can implement proper general hierarchies with unlimited depth. In a *general hierarchy*, you cannot define a maximum depth.

In the first part of this chapter, we are going to show you how specialized hierarchies can be implemented in a SQL Server database. We'll also show you how you can make use of their special property. Our recipe solutions are based on a real-world example of a hierarchical structure used to manage permissions in an online trading system.

Next, our discussion will turn to general hierarchies. Because general hierarchies allow nodes to be nested to any depth, manipulating them requires using generalized solutions. Often, these solutions involve recursion. We'll begin by showing you what you can do using a pure hierarchical model, and we'll show both recursive and nonrecursive algorithms. Then, we'll show you how you can improve the efficiency of a hierarchical model by adding what we term *service information* to it.

Before going further into the chapter, we'd like to review some of the terminology that we use when we discuss hierarchies. Figure 4-1 illustrates a hierarchical structure, and many of the elements are labeled with the terms that we use to refer to them.

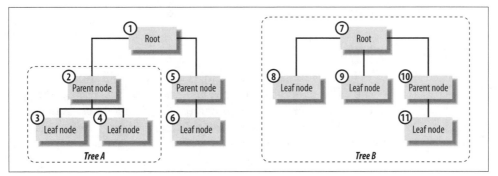

Figure 4-1. A hierarchical structure

The following list contains our definitions for the terms shown in Figure 4-1, as well as for some other terms that we use in this chapter:

Hierarchy
> Refers, generally, to a hierarchical structure. For example, employee relationships in a business represent a hierarchy.

Tree
> Refers to a specific manifestation of a hierarchical structure. A specific organizational chart would be an example of a tree. As Figure 4-1 shows, hierarchically structured data may consist of more than one tree.

Subtree

Refers to a tree that is known to not start at the root node. The term *branch* is sometimes used as a synonym for subtree.

Node

Refers to an element in a tree.

Leaf node

Refers to an element in a tree that does not have any child nodes. A leaf node, sometimes just referred to as a leaf, is a special case of the more generic node.

Root

Refers to the node having no parents. Any given tree will have exactly one root node.

Parent

Refers to a node that has other nodes (child nodes) underneath it.

Child

Refers to a node that falls underneath another node (a parent node).

Vertex

Is a synonym for node.

In a hierarchy, child nodes are subordinate to, and belong to, their parents. If you delete a node, or move a node, that operation affects not only the node on which you are operating, but also all of its children. For example, if you delete node 2, as shown in Figure 4-1, you are also implicitly deleting nodes 3 and 4.

Specialized Hierarchies

Specialized hierarchies can be found in almost any real-world application. However, they aren't always manifested in an obvious way, and programmers often don't even realize that what they are actually doing is programming a hierarchy. When programming for a specialized hierarchy, you can take advantage of limitations such as a limited number of nodes, a limited number of levels, the fact that only leaves hold data, or some other specialized aspect of the hierarchy in question.

As a basis for the recipes in this chapter, we've used a permission-hierarchy example that is taken from an online trading system that is actually in production use. We've simplified our example somewhat for demonstration purposes. The purpose of the mechanism is to implement support for an order-routing system in which traders have different permissions relating to trades that they can make. An automatic system processes orders according to given permission rules. If a trader sends an order through a system for which he is not authorized, the system rejects the order before submitting it to the market. The following data is an example of some of the rules that the system must enforce:

```
Trader    Type     Limit
---------------------------
Alex      Shares    100
Alex      Futures    10
Alex      Bond       10
Cindy     Shares   1000
Cindy     Bonds    1000
Michael   Shares    200
...
```

As you can see, there are several types of permissions granted to each trader. Alex, for example, can trade shares of stock in blocks of no more than 100 shares. Cindy, on the other hand, is allowed to trade in blocks of up to 1,000 shares. If you were designing a database structure to hold rules like these, the simplistic approach would be simply to define permissions for each specific trader using the system. However, it's likely to be more practical to group those permissions so that supervisors can easily grant a set of permissions to a particular trader. For example, you could have permission groups for commodity traders, future traders, and spot market traders. The resulting hierarchy would be the limited hierarchy shown in Figure 4-2.

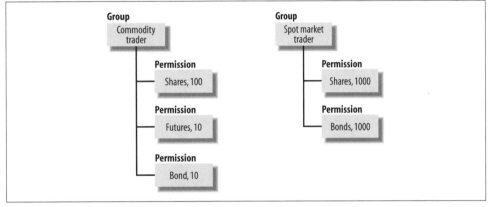

Figure 4-2. The limited-trading permission hierarchy

Some might look at this scheme and see two distinct entities: groups and permissions. That's probably a valid view, but we would argue that, at a higher level of abstraction, this structure represents a limited hierarchy of only two levels. The highest level is the group level, and the level below that is the permission level. When writing code to query and manage this hierarchy, you can take advantage of the fact that it's limited to only two levels of depth. You can use solutions that are specific for that case that are more efficient than those that you would need to navigate a more generalized and unrestricted hierarchy. The recipes we have in this chapter highlight the considerations that you need to take into account, as well as the efficiencies that you gain, when working with a specialized hierarchy such as that shown in Figure 4-2.

General Hierarchies

The standard model for representing general hierarchies is to set up a parent/child relationship. The implementation in Transact-SQL, however, is different from tree-structure implementations in other programming languages. Hierarchical structures implemented in Transact-SQL have two characteristics that distinguish them from hierarchical structures implemented in a programming language such as C:

- A lack of pointers
- An unlimited number of children

Programmers using C, or other procedural languages, to implement hierarchies usually deal with fixed-size structures in which the parent and child nodes are linked with pointers. Moving from one node to another is fairly inexpensive in terms of the resources that are consumed, because such a move involves only the swapping of a couple of pointers in memory. With SQL, on the other hand, a move between nodes usually involves disk I/O, because each node ends up being a row in a table. Disk I/O is expensive in terms of the time and resources consumed, so SQL programmers need to be very careful about the number of visits they make to each node. An advantage of SQL, though, is that it's easy to allow for an unlimited number of children. Unlike the fixed structures often used in procedural languages, database tables have no arbitrary limit on the number of rows they may contain.

The design of a hierarchy is a good example of a case in which how you model your data is much more important than the actual algorithms that you use to manipulate your data. The following CREATE TABLE statement shows the structure most often used to represent general hierarchies in a relational database:

```
CREATE TABLE Hierarchy(
    VertexId INTEGER,
    Parent INTEGER,
    ...
    PRIMARY KEY(VertexId)
)
```

In this structure, each row in the Hierarchy table represents one node. The VertexId field contains a unique address for each node. Each node then points back to its parent by storing the parent's VertexId value in the Parent field. Using such a structure, you can create an unlimited number of children for each parent.

SQL programmers have been using this type of structure for some time, and it looks great from a design point of view. However, SQL has strangely weak support for hierarchies. If you aren't careful, the code you write to manipulate a hierarchical structure, such as the one shown here, can be inefficient and lead to a host of performance problems.

We have several recipes in this chapter that show reasonably efficient solutions for common operations that you'll need to perform on generalized hierarchical data. These solutions are based on the example of a project-tracking database that you manage. In this project-tracking database, you store data about projects and their subprojects. Any given project can be broken up into an arbitrary number of subprojects for planning purposes. Those subprojects can be further broken up into even smaller subprojects. This process can continue for any number of levels of depth. Eventually, you get down to the bottom-level in which the subprojects have no children. A subproject with no children is referred to as a *task*. Your job is to build SQL queries, procedures, and functions in support of a project-tracking application.

Data about projects and subprojects is stored in the Projects table, which is defined as follows:

```
CREATE TABLE Projects(
    Name VARCHAR(20),
    Cost INTEGER,
    Parent INTEGER,
    VertexId INTEGER,
    Primary key(VertexId)
)
```

The first two columns—the Name and Cost columns—represent the actual project and subproject data. In a real application, you would have more information than that, but these two columns will suffice for the purposes of example. The remaining two columns in the table are used to define the hierarchy. The VertexId column contains a unique identifier for each project, subproject, and task. The Parent column in any given row points to the parent project or subproject for that row. Figure 4-3 provides a visual illustration of this hierarchy.

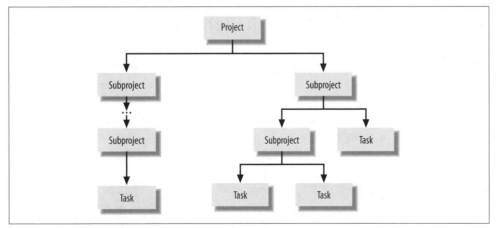

Figure 4-3. The general project-tracking hierarchy

The scripts named *ch04.*.objects.sql* (downloadable from this book's web site) will create and populate all the tables used in this chapter's recipes. When you run the script, you'll get the following data in the Projects table:

```
Name                  Cost         Parent       VertexId
-------------------- ------------ ------------ ------------
New SW                0            0            1
Specifications        0            1            2
Interviews            5            2            3
Drafts                10           2            4
Consolidations        2            2            5
Final document        15           2            6
Presentation          1            6            7
Prototype             0            1            8
UI Design             10           8            9
Calculations          10           8            10
Correctness Testing   3            10           11
Database              10           8            12
Development           30           1            13
UI Implementation     10           13           14
Coding                20           13           15
Initial testing       40           13           16
Beta testing          40           1            17
Final adjustments     5            17           18
Production testing    20           1            19
```

As you can see, the Parent column is used to maintain the hierarchical structure of the project data. Each child has only one parent, so only one Parent column is needed for each row in the table. Consequently, an unlimited number of children can be created for any given project or subproject. Figure 4-4 shows a graphical view of our example project.

4.2   Creating a Permission Hierarchy

Problem

You need to create a system for maintaining a simple permission hierarchy for a trading system. This hierarchy needs to be similar to the one described earlier in "Specialized Hierarchies." Permissions should be manageable in groups so a set of permissions can be granted to a trader easily. In addition, your solution needs to allow for permission types to be added dynamically while the system is in production.

Solution

Define two tables. In the first table, define groups of permissions; in the second table, link those groups to particular traders. Each trader can belong to more than one permission group. The table defining the permission groups can be defined as follows:

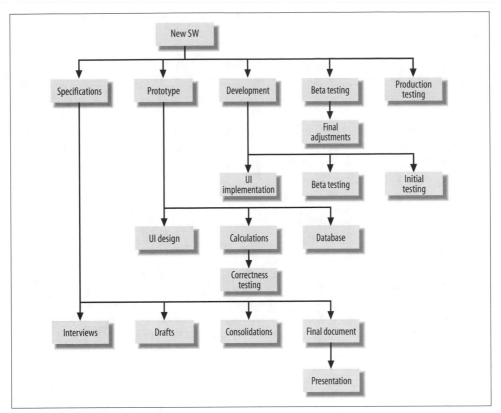

Figure 4-4. The sample project

```
CREATE TABLE GroupPermissions(
    GroupId VARCHAR(20) NOT NULL,
    ProductType VARCHAR(10) NOT NULL,
    Status CHAR(1) CHECK(status in ('V','S')) DEFAULT('V'),
    Limit NUMERIC(10,2) NULL,
    PRIMARY KEY(GroupId,ProductType)
)
```

In our GroupPermissions table, there are two attributes describing trading permissions for each product group. One attribute is a status attribute. The status of each trading permission can be set to valid ('V') or suspended ('S'). The second attribute is an order limit that defines the maximum permitted size for a trade involving the product group. If a trader is authorized to trade bonds and has a trading limit of 1,000, that trader is not allowed to initiate a trade involving more than 1,000 bonds. The following is a representative sample of the type of data that you could store in this table:

```
GroupId              ProductType Status Limit
-------------------- ----------- ------ ------------
Debt                 Bill        V      10000.00
Debt                 Bond        V      10000.00
Derivatives          Future      V      200.00
Derivatives          Option      V      100.00
Equities             Share       V      1000.00
```

The second table needs to keep track of the permission groups assigned to each trader. Its definition can be as follows:

```
CREATE TABLE GroupMembership(
    AccountId VARCHAR(20) NOT NULL,
    GroupId VARCHAR(20) NOT NULL
    PRIMARY KEY(AccountId,GroupId)
)
```

This table simply links accounts with groups. Whenever a trader is assigned to a new group or removed from an existing group, the table must be updated to reflect that fact. The following sample shows the group assignments for three traders:

```
AccountId            GroupId
-------------------- --------------------
Alex0001             Debt
Alex0001             Derivatives
Alex0001             Equities
Betty0002            Derivatives
Charles0003          Debt
```

You can see from this example that a single trader can belong to multiple groups. In this case, Alex0001 belongs to three groups: Debt, Derivatives, and Equities. In the next section, we'll describe one way to handle cases where a trader's permissions from one group conflict with his permissions from another group.

Discussion

The main goal of our solution is to separate the definition of permissions and groups from the assignment of groups to traders. Please note that the GroupPermissions table is not fully normalized. To normalize it, you would have to separate the definition of groups from the definition of products and then use an intersection table to define the Limit and Status attributes. The lack of normalization here simplifies the example somewhat, but it doesn't affect the overall behavior of our design nor does it affect the queries that you'll see in this section.

 The goal of normalization is to provide specific benefits to database design—reduced redundancy being the foremost benefit. However, there are many situations in which reduced redundancy is less valuable than the performance gains you get from a denormalized structure.

Checking permissions for a trader

Queries regarding trading authorizations can easily be performed on the model that we've designed. For example, to list the trading permissions for the account Alex0001, all you need is the following simple join:

```
SELECT m.AccountId, g.ProductType, MIN(g.Limit) Limit
FROM GroupMembership m JOIN GroupPermissions g
   ON m.groupId=g.groupId
WHERE  Status='V' AND AccountId='Alex0001'
GROUP BY m.AccountId, g.ProductType
```

```
AccountId             ProductType Limit
--------------------- ----------- ------------
Alex0001              Bill        10000.00
Alex0001              Bond        10000.00
Alex0001              Future      200.00
Alex0001              Option      100.00
Alex0001              Share       1000.00
```

While the results of this query are straightforward, the use of the GROUP BY clause together with the aggregate function MIN deserves some additional explanation. The grouping allows us to deal with cases where more than one of a trader's permission groups defines a limit for the same product. In our example data, both the Debt and Equities groups define a trading limit for bonds. Alex0001 is a member of both groups, so an ungrouped query would return the following two records:

```
AccountId             ProductType Limit
--------------------- ----------- ------------
Alex0001              Bond        10000.00
Alex0001              Bond        2000.00
```

With two limits for the same product, the question is which limit takes precedence. In our example query, we used the MIN function for the lower limit to take precedence over the higher limit. If you wanted the higher limit to take precedence, you would make that happen simply by using MAX instead of MIN. The GROUP BY clause is a requirement when using aggregate functions in this manner and ensures that only one permission is ultimately returned for each product that the trader is authorized to trade.

Revoking permissions for a group

The Status column in our design allows you to quickly and efficiently revoke a specific permission from a group or to suspend all permissions for a given group. For example, to suspend all trading permissions for the Debt group, you could execute the following statement:

```
UPDATE GroupPermissions SET Status='S' WHERE GroupId='Debt'
```

The previously shown query for checking permissions only looks at valid permissions (Status = 'V'); those you've just suspended (Status = 'S') will automatically be excluded. Their definitions, however, will still exist in the database, so you can easily enable them again when you want to do so.

The solution shown in this recipe is a general solution and can be used for almost any type of permission hierarchy with a limited number of levels. It can be used for security hierarchies where different levels of security authorization are defined, for storing information regarding types of users and their authorizations in a web-based authorization system, or for any other type of permission hierarchy where a large number of users or accounts is used.

4.3 Changing Individual Permissions

Problem

You've implemented the permission solution described in the previous section, and you are happy with the ability to assign permissions to groups of users, but you also want the ability to grant specific exceptions directly to specific traders.

Solution

The solution is twofold. First, create an additional table to record exceptional permissions granted directly to a trader. Second, modify the query that you use to obtain the permissions that are currently valid for a given trader. The additional table could look like the following AccountPermissions table:

```
CREATE TABLE AccountPermissions(
    AccountId VARCHAR(20) NOT NULL,
    ProductType VARCHAR(20) NOT NULL,
    Status CHAR(1) CHECK(Status in ('V','S')) DEFAULT('V'),
    Limit NUMERIC(10,2) NULL,
    PRIMARY KEY(AccountId, ProductType)
)
```

In this table, insert records to record all the permissions that you want to assign to traders that are in addition to the permissions those users inherit from their groups. For example, suppose that Alex0001 had a share limit of 1,000 because he belonged to the equities group. Further suppose that you wanted to make Alex0001 an exception to the rule for that group and raise his share limit to 5,000. To do this, insert the following row into the AccountPermissions table:

AccountId	ProductType	Status	Limit
Alex0001	Share	V	5000.00

With the AccountPermissions table in place, you need to modify the query that you use to retrieve permissions for a given user. That query now needs to take into account this new table. The query in the following example, which returns permissions for Alex0001, will do that:

```
SELECT m.AccountId, g.ProductType,
    CASE WHEN isnull(MIN(a.Limit),0) > MIN(g.Limit)
        THEN MIN(a.Limit)
        ELSE MIN(g.Limit)
    END Limit
FROM GroupMembership m JOIN GroupPermissions g
        ON (m.GroupId=g.GroupId)
    LEFT OUTER JOIN AccountPermissions a
        ON (m.AccountId=a.AccountId AND g.ProductType=a.ProductType)
WHERE  m.AccountId='Alex0001'
GROUP BY m.AccountId, g.ProductType
HAVING MIN(g.status)='V' AND isnull(MIN(a.status),MIN(g.status))='V'
```

```
AccountId              ProductType Limit
--------------------   ----------- -----------
Alex0001               Bill        10000.00
Alex0001               Bond        2000.00
Alex0001               Future      200.00
Alex0001               Option      100.00
Alex0001               Share       5000.00
```

Note the emphasized line in the output. That line represents the permission to trade 5,000 shares that came from the AccountPermissions table.

Discussion

The idea behind the permissions model described in this chapter is to have permissions set through group memberships whenever possible. However, in practice, you'll often find that it is useful to have a tuning facility of sorts that allows you to directly change a specific permission for a specific user. To that end, we created the additional table named AccountPermissions in which such exceptions are recorded. Our new query joins the GroupPermissions table with the GroupMembership table to return permissions set at the group level. Those results are then joined with the AccountPermissions table, which adds account-specific exceptions to the result set. An outer join is used for this third table to make the account-specific exceptions optional.

The GROUP BY clause is again used in this new version of the query, for the same reason as before—we only want one permission to be returned for each product type. There is one difference, though: this time, the GROUP BY function includes more columns in its column list:

```
GROUP BY m.AccountId, g.ProductType
```

The CASE statement that you see in the query is used to decide which value to take if both individual and group permissions for the same account and product are present. It checks both values and reports just one:

```
CASE WHEN isnull(MIN(a.Limit),0) > MIN(g.Limit)
     THEN MIN(a.Limit)
     ELSE MIN(g.Limit)
  END Limit
```

In our case, our authorization policy is that account-specific permissions only take precedence over permissions granted at the group level when the account-specific limit is *greater than* the group-specific limit. The isnull() function takes care of cases where individual permissions are not set. It does this by supplying a zero value for those cases. Using a CASE statement like this is a very flexible approach, because you can easily implement different authorization policies. It would be trivial, for example, to change the CASE statement such that account-specific permissions always took precedence over group-level permissions, regardless of whether the account-specific permission specified a higher or lower limit.

Unlike the query shown previously in this chapter in which the Status flag was checked in the WHERE clause, this query takes the different approach of checking the Status flag in the HAVING clause. In fact, the query checks to be sure that both flags—for the group-level permission and for the account-specific permission—are set:

```
HAVING MIN(g.status)='V' AND isnull(MIN(a.status),MIN(g.status))='V'
```

In this case, if only one of the two applicable flags is set to 'S', the permission is revoked.

The solution shown in this recipe is very useful when you need to make exceptions for existing permissions set at the group level. However, it has one significant problem: you cannot define an account-specific permission for a trader in cases where a permission for the same product has not also been granted at the group level.

4.4   Adding New Individual Permissions

Problem

The previous recipe's solution allows you to define individual exceptions to permissions that a trader already has at the group level. However, you wish to grant permissions to specific traders without regard to whether permissions for the same products have been granted at the group level.

Solution

In the previous recipe, you could define an exception to a permission that a trader had already been granted at the group level. For example, you could create the following two rows in AccountPermissions:

```
AccountId             ProductType           Status Limit
--------------------  --------------------  ------ ------------
Alex0001              Share                 V      5000.00
Betty0002             Share                 V      8000.00
```

The query in the previous recipe, however, will only respect these account-specific permissions in cases where the traders in question have also been granted permission to trade shares at the group level. This limitation, if you wish to call it that, comes about as a result of the three-way join used in the query.

You may wish account-specific permissions to take effect all the time. To do that, you can use the same data model as shown in the previous recipe, but with a different query. The query shown in the following example is a union query and correctly returns both group-level and account-specific permissions for Betty0002:

```
SELECT m.AccountId, g.ProductType, MIN(g.Limit) Limit
FROM GroupMembership m JOIN GroupPermissions g
   ON m.groupId=g.groupId
```

```
WHERE Status='V' AND AccountId='Betty0002'
    AND NOT EXISTS(SELECT * FROM AccountPermissions  a
        WHERE m.AccountId=a.AccountId AND g.ProductType=a.ProductType)
GROUP BY m.AccountId, g.ProductType
UNION
SELECT a.AccountId, a.ProductType,a.Limit
FROM AccountPermissions a
WHERE a.AccountId='Betty0002' AND a.Status='V'


AccountId            ProductType          Limit
-------------------- -------------------- ------------
Betty0002            Share                8000.00
Betty0002            Future               200.00
Betty0002            Option               100.00
```

As you can see, even though Betty0002 has not been granted permission to trade shares at the group level, this query still picked up the account-level share permissions. The query in the previous recipe won't do that.

Discussion

The key to this query is that it is a union query. The first query in the union reports all those permissions that are defined only at the group level. The subquery in that query's WHERE clause ensures that group-level permissions for products are excluded when account-specific permissions exist for those same products. The second query in the union then returns account-specific permissions. The results from the two queries are combined as a result of the UNION clause.

There are two drawbacks to the solution shown in this recipe. One is that this solution is less efficient than the one shown in the previous recipe. This is because there are three SELECT statements involved instead of just one. Another drawback is that this solution is inflexible in terms of which permission to use when permission for the same product is granted at both the group and the account level. In such cases, the account-specific permission always takes precedence over the group-level permission. A way to overcome this latter limitation is to create a more general UNION query that includes both group- and account-level permissions, embed that query in a view, and then manipulate the view with an appropriate query. The following statement creates such a view:

```
CREATE VIEW Permissions
AS
SELECT m.AccountId, g.ProductType, MIN(g.Limit) Limit
    FROM GroupMembership m JOIN GroupPermissions g
        ON m.groupId=g.groupId
    WHERE Status='V'
    GROUP BY m.AccountId, g.ProductType
UNION
    SELECT a.AccountId, a.ProductType,a.Limit
    FROM AccountPermissions a
    WHERE   a.Status='V'
```

This VIEW returns the group permissions expanded for each account and also includes any account-specific permissions that may exist. To list all permissions for a particular account, query the view and apply your interpretation policy in the query. For example:

```
SELECT ProductType, MIN(Limit) Limit FROM permissions
WHERE AccountId='Alex0001'
GROUP BY ProductType

ProductType          Limit
-------------------- ------------
Bill                 10000.00
Bond                 2000.00
Future               200.00
Option               100.00
Share                1000.00
```

This query lists permissions for Alex0001. The MIN function resolves cases where multiple permissions exist for the same product type. When such cases occur, MIN ensures that only the lowest applicable limit is returned. To always return the highest-applicable limit, you could use the MAX function.

The solutions shown in this recipe are flexible, because they allow for easy addition of new levels to the permission structure. All you need is to add UNION clauses to your query or to your view.

4.5   Centralizing Authorization Logic

Problem

You wish to centralize the logic for your authorization policy. You want to be able to query for an individual trader's permissions, but you don't want that query to contain the logic that handles conflicting permissions and individual exceptions. Your goal is to be able to make reasonable changes to your permissions policies and model without forcing a change to queries already running in production programs.

Solution

Create a view into which you embed an authorization query. The benefit of this is that you can easily change the underlying query of the view without having to change the code in all the programs that query the view. The following view implements the authorization logic shown in the first recipe titled "Creating a Permission Hierarchy":

```
CREATE VIEW orderAuthorization
AS
SELECT AccountId, ProductType, MIN(Limit) Limit
FROM GroupMembership m JOIN GroupPermissions g
   ON m.groupId=g.groupId
WHERE Status='V'
GROUP BY AccountId, ProductType
```

Using this view, you can now obtain the permissions for a specific trader by executing a simple query such as the one shown in the following example:

```
SELECT AccountId, ProductType, Limit
FROM OrderAuthorization
WHERE AccountId = 'Alex0001'

AccountId             ProductType Limit
--------------------- ----------- ------------
Alex0001              Bill        10000.00
Alex0001              Bond        2000.00
Alex0001              Future      200.00
Alex0001              Option      100.00
Alex0001              Share       1000.00
```

You can also issue a query against this view to check for a specific permission. For example, suppose an order to trade 3,000 shares for the account Alex0001 comes into the system. You can use the simple query shown in the following example to retrieve the maximum limit for this type of order:

```
SELECT Limit
FROM orderAuthorization
WHERE AccountId='Alex0001' AND productType='Share'

Limit
------------
1000.00
```

By keeping your queries simple and writing them against a view such as this, you can easily modify your permission model and logic. In the event that you make such modifications, the view will insulate your existing queries from the changes.

Discussion

This solution demonstrates a good separation of business logic from the data model. Imagine that these permissions can be any type of permissions for a large amount of accounts. Having the interpretation of the data model embedded within a view is very likely to pay off for you. Changes in real-life systems are frequent, and often unexpected, so it is usually not wise to hand-code the interpretation (embedding the query) of a data model into your application system. With the view-based solution shown in this recipe, you are free to change the underlying permission model and the interpretation policy during production without going through the additional trouble of recompiling the system or changing the code.

4.6   Implementing General Hierarchies

Problem

You want to implement a project-tracking system based on a general hierarchy, and you want to run some basic, single-level hierarchical queries against that hierarchy.

Solution

Use the general parent/child model described earlier in the project-tracking example in the "Types of Hierachies" section as the basis for the project-tracking system. In this model, a project is composed of subprojects or tasks, tasks may be broken into subtasks, and subtasks may themselves be broken up into subtasks. There is no limit to the level of nesting that may occur, and it all occurs within one database table named Projects. Conceptually, a project is simply the highest-level task. The Projects table is defined as follows:

```
CREATE TABLE Projects(
    Name VARCHAR(20),
    Cost INTEGER,
    Parent INTEGER,
    VertexId INTEGER,
    Primary key(VertexId)
)
```

With this solution in mind, let's look at a few problems that are common to hierarchical structures, such as the one used here to define projects:

- List all leaf nodes
- List all nodes that are not leaf nodes
- Find the most expensive vertices
- List the immediate children of a node
- Find the root

The next few sections present SQL Server solutions to each of these problems.

List all leaf nodes

Leaf nodes are nodes without children. The subquery in the following SELECT statement checks each node to see if any other nodes claim it as a parent. If none do, then that node is a leaf node:

```
SELECT Name FROM Projects p
WHERE NOT EXISTS(
    SELECT * FROM Projects
    WHERE Parent=p.VertexId)
```

The result of executing this query is a list of all subprojects (or tasks if you prefer) that have no children:

```
Name
--------------------
Interviews
Drafts
Consolidations
Presentation
```

```
UI Design
Correctness Testing
Database
UI Implementation
Coding
Initial Testing
Final Adjustments
Production Testing
```

List all nodes that are not leaf nodes

To list all nodes that are not leaf nodes—in other words, all nodes that have children—begin with the same query used to list leaf nodes and just convert the NOT EXISTS into an EXISTS:

```
SELECT Name FROM Projects p
WHERE EXISTS(
    SELECT * FROM Projects
    WHERE Parent=p.VertexId)
```

This query lists all nodes with children:

```
Name
--------------------
New SW
Specifications
Final Document
Prototype
Calculating
Development
Beta Testing
```

Find the most expensive vertices

Each task in the project has a cost associated with it. Each task is also a vertex. To find the N most expensive tasks, simply query the table, order the results by cost, and use the TOP operator to limit the results to the top N rows. For example:

```
SELECT TOP 5 Name, Cost
FROM Projects
ORDER BY cost DESC

Name                Cost
------------------- -----------
Inital testing      40
Beta testing        40
Development          30
Coding               20
Production testing   20
```

This is a good example of a case where it is more productive to issue straight SQL queries, rather than attempt to navigate the hierarchy.

Find the immediate children of a node

Given a particular node, you can write a query to return that node's immediate children. The following query, for example, returns the subprojects of the project named Specifications:

```
SELECT Name FROM Projects
WHERE Parent=(
    SELECT VertexId FROM Projects
    WHERE Name='Specifications' )

Name
--------------------
Interviews
Drafts
Consolidations
Final document
```

Only immediate children are returned. The parent record for each of the four records shown here is the record for the "Specifications" task. These records may, themselves, have children, but those children won't show up in the results for this query.

Find the root

The root is the vertex with no parents. The query to return it is simple, because all you need is to return the one node with no parent pointer. For example:

```
SELECT Name FROM Projects WHERE Parent=0

Name
--------------------
New SW
```

In our example, we use a value of zero to indicate that a node does not have a parent. You could just as easily use a NULL to indicate the same thing, in which case you would specify Parent IS NULL as your WHERE clause condition.

Discussion

As you can see, these queries work on a single level where, at most, they refer to one level above (to parents) or below (to children). For these types of queries, you don't need any additional algorithms or data structures to retrieve information. The queries are pretty straightforward, and you just have to remember the definition of your hierarchy and its elements to write them.

4.7   Traversing Hierarchies Recursively

Problem

You need to step through a hierarchy and print out a report listing all vertices. You want the report to show the hierarchical nature of the data by indenting children under their parent node.

Solution

One solution is to use a recursive algorithm to traverse the tree. To do that, encapsulate the algorithm in a stored procedure. The following code creates a stored procedure named TraversProjectsRecursive. The stored procedure takes one argument, specifying from which node to begin. The procedure then works its way down through that node's children, grandchildren, and so forth.

```
CREATE PROCEDURE TraverseProjectsRecursive
@VertexId INTEGER
AS
    /* to change action on each vertex, change these lines */
    DECLARE @Name VARCHAR(20)
    SELECT @Name=(SELECT Name
                    FROM Projects WHERE VertexId=@VertexId)
    PRINT SPACE(@@NESTLEVEL*2)+STR(@VertexId)+' '+@Name
    /* ****** */

    DECLARE subprojects CURSOR LOCAL FOR
        SELECT VertexId FROM Projects WHERE Parent=@VertexId

    OPEN subprojects
        FETCH NEXT FROM subprojects INTO @VertexId
        WHILE @@FETCH_STATUS=0 BEGIN
            EXEC TraverseProjectsRecursive @VertexId
            FETCH NEXT FROM subprojects INTO @VertexId
        END
    CLOSE subprojects
    DEALLOCATE subprojects
```

When calling the procedure, you need to specify the initial node from which you want the procedure to start traversing. If you want to print out the entire hierarchy, then specify the root node (in our case 1). For example:

```
TraverseProjectsRecursive 1

1 New SW
  2 Specifications
    3 Interviews
    4 Drafts
    5 Consolidations
    6 Final document
      7 Presentation
  8 Prototype
    9 UI Design
    10 Calculations
      11 Correctness Testing
    12 Database
  13 Development
    14 UI Implementation
    15 Coding
    16 Inital testing
  17 Beta testing
    18 Final adjustments
  19 Production testing
```

Discussion

The algorithm used by the TraverseProjectsRecursive procedure is a classical tree-traversal method adapted to the specifics of SQL. You can easily adapt this procedure for use with other hierarchical structures besides the projects structure shown in this chapter. To adapt this procedure, change only the SELECT and PRINT statements.

 When you create a recursive procedure such as the one shown here, MS SQL Server will warn you with a message such as the following: "Cannot add rows to sysdepends for the current stored procedure because it depends on the missing object 'TraverseProjectsRecursive.' The stored procedure will still be created." Do not worry about this message. Recursive procedures are a special case, and you can safely ignore the warning.

The first SELECT statement in the procedure retrieves the name associated with the vertex that is passed in as a parameter. That name is placed into the @Name variable, which is then used in the subsequent PRINT statement:

```
PRINT SPACE(@@NESTLEVEL*2)+STR(@VertexId)+' '+@Name
```

In this PRINT statement, we use the @@NESTLEVEL variable. That variable is maintained automatically by SQL Server and returns the current nesting level. This information is a great advantage when working with stored procedures. In our case, we want to indent every project proportionally to its depth. To do that, we multiply the nesting level by two to indent each child two spaces underneath its parent.

After we print the name of the current vertex, we need to go forward to its children. A vertex can have more than one child, so we define a cursor to select these:

```
DECLARE subprojects CURSOR LOCAL FOR
    SELECT VertexId FROM Projects WHERE Parent=@VertexId
```

This cursor definition uses the LOCAL clause, ensuring that the cursor is defined for the current procedure only. By default, cursors are global, which means that any cursor defined is visible from all code executed within the current connection. Since this procedure calls itself repeatedly within the context of one connection, we must specify that this cursor definition be local to each invocation of the procedure.

After opening the subprojects cursor, we simply step through the list of subprojects and recursively invoke the TraverseProjectsRecursive procedure on each one:

```
FETCH NEXT FROM subprojects INTO @VertexId
    WHILE @@FETCH_STATUS=0 BEGIN
        EXEC TraverseProjectsRecursive @VertexId
        FETCH NEXT FROM subprojects INTO @VertexId
    END
```

Even though the recursive mechanisms are very elegant, they are not very efficient. Furthermore, in SQL Server they have a limit of only 32 nesting levels. If you query your hierarchy infrequently, then the overhead of recursion may be acceptable, and you need not bother with other mechanisms. However, if you do this type of thing often, some further optimizations might be necessary to give you adequate performance. Sometimes it's useful to use recursion for prototyping, because recursive solutions are simple to code. Later, you can optimize your code with a nonrecursive solution before you go to production.

4.8   Manipulating Hierarchies Recursively

Problem

You want to add and delete vertices and their subtrees. When you hire a new employee or open a new project in your company, you need to add this information into your system. To maintain the hierarchical structure of your employee information, special procedures must be followed.

Solution

To add a vertex to a hierarchy, you simply insert the row into the table with the proper parent pointer. No other action is necessary. If the vertex you just added has children, you insert those children in the same manner. No additional manipulations are needed.

Things become more complex when you need to delete a vertex, because you not only need to delete the row for the vertex, you need to delete any rows that represent children as well. For this purpose, you can use a modified version of the traversing algorithm shown in the previous recipe. The following RemoveProjectsRecursive procedure will delete a specified vertex and all vertices that fall underneath it:

```
CREATE PROCEDURE RemoveProjectsRecursive
@VertexId INTEGER
AS
    SET NOCOUNT ON
    DECLARE @LocalVertex INTEGER
    SELECT @LocalVertex=@VertexId

    DECLARE subprojects CURSOR LOCAL FOR
        SELECT VertexId FROM Projects WHERE Parent=@VertexId

    OPEN subprojects
        FETCH NEXT FROM subprojects INTO @LocalVertex
        WHILE @@FETCH_STATUS=0 BEGIN
            EXEC RemoveProjectsRecursive @LocalVertex
            FETCH NEXT FROM subprojects INTO @LocalVertex
        END
```

```
CLOSE subprojects
DEALLOCATE subprojects

DELETE FROM Projects WHERE VertexId=@VertexId

PRINT 'Vertex ' +CONVERT(VARCHAR(8),@VertexId) + ' removed!'
```

To delete a vertex, simply invoke the RemoveProjectsRecursive procedure and pass in the vertex ID as a parameter. In the following example, the procedure is used to delete the vertex for Specifications, which happens to be vertex 2:

```
RemoveProjectsRecursive 2

Vertex 3 removed!
Vertex 4 removed!
Vertex 5 removed!
Vertex 7 removed!
Vertex 6 removed!
Vertex 2 removed!
```

Six rows were deleted as a result of deleting the Specifications vertex. Four of the rows are for the four children, one row is for a child of a child, and the sixth row is for the Specifications vertex, itself. This procedure always deletes the parent nodes last to avoid any foreign-key violations.

Discussion

Obviously, adding new members to a hierarchy is fairly easy since a hierarchical structure does not have any limitations on the number of children or levels of hierarchy that you can have. Inserting a new row under a parent is easy.

For deleting, we used the traversing algorithm from the previous recipe. When we adapted that algorithm for deleting a vertex, we were careful to have it remove all children before finally removing a parent node. If a parent is removed before its children, the table would contain nodes with no parents. Such nodes would need to be collected and eliminated using a specially coded garbage-collection mechanism. While such a mechanism is possible, you have the problem of how to differentiate valid parent-free nodes (project roots) from the orphan nodes that remain because you deleted their parents.

The algorithm shown in this recipe is fairly efficient; it removes leaf nodes and parent nodes with the same procedure, and it does not result in significant overhead if you are removing just a leaf vertex.

4.9   Aggregating Hierarchies

Problem

You want to aggregate hierarchical data. For example, you wish to sum the cost of a project or task, beginning from a specific vertex and working your way down through all levels of the hierarchy underneath that vertex.

Solution

With respect to the projects example that we have been using for these general hierarchy recipes, you can use the following stored procedure to summarize the costs of all subprojects for a specific project. You specify the project by passing its vertex ID as a parameter to the procedure.

```
CREATE PROCEDURE AggregateProjects
@VertexId INTEGER
AS
SET NOCOUNT ON
    DECLARE @lvl INTEGER
    DECLARE @Name VARCHAR(20)
    DECLARE @Cost INTEGER
    DECLARE @Sum INTEGER

    CREATE TABLE #stack (
        VertexId INTEGER,
        Name VARCHAR(20),
        Cost INTEGER,
        Lvl INTEGER
    )

    SELECT @Sum=0
    SELECT @Lvl = 1

    INSERT INTO #stack
        SELECT VertexId, Name, Cost, 1 FROM Projects
        WHERE VertexID=@VertexId

    WHILE @Lvl > 0 BEGIN
        IF EXISTS (SELECT * FROM #stack WHERE lvl = @lvl) BEGIN

            SELECT TOP 1 @VertexId = VertexId, @Name=Name, @Cost=Cost
                FROM #stack WHERE lvl = @lvl
                ORDER BY VertexId

            /* to change action each vertex, change this line */
            SELECT @Sum=@Sum+@Cost
            /* ******* */

            DELETE FROM #stack WHERE vertexId = @VertexId

            INSERT #stack
                SELECT VertexId, Name, Cost, @lvl + 1
                FROM Projects WHERE parent = @VertexId

            IF @@ROWCOUNT > 0
                SELECT @lvl = @lvl + 1
        END ELSE
            SELECT @lvl = @lvl - 1

    END
    PRINT 'Sum of project costs is '+STR(@Sum)+'.'
    DROP TABLE #stack
SET NOCOUNT OFF
```

The following examples show the results of executing this procedure for all projects (VertexId=1) and for the Specifications project (VertexId=2).

```
AggregateProjects 1
Sum of project costs is        231.

AggregateProjects 2
Sum of project costs is         33.
```

Discussion

The algorithm shown here is adapted from the SQL Server Books Online recommendation for expanding hierarchies. Those familiar with algorithms and data structures will notice that it is a nonrecursive implementation of a recursive traversing algorithm. The code uses an internal stack implemented as a temporary table. The stack holds interesting information from the hierarchical Projects table, plus an additional column named lvl. The lvl column records the level that each entry holds in the hierarchy. The stack definition is as follows:

```
CREATE TABLE #stack (
        VertexId INTEGER,
        Name VARCHAR(20),
        Cost INTEGER,
        Lvl INTEGER
    )
```

After the #stack table is created, two variables are initialized. The @lvl variable tracks the current level on which the code is operating, while the @sum variable accumulates the sum of all costs. Next, an INSERT statement is used to store the root onto the stack. Note that the root in our case is the vertex identified by @VertexId.

The code then loops through each element on the stack. The loop begins by popping one element from the stack. The retrieved data contains a cost, which is added to the total cost being accumulated in @sum:

```
SELECT TOP 1 @VertexId = VertexId, @Name=Name, @Cost=Cost
    FROM #stack WHERE lvl = @lvl
    ORDER BY VertexId

SELECT @Sum=@Sum+@Cost
```

After accumulating the cost for the vertex just pulled from the stack, the code deletes that read vertex and adds all of its children to the stack:

```
DELETE FROM #stack WHERE vertexId = @VertexId

INSERT #stack
    SELECT VertexId, Name, Cost, @lvl + 1
    FROM Projects WHERE parent = @VertexId

IF @@ROWCOUNT > 0
    SELECT @lvl = @lvl + 1
```

The IF statement that you see in this code ensures that if the vertex just deleted from the stack has any children, the @lvl value is increased to indicate that the code is moving one level down in the hierarchy.

The IF EXISTS clause at the beginning of the loop ensures that so long as there are some candidates available on the current level, the loop repeats and browses through them all. The SET NOCOUNT ON directive at the beginning of the procedure just limits the number of messages displayed from the procedure. It does not affect the logic of the algorithm. Without SET NOCOUNT ON, you'll see a steady stream of "(1 row(s) affected)" messages as the code executes.

This algorithm is general enough that it can be used for any kind of operation for which you prefer traversing the hierarchy in a nonrecursive manner. If you want to change the operation that is performed on each node, change the code where current cost is added to the total sum.

The code demonstrates why the general model for hierarchies has a limited application in SQL. When you need to traverse over more than one level efficiently, the code starts to expand to an almost unreadable size.

4.10   Preparing Multilevel Operations

Problem

Your system performs many multilevel, hierarchical operations, and the performance of those operations has not been satisfactory. You need to improve that poor performance.

Solution

One solution is to store additional accessibility information into a service table, and then use that information when querying your hierarchical table. For example, the following ProjectPaths table records the path to, and the depth of, each vertex in the Projects table:

```
CREATE TABLE ProjectPaths(
   VertexId INTEGER,
   Depth INTEGER,
   Path VARCHAR(300)
)
```

After creating the ProjectPaths table, you can use the following procedure to fill the table with the depth and path information for each vertex in the Projects table:

```
CREATE PROCEDURE BuildProjectPathsRecursive
@VertexId INTEGER
AS
SET NOCOUNT ON
   DECLARE @Path VARCHAR(300)
   DECLARE @Depth INTEGER
```

```
    SELECT @Depth=a.Depth,@Path=a.Path
    FROM ProjectPaths a JOIN Projects p ON p.parent=a.vertexId
    WHERE @vertexId=p.vertexId

    DELETE FROM ProjectPaths WHERE VertexId=@VertexId
    INSERT INTO ProjectPaths VALUES(
        @VertexId,
        isnull(@Depth,0)+1,
        isnull(@Path,'.')+CAST(@VertexId AS VARCHAR(15))+'.')

    DECLARE subprojects CURSOR LOCAL FOR
        SELECT VertexId FROM Projects p WHERE Parent=@VertexId
    OPEN subprojects

        FETCH NEXT FROM subprojects INTO @VertexId
        WHILE @@FETCH_STATUS=0 BEGIN

        EXEC BuildProjectPathsRecursive @VertexId
        FETCH NEXT FROM subprojects INTO @VertexId
    END
    CLOSE subprojects
    DEALLOCATE subprojects
SET NOCOUNT OFF
```

This procedure takes one parameter, which tells the procedure with which node to start. The procedure then works its way down the hierarchy. To process all nodes in the Projects table, invoke this procedure and pass a value of 1 as follows:

```
BuildProjectPathsRecursive 1
```

The procedure fills the ProjectPaths table with additional information for every vertex. The Depth column records the depth of each vertex. The Path column records the path to each vertex. In the path, the vertex numbers are separated by dots. The ProjectPaths table that will be built contains the following rows:

```
VertexId    Depth       Path
----------- ----------- -----------
1           1           .1.
2           2           .1.2.
3           3           .1.2.3.
4           3           .1.2.4.
5           3           .1.2.5.
6           3           .1.2.6.
7           4           .1.2.6.7.
8           2           .1.8.
9           3           .1.8.9.
10          3           .1.8.10.
11          4           .1.8.10.11.
12          3           .1.8.12.
13          2           .1.13.
14          3           .1.13.14.
15          3           .1.13.15.
16          3           .1.13.16.
17          2           .1.17.
18          3           .1.17.18.
19          2           .1.19.
```

Discussion

The idea for this recipe has been taken from an article published by Itzik Ben-Gan (*SQL Server Magazine*, June, 2000). His development of this technique is a recent achievement resulting from his search for an ultimate support structure to improve the efficiency of the classical hierarchical model. Although it was originally promoted as an add-on to an existing hierarchy table, we see no reason why you shouldn't normalize properly and separate the hierarchy and its data from the support structure.

The path leading to every vertex is stored in the ProjectPaths table. This represents the work of traversing the hierarchy, and because it is stored in the ProjectPaths table, it only needs to be done once. Please note that the length of the Path field can be changed according to your needs. It does, however, make sense to keep it reasonably small, especially if you want to index it.

The stored procedure named BuildProjectPathsRecursive fills the ProjectPaths table with the paths to each vertex in the subtree. It uses the recursive traversal algorithm introduced earlier in this chapter and runs the following code for each vertex:

```
SELECT @Depth=a.Depth,@Path=a.Path
FROM ProjectPaths a JOIN Projects p ON p.parent=a.vertexId
WHERE @vertexId=p.vertexId

DELETE FROM ProjectPaths WHERE VertexId=@VertexId
INSERT INTO ProjectPaths VALUES(
    @VertexId,
    isnull(@Depth,0)+1,
    isnull(@Path,'.')+CAST(@VertexId AS VARCHAR(15))+'.')
```

The SELECT statement reads the depth and path data from the parent. Next, any old information for the vertex is deleted from the ProjectPaths table, and new data is inserted. If the @Depth or @Path variables are null, indicating that no access path for the parent exists, then an initial value of 0 is set for the depth, and an initial value of a dot (.) is set for the path. Regardless of how the depth gets set, it is increased by one. That's because the @Depth variable represents the depth of the current node's parent. You have to increment that depth by 1 to get the current node's depth. Similarly, the @Path variable contains the path to the parent. The current vertex ID is appended onto that path to yield the path to the current node. These new depth and path values are then inserted into the ProjectPaths table.

If you prefer nonrecursive algorithms, you can rewrite the recursive BuildProject-PathsRecursive procedure as a nonrecursive procedure. This code is as follows and uses the stack-based technique shown earlier in the recipe titled "Aggregating Hierarchies":

```
CREATE PROCEDURE BuildProjectsPaths
@VertexId INTEGER
AS
SET NOCOUNT ON
```

```
DECLARE @lvl INTEGER

CREATE TABLE #stack (
    VertexId INTEGER,
    Lvl INTEGER
)

SELECT @Lvl = 1

INSERT INTO #stack
    SELECT VertexId,1 FROM Projects WHERE VertexId=@VertexID

WHILE @Lvl > O BEGIN
    IF EXISTS (SELECT * FROM #stack WHERE lvl = @lvl) BEGIN

        SELECT TOP 1 @VertexId = VertexId FROM #stack
            WHERE lvl = @lvl
            ORDER BY VertexId

         DELETE FROM ProjectPaths WHERE VertexId=@VertexId
         INSERT INTO ProjectPaths
           SELECT p.vertexId,
               isnull(a.Depth,O)+1,
               isnull(a.Path,'.')+CAST(p.VertexId AS VARCHAR(15))+'.'
               FROM ProjectPaths a,Projects p
               WHERE @vertexId=p.vertexId AND p.parent*=a.vertexId

        DELETE FROM #stack WHERE vertexId = @VertexId

        INSERT #stack
            SELECT VertexId, @lvl + 1 FROM Projects
            WHERE parent = @VertexId

        IF @@ROWCOUNT > O
            SELECT @lvl = @lvl + 1
    END ELSE
        SELECT @lvl = @lvl - 1

    END
SET NOCOUNT OFF
```

4.11   Aggregating Hierarchies Revised

Problem

You want to perform aggregation on your hierarchy. As before, you wish to sum the cost of a project or task by beginning from a specific vertex and working your way through all levels of the hierarchy. This time, though, you wish to enhance the efficiency of your aggregation by using the ProjectPaths service table created in the previous recipe. In addition to summarizing the cost, you also wish to list the hierarchy in an indented format.

Solution

Recall that the previous aggregation procedure was fairly complex and made use of a temporary table named #stack. With the ProjectsPaths table, that same aggregation process becomes simple enough that you can perform it with the SQL query shown in the following example:

```
SELECT SUM(cost) Total
FROM ProjectPaths a JOIN Projects p
    ON a.VertexId=p.VertexId
WHERE
    Path LIKE (SELECT Path FROM ProjectPaths WHERE VertexId=1)+'%'

Total
-----------
231
```

The query in this example summarizes the costs of all projects and tasks under VertexId 1. As you can see, the result of 231 was obtained without the need for recursion and without the need for a temporary stack table. It was obtained with only a four-line SELECT statement, as opposed to the 48 lines of procedural code required for the earlier version of the aggregation solution.

You can also make use of the ProjectPaths table to list the project in a hierarchical manner:

```
SELECT Space(Depth*2)+Name Project
FROM ProjectPaths a JOIN Projects p
ON a.VertexId=p.VertexId
WHERE
    Path LIKE (SELECT Path FROM ProjectPaths WHERE VertexId=1)+'%'
ORDER BY a.Path

Project
---------------------------------
  New SW
    Development
      UI Implementation
      Coding
      Initial testing
    Beta testing
      Final adjustments
    Production testing
    Specifications
      Interviews
      Drafts
      Consolidations
      Final document
        Presentation
    Prototype
      Calculations
        Correctness Testing
      Database
      UI Design
```

Again, the ProjectPaths table enabled the desired result to be generated using only a short SQL query, as opposed to the rather long procedure that would otherwise be required. Please note that the order in which tasks are listed in the result might not be the same as you get with the TraverseProjectsRecursive procedure. However, the hierarchical structure of the information is still preserved.

Discussion

The first query joins the ProjectPaths and Projects tables. This is a one-to-one join, since both tables have an equal number of rows. The secret to the query lies in the second part of the WHERE clause:

```
Path LIKE (SELECT Path FROM ProjectPaths WHERE VertexId=1)+'%'
```

The WHERE clause gathers all vertices for which the beginning of the path string is equal to the root vertex (in our case, it is .1.). The summation of all costs is then just a simple matter of applying the SUM function to those rows.

Multilevel operations can now be performed efficiently using the ProjectPaths table. Once you know the path to the parent node, you know the paths to all of that node's children. Had you wished to summarize the cost for the Specifications subproject, you could modify the second part of the WHERE clause as follows:

```
Path LIKE (SELECT Path FROM ProjectPaths WHERE VertexId=2)+'%'
```

When writing queries using a table like the ProjectPaths table, you need to remember two rules. First, if you wish to perform an operation on a parent vertex together with all its children, you should use the % pattern match operator at the end of the search string in your LIKE predicate. Second, if you wish to exclude the parent from the result set, you should use the _% pattern. The additional underscore in the pattern match string *requires* that a character be present. Thus, if the parent's path is .1., it will not match a pattern of .1._%. Any children, however, will have a character following the second dot, so they *will* match the pattern.

The Depth column in the ProjectPaths table allows you to zero in easily on vertices of a given depth. For example, the following query will return a list of all level two projects in the Projects table:

```
SELECT SUM(cost) Total
FROM ProjectPaths a JOIN Projects p
    ON a.VertexId=p.VertexId
WHERE a.Depth=2
```

The Depth column can also be used to compute indention, as you saw earlier in this recipe's second query:

```
SELECT Space(Depth*2)+Name Project
```

In this case, the Depth column value was multiplied by two to determine the correct number of leading spaces for each line of output.

CHAPTER 5

Temporal Data

Almost any computer system uses some sort of *temporal*, or time-based, data. Temporal data could be in the form of contract dates, dates corresponding to school athletic results, or periods of time in which employees are booked in meetings. In any case, with the use of temporal data, database records have a given place on a timeline. However, a database can store only discrete time values, while time itself is continuous. This makes working with temporal data a bit of a challenge.

In this chapter, we'll discuss the fundamentals of working with temporal data, and we'll show how you can implement the three basic temporal types: instants, durations, and periods. We'll also briefly show Transact-SQL functions that manipulate temporal data.

Our recipes demonstrate a mechanism for enforcing granularity rules, how to handle calendar information, and how to extend date datatypes beyond their default scope. We show techniques for manipulating instants, durations, and periods that can be used in any temporal-database problem.

The selection of recipes for this chapter reveals both the complexity of working with temporal data and also the range of possible solutions for temporal-data problems. Temporal data is not just the same as any other type of data. Temporal data has specific characteristics that can trip you up if you don't fully understand what you are doing.

5.1   Introduction

Representing temporal data in a database is probably one of the most unnatural concepts for a human to comprehend. The reason is that we use temporal information with very vague and undefined terms. For example, when we say that something should be done "until tomorrow," do we mean exactly until tomorrow midnight? Or, rather until tomorrow within normal working hours? Does "until tomorrow" mean that something is done through the last instant of today, or does it really mean that we must progress over the threshold to tomorrow? Similar questions puzzle database designers when working with temporal data. Humans often use temporal information within an implicit context, which can sometimes be very difficult to represent in program code.

In the next few sections, we'll talk about some concepts that you need to understand when working with temporal data. We'll also talk about the datatypes that SQL Server provides for use with temporal data.

Granularity

The concept of *granularity* is important when dealing with temporal data. Granularity refers to the smallest unit of time that you wish to deal with and that you wish to store. As you know, the data represented in a database is just an approximation of the real world. While time in our lives is linear, the time information stored in a database is discrete and accurate to a given granularity. If your granularity is a day, you'll store only dates. If your granularity is a second, you will store values that are accurate to the second.

You should be aware of two types of granularities when working with temporal data. The first type of granularity is commonly referred to as *precision*. Precision is explicit and is defined by the datatype you use to store temporal data. Precision refers to the finest granularity that a datatype can handle. For example, the precision of SQL Server's DATETIME type is 3.3 milliseconds. Every DATETIME value really represents a specific millisecond point in time. For example:

```
INSERT INTO ContractorsSchedules
  (JobID, ContractorID, JobStart)
  VALUES ('RF10023','Jenny','2001-10-18')

(1 row(s) affected)

SELECT JobID, ContractorID, JobStart
FROM ContractorsSchedules
WHERE ContractorID='Jenny';

JobID      ContractorID JobStart
---------- ------------ ---------------------------
RF10023    Jenny        2001-10-18 00:00:00.000
```

In this example, only a date is inserted into the database. Look, however, at the date as it is retrieved. You'll see that it now contains a time component resolved down to the millisecond.

There is a trap in SQL that you must watch for when working with dates. It's easy to be drawn into the assumption that when you insert a date into a database, you have stored a value that encompasses the full day. In fact, due to the manner in which temporal data is physically stored, you are storing just a single point in the day. Misunderstanding this issue can be a source of great confusion.

The second type of granularity is a bit more subtle. It's the granularity that you care about, as opposed to what is actually stored. For example, if you are interested in events accurate up to one second, your granularity is set to one second, regardless of the precision your datatype allows. You should be aware of, and define clear rules for, the granularity used in all temporal operations within a database.

Dealing with this second type of granularity can be challenging. You'll usually need additional programming to bridge the gap between the granularity you want at a business-rule level and the granularity (precision) of the datatypes that you are using. It's all too easy to compare two data values that happen to use different granularities, only to get an erroneous result.

Let's look at an example to demonstrate a common error made by SQL programmers. A programmer designed software for an online library reservation system in which a reader can make reservations for books. The programmer used the DATETIME datatype to store the dates:

```
CREATE TABLE LibraryReservations(
    BookId CHAR(10),
    UserId CHAR(10),
    ReservedFrom DATETIME,
    ReservedTo DATETIME
)
```

The programmer created an online interface that allows users to add new reservations or check for a book's availability. Users can specify only dates when they make a reservation, or they can specify times along with those dates. Say that one user reserves a book from November 5, 2001 until November 6, 2001. The system might record the reservation using an INSERT, such as the following:

```
INSERT INTO LibraryReservations
    (BookId, UserId, ReservedFrom, ReservedTo)
    VALUES ('XF101','Jeff','2001-11-5','2001-11-6')
```

Now, let's say that a second user checks to see whether the same book is available from November 6, 2001, 15:00 onward. To implement this check, the programmer uses the following query to see whether the desired time falls into any of the reservation intervals for the book:

```
SELECT BookId FROM LibraryReservations
WHERE BookId='XF101' AND
    'Nov 6 2001 15:00' BETWEEN ReservedFrom AND ReservedTo
```

If you run through this scenario and execute this query, you'll get a result that is incorrect from a business perspective. Why? Because the programmer didn't understand and take into account SQL Server's handling of default time values. Let's look at the actual row inserted when the first user reserved the book:

```
SELECT *
FROM LibraryReservations
WHERE BookId='XF101' and UserId='Jeff'
```

BookId	UserId	ReservedFrom	ReservedTo
XF101	Jeff	2001-11-05 00:00:00.000	2001-11-06 00:00:00.000

Notice the time values associated with each date? Do you see that 2001-11-06 15:00 falls outside the reservation range? The first user intended to keep the book for the entire day, but the programmer didn't take that into account. Instead, the programmer allowed the database to supply the default time value, which represents the *beginning* of the day, not the end.

The solution to the problem illustrated by the previous example is in two parts. First, you need to strongly enforce the business rules that you've defined for temporal data in your application. Second, you may need to write code that protects you against problems. We'll talk about this second aspect in some of our recipes.

Temporal Datatypes in Transact-SQL

Transact-SQL uses two datatypes to store temporal data: DATETIME and SMALL-DATETIME. Both store date and time data. The differences are only in the precision and the range of values available and come about because of differences in the storage capacities of the two datatypes.

DATETIME is a higher granularity datatype. It uses 8 bytes for each instance. 4 of those bytes are used to represent the date, and the other 4 are used to represent milliseconds past midnight. The DATETIME datatype can store values from January 1, 1753 through December 31, 9999, which is more than enough for business purposes.

A lower granularity datatype is SMALLDATETIME. It uses only 4 bytes of storage, and it can only handle dates between January 1, 1900 and June 6, 2079. In addition, the granularity of SMALLDATETIME is only to the minute. You can't represent seconds and milliseconds using SMALLDATETIME like you can using DATETIME.

Contrary to what you might think, there is no native way in Transact-SQL to store date and time data separately—you have to store both types of information within the same two datatypes. As you might imagine, this can be a source of a great confusion if you don't use the types carefully.

A common misconception with respect to temporal datatypes is that the TIMESTAMP datatype represents a third type that can be used for temporal data. The fact that there is a CURRENT_TIMESTAMP function to return the current date and time only adds to the confusion. The name is misleading. TIMESTAMP is *not* a temporal datatype. TIMESTAMP is a binary datatype used to version stamp rows in a table with unique, 8-byte, binary numbers. You cannot use TIMESTAMP for temporal operations. To further confuse things, the TIMESTAMP datatype in Transact-SQL is not the same as the TIMESTAMP datatype defined in the ANSI SQL-92 standard. A SQL-92 TIMESTAMP is actually similar to the Transact-SQL DATETIME datatype.

Date and Time Input

With Transact-SQL you can use a variety of input formats for date and time values. However, if you aren't careful, this can become a major source of confusion and errors. We strongly recommend you use only one standardized format for all date/time values that are input to, and output from, SQL Server. This doesn't mean your users must be limited to that one format. Your frontend tools can use any presentation format you desire, but it'll be less confusing if those tools, in turn, use only one format to communicate with the database. It is probably best to use an international standard date format such as ISO 8601, which we are going to use in all our recipes.

ISO 8601 defines international standard date notation as YYYY-MM-DD HH:MM: SS.MMM. Such a date can be used in a Transact-SQL string and is converted automatically from a string to a date value without the need to use explicit conversion functions. You don't need to use the full notation. You can use any subset of leading parts; for example, use the notation YYYY-MM-DD if you are working only with dates, not times. It is convenient that SQL Server can convert an ISO 8601 date automatically since it avoids readability problems resulting from explicit use of CONVERT or CAST functions.

For example, if you want to compare a date parameter in a query with a constant, you can use the simplified ISO notation:

```
WHERE '2001-2-2 17:04' < JobStart
```

The server will cast the string into a date automatically. It's not necessary to use the CONVERT function:

```
WHERE CONVERT(DATETIME,'Feb 2 2001 5:04PM') < JobStart
```

As you can see, the version of the query that doesn't use the CONVERT function is the more readable of the two.

Another advantage of the ISO 8601 date format is that it ensures the internationality of constant values. For example, the date '2/3/2001' can't be correctly interpreted without some additional information. You need to know whether the European or U.S. convention for ordering the day and month applies. Without that information, it is not clear whether we are talking about March 2, 2001 or February 3, 2001.

Temporal Types

When working with date and time data, you'll find that there are three basic types of temporal data to be concerned with:

Instant
    A single point in time

Duration
    An interval or length of time

Period
    An interval of time that begins at a specific instant

In literature, you'll find different names for these types, names such as *event* and *intervals*, but those names all indicate one of the three basic types listed here.

Don't confuse the temporal types we've listed here with datatypes you use in a particular SQL dialect. These temporal types represent real-world uses for time and date data; they transcend any specific database implementation.

Instants

An *instant*, also called an event, is a single point in time with reference to a specific granularity. If the granularity of a problem is in terms of days, an instant ends up being a specific date. If the granularity is in terms of hours, an instant is defined as a specific hour of a specific day. For example, a calendar maker is only interested in dates and would note that the millennium started on January 1, 2001.

In Transact-SQL, instants are represented with a value stored in one of the two available datatypes: DATETIME or SMALLDATETIME. For example:

```
...
ContractStart SMALLDATETIME,
...
InvoiceIssued DATETIME,
...
```

There are several functions applicable to instants:

- GETDATE
- CURRENT_TIMESTAMP
- GETUTCDATE
- DATENAME
- DATEPART
- DAY
- MONTH
- YEAR

The GETDATE and CURRENT_TIMESTAMP functions provide equivalent functionality. GETDATE exists for historical reasons, while CURRENT_TIMESTAMP follows the SQL standard. Both functions simply return the current instant at the time of their invocation. The resolution of these functions is in milleseconds.

The GETUTCDATE function is of a similar nature; however, it returns the current UTC (Coordinated Universal Time) time resolved to the millisecond. You should be aware that using this function requires great confidence that the base system is installed properly and that date modifications (such as switching to daylight saving time) are handled correctly. In general, we do not recommend using this function unless absolutely necessary.

The DATENAME function returns a named portion of a temporal value. For example, you could use DATENAME to return the name of the month in which a given date falls. Again, the validity of this function is subject to specific settings on the server, particularly the language setting. Consequently, using DATENAME can be confusing. In our recipes for this chapter, we give an alternative solution to the use of DATENAME that is a bit more stable and that is not affected by any settings on the server.

The remaining functions in the list—DATEPART, DAY, MONTH, and YEAR—are all variations on the same theme and return different parts of a temporal value. For example, the YEAR function returns the year in which a given date falls.

Duration

A *duration*, sometimes called an interval, is a distance measure of time. For example, when you say that that a meeting lasts for "one hour," the "one hour" represents a duration. If you add a duration to an event, you get a second event; if you add one hour to the instant that the meeting starts, you end up with the instant on which the meeting ends. We use durations every day when we try to describe how long something lasted or when something happened relative to an instant in time. For example, the world 100-meter sprint record is 9.79 seconds (Maurice Greene, IAAF World Championships in Athletics, 1999) and dough for biscuits has to rise for 1 hour before baking.

Interestingly, durations have a direction; they can be in the future or in the past. The most natural way to present a duration that extends into the past is to assign it a negative value. This might sound a bit strange at first; however, it has significant advantages when using the value in applications.

For example, you could specify that you are going to arrive 5 minutes prior to a meeting that has yet to be scheduled. You could represent that as a duration of –5 minutes. Until the meeting is actually scheduled, you know only that you have a duration of –5 minutes. When the meeting is finally scheduled, you'll have a starting point and you can then think of your duration as a period. There will be more on periods in the next section.

Storing durations is not as easy as it sounds. You cannot use temporal datatypes for storing duration information because temporal datatypes are designed to represent only as instant in time. Usually, to record a duration, you use INTEGER or some other numeric datatype. For example:

```
...
ScoreInSeconds INTEGER,
...
```

Notice in this example that the granularity, or units, is implied. The score (from a track meet, possibly) is an INTEGER that represents a number of seconds, but the fact that the unit is seconds is not part of the variable's declaration. When working with durations, you must be aware of the granularity and you must both store and retrieve the information consistently. If your granularity is one second, you should internally represent all durations in seconds and only convert them to more human-readable forms such as HH:MM:SS when needed.

The one Transact-SQL function related to durations is the DATEDIFF function. DATEDIFF takes two date values, or instants, and returns the duration between them in terms of a granularity that you specify.

The DATETIME datatype represents a special case when computing durations between dates: you can use the minus sign between two DATETIME values, and you'll get the duration in days. If you want to calculate the duration in terms of any other granularity, you still need to use the DATEDIFF function where you explicitly specify the unit that you want to use in your result.

Eternity

Eternity is perhaps the longest interval of them all. A representation for eternity is not defined in Transact-SQL. The best approximation we can get is to use the maximum or minimal values in whatever date/time datatype we are using. For DATETIME, these values are '1753-1-1 00:00' and '9999-12-13 23:59'. Similarly, for SMALLDATETME, the values are '1900-1-1 00:00' and '2079-12-31 23:59'. Thus, to represent future eternity as a DATETIME value, we would use '9999-12-13 23:59'.

Periods

A *period* is a duration that is located in time. For a period, you need an instant and a duration from that instant. A typical example of a period is when you say that a meeting started at 8:00 a.m. and lasted for two hours. Another way of expressing a period is to specify two endpoints, such as saying that a meeting started at 8:00 a.m. and ended at 10:00 a.m. Regardless of how you express the period, you end up with a duration beginning at a specific point in time.

There are three possibilities for representing periods in a relational database:

Fully normalized
Insert one row to represent the beginning of a period and another row to mark the end of a period.

Margins
Record both the beginning and ending instants in a single table row.

Margin and duration
Record the beginning instant together with the duration in a single table row.

The fully normalized presentation is to represent each period with two rows in a table:

```
CREATE TABLE ...
    ...
    Instant DATETIME,
    ...
```

Two instants, contained in two separate rows, represent the beginning and end of each period. This representation has some advantages over the others. For example, if you want to record events within periods, you might want to use the fully normalized representation. However, the code required can be complex, because the information about a period is spread over two or more rows. Consequently, this approach is usually not used.

The *margins* and *margin and duration* representations are conceptually equivalent. The difference between the two is more artistic than technical. The representation with margins requires two instants, one marking the beginning of the period and the other marking the end of the period:

```
CREATE TABLE ...
    ...
    JobStart DATETIME,
    JobEnd DATETIME,
    ...
```

The representation of a period with a margin and a duration is similar, requiring just one instant (it can be the beginning or the end) together with a duration in a given granularity:

```
CREATE TABLE ...
    ...
    JobStart DATETIME,
    Lasting INTEGER,
    ...
```

When specifying a period using an instant and a duration, you can use the DATEADD function to calculate the second instant based on the known instant and duration values. A benefit of this approach is that the use of DATEADD forces you to state the granularity of your interval value explicitly, so your code becomes somewhat self-documenting. Given an instant and an interval, the DATEADD function returns a DATETIME value as a result.

 You can use the DATEDIFF function to derive the interval between two instants.

5.2 The Schedules Example

Schedules are one of the most used forms of temporal data. For our example used for the recipes in this chapter, we are going to create a database for a service company to use in coordinating contractors and maintaining their schedules. The core table in that database is as follows:

```
CREATE TABLE ContractorsSchedules(
    JobID CHAR(10),
    ContractorID CHAR(10),
    JobStart DATETIME,
    JobEnd DATETIME,
    JobType CHAR(1) CHECK(JobType in ('B','H')),
    PRIMARY KEY(ContractorId, JobStart)
)
```

Each contractor in our example database is identified by a ContractorID value. In a real-world application, this would likely be a numeric ID code, but, in our example, we'll simply use the contractor's name as the ID. The JobStart and JobEnd attributes define a period in the contractor's calendar during which he is unavailable. A contractor is unavailable if he is booked (JobType 'B') or if he is on holiday (JobType 'H').

The following data, which happens to be for the contractor named Alex, is an example of a contractor schedule:

```
JobId        ContractorId JobStart     JobEnd       JobType
----------   ------------ -----------  -----------  -------
             Alex         Jan  1 2001  Jan 10 2001  H
RF10001      Alex         Jan 11 2001  Jan 20 2001  B
RF10002      Alex         Jan 21 2001  Jan 30 2001  B
RF10020      Alex         Feb  1 2001  Feb  5 2001  B
RF10034      Alex         Feb 11 2001  Feb 20 2001  B
```

Please note that there is no JobId for holidays. This violates the rule of database design of giving each record a unique identifier known as a primary key, but it gives us a nice playing field on which to demonstrate some tricks to use when you don't have a unique identifier for your data. Normally, you would have JobId as a unique identifier and simply assign unique JobId values for holidays.

5.3 Enforcing Granularity Rules

Problem

As a designer of a database, you don't trust your user-interface programmers, and you want to explicitly enforce the granularity of one day in your database. Bottom line: you are using the DATETIME to store dates, and you want to prevent programmers from mistakenly storing time-of-day values in your DATETIME fields.

Solution

Use a trigger to intercept all inserts and updates and have that trigger remove any inadvertent time-of-day values:

```
CREATE TRIGGER ContractorSchedulesUpdate
ON ContractorsSchedules
FOR UPDATE, INSERT
AS
    UPDATE ContractorsSchedules
    SET JobStart=CONVERT(CHAR(10),i.JobStart,120),
      JobEnd=CONVERT(CHAR(10),i.JobEnd,120)
    FROM ContractorsSchedules c, inserted i
    WHERE c.JobId=i.JobId
```

With this trigger in place, programmers are restricted to storing only date values in the JobStart and JobEnd columns. They can try to insert a date and a time, but the time will be ignored. For example, consider the following INSERT statement:

```
INSERT INTO ContractorsSchedules(JobID, ContractorID, JobStart,
JobEnd, JobType)
VALUES('', 'Cindy', '2001-1-1 05:12','2001-1-10 19:15', 'H')
```

Even though this INSERT statement specifies both a date and a time for JobStart and JobEnd, only the dates were accepted:

```
SELECT ContractorId, JobStart, JobEnd
FROM ContractorsSchedules WHERE ContractorId='Cindy'

ContractorId JobStart               JobEnd
------------ ---------------------- ----------------------
Cindy        2001-01-01 00:00:00.000 2001-01-10 00:00:00.000
```

As you can see, the server cut off the time information that was mistakenly included in the INSERT statement.

 If you're following along with our examples, please delete the previously inserted row after you finish studying this recipe. Use the command: DELETE FROM ContractorsSchedules WHERE ContractorId='Cindy'.

Discussion

The trigger brings additional overhead to INSERT and UPDATE operations; however, it provides you with the security of knowing for sure that all temporal information is stored with the required granularity. You control the granularity by adjusting the constant in the CONVERT clause. For example, if you want to set the granularity to hours, you would extend the constant by three more characters:

```
CREATE TRIGGER ContractorSchedulesUpdate
ON ContractorsSchedules
FOR UPDATE, INSERT
AS
```

```
UPDATE ContractorsSchedules
SET JobStart=CONVERT(CHAR(13),i.JobStart,121)+':00',
   JobEnd=CONVERT(CHAR(13),i.JobEnd,121)+':00'
FROM ContractorsSchedules c, inserted i
WHERE c.JobId=i.JobId
```

With this trigger in place and using the same insert as shown in the recipe, the results will be as follows:

```
ContractorId JobStart                JobEnd
------------ ----------------------- -----------------------
  Cindy        2001-01-01 05:00:00.000 2001-01-10 19:00:00.000
```

Setting the scope of the CHAR type effectively chops off the unwanted characters from the ISO format YYYY-MM-DD HH:MI:SS.MMM, so that we are left with YYYY-MM-DD HH. However, after that we are violating the required ISO format, so we add the string ':00' to comply with the required form, which requires at least the minutes along with the hour. In this way, you can easily restrict the granularity in a table to any degree you desire.

 Please note that this solution does not prevent you from using the wrong temporal granularity in queries; i.e., in SELECT statements, it just prevents you from storing information with a granularity finer than you require.

5.4   Storing Out-of-Range Temporal Values

Problem

You are creating a database for an archeologist, and the archeologist needs to store dates that are outside the range of Transact-SQL's temporal datatypes.

Solution

Use the ISO 8601 format, preferably without the dashes between date elements, and store the data as string:

```
CREATE TABLE Archive(
   EventId CHAR(40),
   EventDate CHAR(8)
)
```

Now, insert a few dates and note the results:

```
INSERT INTO Archive
   VALUES ('Columbus departs from Palos, Spain', '14920802')
INSERT INTO Archive
   VALUES ('Columbus arrives at Cuba', '14921029')
INSERT INTO Archive
   VALUES ('Columbus returns to Spain', '14930315')
```

```
SELECT * FROM Archive

EventId                             EventDate
----------------------------------- ----------
Columbus departs from Palos, Spain  14920802
Columbus arrives at Cuba            14921029
Columbus returns to Spain           14930315
```

Discussion

This is, of course, the old programmer's trick for representing temporal data in languages that don't have native support for it. It's designed for AD dates and such dates can easily be sorted properly. There are, however, two additional issues that need emphasizing.

First, don't use the 'YYYY-MM-DD' format when using the technique illustrated in this recipe. If you do use that format, don't forget to include leading zeros for all date elements. Dates such as '1492-8-2' cannot be sorted properly with respect to '1492-10-12'. If you must include dashes in your dates, you should include leading zeros, as in: '1492-08-02'.

The second issue, more of a feature than a problem, is that you can easily extend this format to include hours, minutes, and even seconds. Simply include the requisite number of digits in the date string. This isn't to say, though, that we understand the need for such precise temporal values for dates prior to the 18th century.

5.5 Deriving the First and Last Dates of the Month

Problem

Given an arbitrary date, find the first and last day of the month in which that date falls.

Solution

Use the following query in which CURRENT_TIMESTAMP represents the arbitrary input date:

```
SELECT
   CONVERT(CHAR(8),CURRENT_TIMESTAMP,120)+'01' First_date,
   CAST(SPACE(
      DATEPART(weekday,
         CONVERT(CHAR(8),CURRENT_TIMESTAMP,120)+'01'
      )-1)+'*' as CHAR(8)) "SMTWTFS",
```

```
CONVERT(CHAR(10),
    DATEADD(day,-1,
        DATEADD(month,1,CONVERT(CHAR(8),CURRENT_TIMESTAMP,120)+'01')
    ),120) Last_date,
CAST(SPACE(
    DATEPART(weekday,
        DATEADD(day,-1,DATEADD(m,1,
            CONVERT(CHAR(8),CURRENT_TIMESTAMP,120)+'01')
        )
    )-1)+'*' AS CHAR(8)) "SMTWTFS "
```

This query is a bit complicated because rather than just return two date values, we've chosen also to return a graphical indication of the day-of-the-week on which the first and last dates of the month fall:

```
First_date SMTWTFS  Last_date  SMTWTFS
---------- --------  ---------- --------
2001-07-01 *        2001-07-31  *
```

We ran this query sometime during July, 2001. You can see that the first day of the month was July 1 (obvious) and that the last day of the month was July 31. The other two columns of output indicate that the first day of the month fell on a Sunday, while the last day of the month fell on a Tuesday.

It may seem obvious that the first day of any month is the first, but we've often found it necessary to write SQL queries that automatically calculate that date based on any arbitrary input date.

 We've used CURRENT_TIMESTAMP in this solution to provide an input date value. However, you can replace CURRENT_TIMESTAMP with any arbitrary date value, whether from a function, a column, a bind variable, or even a constant.

Discussion

Transact-SQL is quite strong in that it offers many ways to manipulate information about one point in time. The query in this recipe is a typical example of what you can do using Transact-SQL's built-in date functionality.

The first item in the query's select list translates the input date into a string to cut off the day part, which is then replaced with the constant '01':

```
CONVERT(CHAR(8), CURRENT_TIMESTAMP, 120)+'01'
```

The result of this expression is a string such as '2001-07-01'. The CONVERT function can return results in several different styles. Style 120, which we use here, is ISO compliant and takes the form YYYY-MM-DD HH:MI:SS. We keep just the first eight characters, resulting in a value in YYYY-MM- format. Then we add the '01' string, and the result is the date of the first day of the month.

To find out the day of the week on which a given day falls, we use the DATEPART function with the weekday parameter. That function returns 1 for Sunday, 2 for Monday, and so on. To print the result in a graphical format, we used the numeric day of the week value, along with the SPACE function to set the asterisk (*) in the right spot:

```
SPACE(
    DATEPART(weekday,
        CONVERT(CHAR(8),CURRENT_TIMESTAMP,120)+'01'
    )-1)+'*'
```

Calculating the last day of the month is trickier. The following logic is used in the query:

```
DATEADD(day,-1,DATEADD(month,1,
    CONVERT(CHAR(8),CURRENT_TIMESTAMP,120)+'01')
```

We take the current date (retrieved by CURRENT_TIMESTAMP), set it to the first day of the month, add one month to the result to get the first day of the following month, and, finally, subtract one day to get the last day of the current month.

There is one other little trick to this query that we should point out. Notice that we appear to have two columns of output labeled "SMTWTFS". As you know, SQL Server won't let you use two labels with the same name. A trick you can use in such cases is to add an additional space to the second label. To the server, "SMTWTFS" and "SMTWTFS " are not the same labels, but, to the user, they look the same.

5.6   Printing Calendars

Problem

You want to print a calendar, possibly for the entire year, in a nice-looking format.

Solution

The following query, which uses the Pivot table first introduced in Chapter 1, generates a set of sequential numbers, which are then transformed into dates and printed as a calendar:

```
SELECT
    STR(YEAR(CAST('2001-1-1' AS DATETIME)+i-6))+ SPACE(1)+
        SUBSTRING('JANFEBMARAPRMAYJUNJULAUGSEPOCTNOVDEC',
        MONTH(CAST('2001-1-1' AS DATETIME)+i)*3-2,3) Month,
    DAY(CAST('2001-1-1' AS DATETIME)+i-6) AS S,
    DAY(CAST('2001-1-1' AS DATETIME)+i-5) AS M,
    DAY(CAST('2001-1-1' AS DATETIME)+i-4) AS T,
    DAY(CAST('2001-1-1' AS DATETIME)+i-3) AS W,
    DAY(CAST('2001-1-1' AS DATETIME)+i-2) AS T,
    DAY(CAST('2001-1-1' AS DATETIME)+i-1) AS F,
    DAY(CAST('2001-1-1' AS DATETIME)+i) AS S
```

```
FROM Pivot
WHERE  DATEPART(dw,CAST('2001-1-1' AS DATETIME)+i)%7=0
ORDER BY i
```

The output from this query is a calendar, starting with the week of the initial date, which in this case is 2001-1-1:

```
Month           S    M    T    W    T    F    S
--------------  ---- ---- ---- ---- ---- ---- ----
     2000 DEC 30  31   1    2    3    4    5
     2001 JAN 6   7    8    9    10   11   12
     2001 JAN 13  14   15   16   17   18   19
     2001 JAN 20  21   22   23   24   25   26
     2001 JAN 27  28   29   30   31   1    2
     2001 FEB 3   4    5    6    7    8    9
     2001 FEB 10  11   12   13   14   15   16
     2001 FEB 17  18   19   20   21   22   23
     2001 FEB 24  25   26   27   28   1    2
     2001 MAR 3   4    5    6    7    8    9
...
```

Discussion

This solution demonstrates the use of a Pivot table (named Pivot in our example) to generate a sequence of dates. Look carefully at this query, and you'll see where we added a constant number to a set of DATETIME values rather than using the DATEADD function. We did this for readability. For example, rather than use DAY(CAST('2001-1-1' AS DATETIME)+i-6), we could have used DATEADD(day,i+6, CAST('2001-1-1' AS DATETIME)).

The first line of the SELECT statement extracts year information from the input date. Similarly, it extracts the month and then takes the appropriate month abbreviation from the string containing all possible abbreviations. The year and month information are then combined to form a label for each row of output.

In each row of output, you see the dates for the seven days of the week in question. We directly print only every seventh date (the Saturday), while all other days are calculated by subtracting the appropriate number of days from it.

Your initial reaction to this recipe might be to wonder why we didn't use addition instead of subtraction when calculating the dates for the different days of the week. Here, subtraction is more appropriate than addition. The WHERE clause results in a set of values from the Pivot table that, when added to the input date, yield a list of Saturdays. The first date returned will be that of the Saturday immediately following the input date. Subtraction is used to work backwards through the other days in that week. If addition were used, the days between the first Saturday and the initial date would be skipped. By using subtraction, we get dates for all days in the first week.

Rather than extracting the month abbreviation from a string constant, we could also use the DATENAME function. However, there are some problems with its use. The most important problem is that DATENAME returns names of months according to your current operating system language settings. Language settings can sometimes be wrong, so we prefer to use a string constant containing the month abbreviations. Nevertheless, in case you prefer to use DATENAME, the following is a DATE-NAME version of this recipe's solution:

```
SELECT
    STR(YEAR(CAST('2001-1-1' AS DATETIME)+i-6))+ SPACE(1)+
    DATENAME(month, CAST('2001-1-1' AS DATETIME)+i) Month,
    DAY(CAST('2001-1-1' AS DATETIME)+i-6) AS S,
    DAY(CAST('2001-1-1' AS DATETIME)+i-5) AS M,
    DAY(CAST('2001-1-1' AS DATETIME)+i-4) AS T,
    DAY(CAST('2001-1-1' AS DATETIME)+i-3) AS W,
    DAY(CAST('2001-1-1' AS DATETIME)+i-2) AS T,
    DAY(CAST('2001-1-1' AS DATETIME)+i-1) AS F,
    DAY(CAST('2001-1-1' AS DATETIME)+i) AS S
FROM Pivot
WHERE  DATEPART(dw,CAST('2001-1-1' AS DATETIME)+i)%7=0
ORDER BY i
```

Following is the result if the system has a different language set (in this case Slovenian) and runs the above query:

Month	S	M	T	W	T	F	S
2000 December	30	31	1	2	3	4	5
2001 Januar	6	7	8	9	10	11	12
2001 Januar	13	14	15	16	17	18	19
2001 Januar	20	21	22	23	24	25	26
2001 Januar	27	28	29	30	31	1	2
2001 Februar	3	4	5	6	7	8	9
2001 Februar	10	11	12	13	14	15	16
2001 Februar	17	18	19	20	21	22	23
2001 Februar	24	25	26	27	28	1	2
2001 Marec	3	4	5	6	7	8	9

...

Check the same code on your system, and you might get a different result if your system is set to a different language. This code clearly demonstrates how operating-system settings can affect results from date functions. We recommend that you use code dependent on operating-system settings only when you control those settings or when you need the settings to get the desired results.

5.7 Calculating Durations

Problem

You want to find out how many seconds, minutes, hours, days, or months have passed between two dates. Additionally, you want to calculate interest at a 5% yearly interest rate for 100 USD between those same two dates.

Solution

The first part of this problem is a typical date-arithmetic assignment, and the results can be calculated using the DATEDIFF function. In the following example, 2001-1-1 is used for the beginning date, and CURRENT_TIMESTAMP supplies the current date as the ending date.

```
SELECT
    DATEDIFF(second, '2001-1-1',CURRENT_TIMESTAMP) seconds,
    DATEDIFF(minute, '2001-1-1',CURRENT_TIMESTAMP) minutes,
    DATEDIFF(hour, '2001-1-1',CURRENT_TIMESTAMP) hours,
    DATEDIFF(day, '2001-1-1',CURRENT_TIMESTAMP) days,
    DATEDIFF(month, '2001-1-1',CURRENT_TIMESTAMP) months

seconds     minutes     hours       days        months
----------- ----------- ----------- ----------- -----------
26753371    445889      7431        309         10
```

DATEDIFF Returns Whole Units

Be careful when interpreting the results of a call to DATEDIFF. That function only returns whole units; any fractional values are truncated. For example, you can execute DATEDIFF(month, '2001-1-1',CURRENT_TIMESTAMP) anytime during the month of November and get the same value: 10. That's because until you reach December 1, 2001, a full 11 months have not passed. Fractional values are also not reported for seconds, minutes, hours, and days, but the lack thereof is most noticeable with large units, such as months.

The interest calculation is a bit more noteworthy:

```
SELECT
    100*(POWER(1.0500, CONVERT(NUMERIC(10,4),DATEDIFF(d, '2001-1-1',
        CURRENT_TIMESTAMP)/365.0000)))-100 Interest

Interest
----------------------------------------
4.2900
```

The result is in money units per 100 units, which, in this case, works out to $4.29 interest on our original amount of $100.00. Obviously, you'll get a different result depending on which day you run the query.

Discussion

The DATEDIFF function is a perfect tool for computing durations between two instants (dates). As a rule of thumb, you should always consider using it when dealing with calculations involving periods of time.

In the second query, the DATEDIFF function is used to calculate the number of days from January 1, 2001. With that information, the interest is calculated using the following formula:

```
Amount*1.0500^(NumDays/365.0000)
```

Please note, we wrote 365.0000 in the query, and not 365, on purpose. Using the latter value will result in integer arithmetic: decimal values will be truncated, reducing the interest rate to 0.

Similarly, we had to CAST the DATEDIFF result to the numeric type NUMERIC(10,4). The POWER function requires both arguments to have the same precision, so we expressed the interest rate as 1.0500. Because we are calculating interest, we need such precision to calculate meaningful results.

5.8   Reporting Durations

Problem

You have durations stored in terms of seconds, and you want to report those durations in a human-readable form. For example, you want to report a value such as 12345678 seconds in terms of days, hours, minutes, and seconds.

Solution

Use a little bit of math and some string formatting to report the result:

```
SELECT
    12345678/86400/30 months,
    (12345678/86400)%30 days,
    (1234567%86400)/3600 hours,
    (12345678%3600)/60 minutes,
    12345678%60 seconds
```

months	days	hours	minutes	seconds
4	22	6	21	18

Discussion

Obviously, this is a very simple mathematical problem. To calculate hours from seconds, for example, you only need to divide the number of seconds by 3600 (the number of seconds in one hour). If you need a cascading report, such as the one shown in our solution, you first divide the number of seconds by the number of seconds in a month. Then, you take the remainder of that value and divide by the number of seconds in a day to get the number of days. Continue the process until you work your way down to seconds.

The following is a walkthrough of our solution query:

`12345678/86400/30 months`

> Divides the duration by the number of seconds in a day (86400) to get days and divides that result by 30 to get a value for months. Since we don't know exactly which months we are talking about, we use an arbitrary 30-day month.

`(12345678/86400)%30 days`

> Divides the duration by the number of seconds in a day to get the number of days and then uses the remainder operator (%) to get the number of days left over after dividing by 30 to get months.

`(1234567%86400)/3600 hours`

> Uses the remainder operator to determine the number of seconds left over after dividing by days and divides that value by the number of seconds in an hour (3600) to get hours.

`(12345678%3600)/60 minutes`

> Uses the remainder operator to determine the number of seconds left over after dividing by hours and divides that value by 60 to get minutes.

`12345678%60 seconds`

> Computes seconds remaining after removing all the full minutes from the input value.

 Calculating the number of months in a duration can be tricky, since you really need dates to make such a calculation accurate. In our solution, we assume that each month has 30 days.

5.9   Querying Periods

Problem

You want to find all periods that include a particular date. With respect to our example, we might be interested in finding all contractors that worked on February 12, 2001. February 12, 2001 would be the date in question, and the JobStart and JobEnd dates from each schedule record would define the periods.

Solution

Use the BETWEEN operator to find the periods that include selected date:

```
SELECT
    JobId, ContractorId, CAST(JobStart AS CHAR(12)) JobStart,
    CAST(JobEnd AS CHAR(12)) JobEnd, JobType
FROM ContractorsSchedules
WHERE '2001-2-12' BETWEEN JobStart AND JobEnd
```

```
JobId       ContractorId JobStart     JobEnd       JobType
----------  ------------ ------------ ------------ -------
RF10022     Bob          Feb  5 2001  Feb 15 2001  B
RF10034     Alex         Feb 11 2001  Feb 20 2001  B
```

The results of the query indicate that both Alex and Bob were booked on February 12, 2001.

Discussion

The BETWEEN operator is an inclusive operator. It is equivalent to using both the greater-than-or-equal-to (>=) and less-than-or-equal-to (<=) operators. If your problems require exclusive, or partially exclusive, results, you should use the greater-than (>) or less-than (<) operators. For example, use the following query to find all projects that started before January 12, 2001 and that ended after January 12, 2001, but which did not start or end on exactly those dates:

```
SELECT
    JobId, ContractorId, CAST(JobStart AS CHAR(12)) JobStart,
    CAST(JobEnd AS CHAR(12)) JobEnd, JobType
FROM ContractorsSchedules
WHERE '2001-1-12' > JobStart
  AND JobEnd > '2001-1-12'

JobId       ContractorId JobStart     JobEnd       JobType
----------  ------------ ------------ ------------ -------
RF10001     Alex         Jan 11 2001  Jan 20 2001  B
RF10003     Bob          Jan  5 2001  Jan 15 2001  B
```

Note that we are representing date constants using strings. Using strings this way causes implicit casting (of string values to DATETIME values) in Transact-SQL. The server knows when standardized formats are in use and converts dates accordingly.

5.10   Querying Periods and Respecting Granularity

Problem

As in the previous recipe, you want to find all periods that include a particular date. However, you do not entirely trust the data within your database. Programmers are supposed to ensure that DATETIME values contain only dates (not times), but your experience has been that many DATETIME values do contain time-of-day components. You wish to write your query to avoid problems from time-of-day values.

With respect to our example, the date you are interested in is January 11, 2001, and you wish to find all contractors who are currently scheduled to work on that date.

Solution

Use the following query, which carefully avoids applying any functions to the two database columns, JobStart and JobEnd:

```
SELECT
    JobId, ContractorId, JobStart, JobEnd
FROM ContractorsSchedules
WHERE JobStart < (CAST('2001-1-11' AS DATETIME)+1)
  AND JobEnd >= CAST('2001-1-11' AS DATETIME)
```

```
JobId      ContractorId JobStart                 JobEnd
---------- ------------ ------------------------ --------------------------
RF10001    Alex         2001-01-11 00:00:00.000  2001-01-20 00:00:00.000
RF10003    Bob          2001-01-05 00:00:00.000  2001-01-15 00:00:00.000
```

Discussion

Why such a convoluted query? And why the need to avoid applying functions to database columns? Let's answer one question at a time. First, let's talk about the complexity. Your first thought when faced with the task of writing such a query that involves date ranges might be to use the following, simpler approach:

```
SELECT
    JobId, ContractorId, JobStart, JobEnd
FROM ContractorsSchedules
WHERE JobStart <= '2001-1-11'
  AND JobEnd >= '2001-1-11'
```

This approach is perfectly fine except for the implicit assumption that the time-of-day components of JobStart and JobEnd are always 00:00:00.000. But, if you had a JobStart date such as the one in the following record:

```
RF10001    Alex         2001-01-11 15:30:00.000   2001-01-20 00:00:00.000
```

the WHERE condition that SQL Server would evaluate would be:

```
JobStart <= '2001-1-11'
'2001-01-11 15:30:00.000' <= '2001-01-11 00:00:00.000'
```

The first line represents the condition as you wrote it, while the second line represents the actual values, after the implicit conversion of your input date, that SQL Server evaluates. Clearly, this condition will fail, resulting in the exclusion of job RF10001 from the query results. Yet, the job does begin on January 11, 2001, and you really do want it to appear in the list of jobs underway as of that date. What then, do you do?

Now you might think to apply a function to the JobStart date in the database to truncate any time-of-day component. For example:

```
CONVERT(CHAR(10),JobStart,120) <= CAST('2001-1-11' AS DATETIME)
```

This approach will work, but it has the unfortunate side effect of applying a function (CONVERT in this case) to a database column. That potentially precludes the use of any index that happens to exist on the column in question. For large tables, this can be a significant performance issue. If you happen to index the JobStart column and you wish to allow SQL Server the possibility of using that index, you'll need to take an approach such as the following:

```
JobStart < (CAST('2001-1-11' AS DATETIME)+1)
```

Here, the JobStart column is left untouched. Instead, we manipulate the date value that we are supplying to the query. First, we CAST our date into a DATETIME value. Then, we add 1 to the result. Because we have been sure not to include any time-of-day component in our constant, the result will be the first instant of the following day:

```
(CAST('2001-1-11' AS DATETIME)+1) = '2001-1-12 00:00:00.000'
```

The maximum granularity of a DATETIME value is in milliseconds. There can be no earlier time recorded for our DATETIME value than 00:00:00.000. This means that any DATETIME value that is less than (but not less than or equal to) the value returned by our expression must, in fact, fall sometime during or before January 11, 2001. Thus, we use the less-than operator (<) in our WHERE condition.

For the JobEnd date, we still use greater-than-or-equal (>=) operator:

```
AND JobEnd >= CAST('2001-1-11' AS DATETIME)
```

The comparison that SQL Server makes in this case is:

```
AND JobEnd >= '2001-1-11 00:00:00.000'
```

Again, our expression evaluates to the earliest possible time of day on January 11, 2001. Any time-of-day component associated with a JobEnd date of January 11, 2001 must, by necessity, be equal to or greater than the result of our expression. Hence, we use the greater-than-or-equal (>=) operator in this case.

The result of our careful approach is a query that ignores any time-of-day values for JobStart and JobEnd, does not preclude the use of any indices on those columns, but still returns any jobs underway as of our specified date.

5.11   Finding Available Periods

Problem

You want to derive a list of dates that are not marked as reserved in the Contractors-Schedules table. Such a query would be useful for finding days on which there is at least one contractor available. If a client calls and needs a contractor in January or February, the query should list dates during those months when contractors are available.

Solution

The Pivot table is part of the solution to this problem, because we need to generate a complete list of dates in a given period. The complete solution query is as follows:

```
SELECT
    CAST(DATEADD(day,i,'2001-1-1') AS CHAR(12)) Date
FROM Pivot, ContractorsSchedules c1
WHERE
    DATEADD(d,i,'2001-1-1') BETWEEN '2001-1-1' AND '2001-2-28'
GROUP BY i
HAVING (
    SELECT COUNT(DISTINCT c2.ContractorId)
    FROM ContractorsSchedules c2
    WHERE DATEADD(day,i,'2001-1-1')
        BETWEEN c2.JobStart AND c2.JobEnd)
    <
    COUNT(DISTINCT c1.ContractorId)
```

```
Date
------------
Jan  1 2001
Jan  2 2001
Jan  3 2001
Jan  4 2001
Jan 16 2001
Jan 17 2001
Jan 18 2001
Jan 19 2001
Jan 20 2001
...
```

Discussion

The query adds the Pivot value (the i column) to the beginning date of our period (2001-1-1) and restricts the results to those dates that fall between 2001-1-1 and 2001-2-28. Note that the Pivot numbers begin with 0. The following expression computes the complete set of dates:

```
CAST(DATEADD(day,i,'2001-1-1') AS CHAR(12)) Date
```

and the following condition restricts the list of dates to those falling in January and February:

```
WHERE
    DATEADD(d,i,'2001-1-1') BETWEEN '2001-1-1' AND '2001-2-28'
```

The query then joins each candidate date with rows from the ContractorsSchedules table. Together with the GROUP BY clause, a Cartesian join is created of all booked periods for each candidate date. The actual selection of the result dates is made within the HAVING clause:

```
HAVING (
    SELECT COUNT(DISTINCT c2.ContractorId)
    FROM ContractorsSchedules c2
    WHERE DATEADD(day,i,'2001-1-1')
        BETWEEN c2.JobStart AND c2.JobEnd)
    <
    COUNT(DISTINCT c1.ContractorId)
```

The HAVING clause looks complex. It works by querying for the number of contractors booked on the day in question and comparing to see whether that value is less than the total number of contractors. The subquery counts contractors booked on the day in question:

```
SELECT COUNT(DISTINCT c2.ContractorId)
FROM ContractorsSchedules c2
WHERE DATEADD(day,i,'2001-1-1') BETWEEN c2.JobStart AND c2.JobEnd
```

The second COUNT returns the number of all contractors in the Cartesian product:

```
COUNT(DISTINCT c1.ContractorId)
```

The comparison operator checks to see whether all contractors are actually booked on the date in question. If the number of booked periods within one group (representing a candidate date) is equal to the total number of contractors, the check fails and the candidate date is not reported. On the other hand, if not all contractors are booked, there must be some available, so the candidate date is returned in the result set.

Extending the query to report only those dates where there is a team of at least N contractors available is easy. You simply have to add N–1 to the subquery of the counted booked contractors. For example, use the following version of the subquery to return dates on which at least two contractors are available:

```
SELECT COUNT(DISTINCT c2.ContractorId) + 1
FROM ContractorsSchedules c2
WHERE DATEADD(day,i,'2001-1-1') BETWEEN c2.JobStart AND c2.JobEnd
```

5.12   Finding Common Available Periods

Problem

Similar to group schedulers, such as MS Exchange, you want to find common availability dates for a group of people. With respect to our example, let's say we want to find days in January and February on which both Alex and Bob are available.

Solution

Using logic similar to that used in the "Finding Available Periods" solution, we use the Pivot table to generate candidate dates. We then add a subquery to see whether both Bob and Alex are available for a given date:

```
SELECT
    CAST(DATEADD(day,i,'2001-1-1') AS CHAR(12)) Date
FROM Pivot
WHERE
    DATEADD(day,i,'2001-1-1')
        BETWEEN '2001-1-1' AND '2001-2-28' AND
    NOT EXISTS(
        SELECT * FROM ContractorsSchedules
        WHERE (ContractorId='Alex' OR ContractorId='Bob') AND
            DATEADD(day,i,'2001-1-1') BETWEEN JobStart AND JobEnd
    )

Date
------------
Jan 31 2001
Feb 21 2001
Feb 22 2001
Feb 23 2001
Feb 24 2001
Feb 25 2001
Feb 26 2001
Feb 27 2001
Feb 28 2001
```

Discussion

The problem of needing to find available periods within known schedules occurs frequently, and the solution is actually quite straightforward. The solution query uses the Pivot table to generate a list of all possible dates within the period of interest (February 1–28, 2001, in this case).

The first part of the WHERE clause limits the dates so that they fall within the given period. The second part of the WHERE clause is a correlated subquery that checks, for each date, to see whether either Alex or Bob are booked. If neither Alex nor Bob are booked, the subquery will return no rows, the NOT EXISTS clause will be satisfied, and the date in question will be added to the query's result set.

5.13   Excluding Recurrent Events

Problem

You have two dates, and you want to calculate the number of working days between them. This means that you must exclude Saturdays and Sundays from the calculation. For example, let's calculate the number of working days between January 1, 2001 and March 1, 2001.

Solution

Use the following query, which makes use of the Pivot table and the DATEPART function to exclude weekend days:

```
SELECT
    COUNT(*) No_working_days,
    DATEDIFF(day,'2002-1-1','2002-3-1') No_days
FROM Pivot
WHERE
    DATEADD(day,i,'2002-1-1') BETWEEN '2002-1-1' AND '2002-3-1' AND
    DATEPART(weekday, DATEADD(d,i,'2002-1-1')) BETWEEN 2 AND 6
```

The query calculates the number of working and calendar days between the two dates:

```
No_working_days No_days
--------------- -----------
44              59
```

Discussion

Querying the Pivot table generates sequential numbers that are then translated into dates using the DATEADD function. The first part of the WHERE clause uses BETWEEN to restrict the result set to only those dates between the two dates of interest. The second part of the WHERE clause makes use of the DATEPART function to determine which dates represent Saturdays and Sundays and eliminates those dates from the result. You are left with the working days.

The COUNT(*) function in the SELECT list counts up the working days between the two dates, and the DATEDIFF function in the SELECT list returns the number of calendar days between the two dates.

> DATEDIFF is a simple function and returns the number of calendar dates between two dates when used with the DAY parameter.

5.14   Excluding Nonrecurring Events

Problem

You want to include calendar information in your queries, and you wish to exclude national holidays and other nonworking days. Unlike weekends, which recur on a weekly basis, holidays can be characterized as nonrecurring events.

Some holidays do recur on a yearly basis, even on the same date each year, but it's still convenient to treat them as nonrecurring events.

Solution

To implement support for holidays and other special dates, you have to store them in your database. You'll need a table such as the following:

```
CREATE TABLE Holidays(
    Holiday DATETIME,
    HolidayName CHAR(30)
)
```

After creating the table, populate it with a list of applicable holidays. For recipes in this chapter, we will use the following Slovene holidays:

```
SELECT CONVERT(CHAR(10),Holiday,120) Holiday,HolidayName FROM Holidays

Holiday     HolidayName
---------- ------------------------------
2001-01-01 New Year Holiday
2001-01-02 New Year Holiday
2001-02-08 Slovene Culture Holiday
2001-04-16 Easter Monday
2001-04-27 Resistance Day
2001-05-01 Labour Holiday
2001-05-02 Labour Holiday
2001-06-25 Day of the Republic
2001-08-15 Assumption of Mary
2001-10-31 Reformation Day
2001-12-25 Christmas
2001-12-26 Independance Day
```

To calculate working days between January 1 and March 1, excluding holidays and weekends, use the following query:

```
SELECT
    COUNT(*) No_working_days,
    DATEDIFF(day,'2001-1-1','2001-3-1') No_days
FROM Pivot
WHERE
    DATEADD(day,i,'2001-1-1') BETWEEN '2001-1-1' AND '2001-3-1' AND
    DATEPART(weekday, DATEADD(d,i,'2001-1-1')) BETWEEN 2 AND 6 AND
    NOT EXISTS(SELECT * FROM Holidays
        WHERE holiday=DATEADD(day,i,'2001-1-1'))

No_working_days No_days
--------------- -----------
41              59
```

Note that in the table, there are three holidays between the dates specified in the query, January 1, 2001 and March 1, 2001, and that the query returns 41, which is exactly 3 days less than the result we calculated when we didn't use the Holidays table.

Discussion

This solution query is just an extension from the one used in the previous recipe; it differs only in the last part of the WHERE clause where support for holidays is added. The first part of the query generates the candidate dates and excludes all recurring events (weekends). The last part of the WHERE clause is a subquery that further excludes any dates listed in the Holidays table:

```
NOT EXISTS(SELECT * FROM Holidays
    WHERE holiday=DATEADD(day,i,'2001-1-1'))
```

This subquery can be used in any query from which you want to exclude holidays. If you have types of dates other than holidays to exclude, you can easily extend this pattern by creating other date-exclusion tables. For example, you could build a separate table to reflect planned downtime for a factory.

You can easily add columns to the Holidays table if you need to track more information about each holiday. The key problem with this solution is that users need to keep the Holidays table up-to-date with enough holiday information to at least cover any period you anticipate using in a query. If populated just for one year, the results are correct only if all queries include only periods within that year. If you query for data beyond the scope of the rows currently in the Holidays table, you will get results, but those results will not be correct.

As in other code recipes, the DATEADD function is just a tool that generates dates from the Pivot table. We used it here, because we needed to generate a row for each date between our two dates. If you build your queries to run against a table with dates in each record, and for which you do not need to generate missing dates on the fly, simply replace the i column from the Pivot table with your own date column:

```
DATEPART(dw,SampleDate) BETWEEN 2 AND 6 AND
NOT EXISTS(SELECT * FROM Holidays
    WHERE holiday=SampleDate)
```

5.15   Finding Continuous Periods

Problem

You want to find continuous periods from a list of periods in the database. In our example, you want to list all periods during which a contractor is booked and you wish to merge all neighboring periods into one.

Solution

Use the following query to obtain a list of periods during which contractors are booked:

```
SELECT
    c1.ContractorId ContractorId,
    CAST(c1.JobStart AS CHAR(12)) JobStart,
    CAST(c2.JobEnd AS CHAR(12)) JobEnd,
    DATEDIFF(d,c1.JobStart, c2.JobEnd)+1 Length
FROM
    ContractorsSchedules c1,
    ContractorsSchedules c2,
    ContractorsSchedules c3
WHERE
    c1.ContractorId=c2.ContractorId AND c1.JobStart <= c2.JobStart AND
    c1.ContractorId=c3.ContractorId AND
        c3.JobStart BETWEEN c1.JobStart AND c2.JobEnd AND
    NOT EXISTS(
        SELECT * FROM ContractorsSchedules c4
        WHERE c4.ContractorId=c1.ContractorId AND
            c2.JobEnd+1 BETWEEN c4.JobStart AND c4.JobEnd) AND
    NOT EXISTS(
        SELECT * FROM ContractorsSchedules c5
        WHERE c5.ContractorId=c1.ContractorId AND
            c1.JobStart-1 BETWEEN c5.JobStart AND c5.JobEnd)
GROUP BY c1.ContractorId, c1.JobStart, c2.JobEnd
HAVING
    SUM(DATEDIFF(d,c3.JobStart,c3.JobEnd)) + COUNT(*)
    =
    DATEDIFF(d,c1.JobStart,c2.JobEnd) + 1
ORDER BY ContractorId, c1. JobStart
```

The results should appear as follows:

```
ContractorId JobStart     JobEnd       Length
------------ ------------ ------------ ----------
Alex         Feb  1 2001  Feb  5 2001  5
Alex         Feb 11 2001  Feb 20 2001  10
Alex         Jan  1 2001  Jan 30 2001  30
Bob          Feb  5 2001  Feb 15 2001  11
Bob          Jan  5 2001  Jan 15 2001  11
```

Discussion

This problem may sound simple at first; however, there are some aspects to it that make it a good example of periodic manipulation. The key problem is in the handling of neighboring periods. If two periods are neighbors, the beginning of one period will be one temporal unit apart from the end of the other period. In our example, the temporal unit is one day, so a contractor might stop work on one project on a given day only to begin work on another project the very next day. For the purposes of this report, we want to report an extended time period that covers both projects. How do we accomplish this?

Let's think about the definition of a period for a moment. A period is defined as a duration with definite beginning and end points. All contractor jobs begin on a specific date, and they all end on a specific date. Let's apply the same concept to a sequence of adjacent periods. If a contractor has several projects that come in succession, there will always be one project that comes first and one project that comes last. We are interested in the JobStart date from the first project and the JobEnd date from the last project.

The key to our query now is to identify correctly the first and last projects in a series of adjacent projects. We can begin by joining the ContractorsSchedules table to itself, thereby generating all possible combinations of JobStart and JobEnd dates. In this recipe, we'll refer to each such combination as a *candidate*. The following set of characteristics can then be used to narrow the results down to only those candidates that represent the beginning and end of a series of adjacent projects for a given contractor:

- The candidate JobEnd date must not immediately precede the JobStart date of another project.
- The candidate JobStart date must not immediately follow the JobEnd date of another project.
- The JobStart date from the first project in the series must be less than the JobEnd date from the last project in the series.
- There must be no unassigned days (i.e., not within a project) within a candidate date range.

We begin writing our solution query by joining ContractorsSchedules to itself, thus generating all possible combinations of JobStart dates from one project with JobEnd dates from a second project. We join ContractorsSchedules to itself a third time to include all possible combinations of intervening projects. The following SELECT represents the beginnings of our query. We've added columns to display the dates from c3 to make it easier for you to follow our logic as we walk through the remainder of the query. We've also modified the headings slightly to make it clear from which alias (c1, c2, or c3) each date is drawn.

```
SELECT
    c1.ContractorId ContractorId,
    CAST(c1.JobStart AS CHAR(12)) JobStart1,
    CAST(c2.JobEnd AS CHAR(12)) JobEnd2,
    DATEDIFF(d,c1.JobStart, c2.JobEnd)+1 Length,
    CAST(c3.JobStart as CHAR(12)) JobStart3,
    CAST(c3.JobEnd as CHAR(12)) JobEnd3
FROM
    ContractorsSchedules c1,
    ContractorsSchedules c2,
    ContractorsSchedules c3
WHERE
    c1.ContractorId=c2.ContractorId AND c1.JobStart <= c2.JobStart AND
    c1.ContractorId=c3.ContractorId AND
        c3.JobStart BETWEEN c1.JobStart AND c2.JobEnd
```

ContractorId	JobStart1	JobEnd2	Length	JobStart3	JobEnd3
Alex	Jan 1 2001	Jan 10 2001	10	Jan 1 2001	Jan 10 2001
Alex	Jan 1 2001	Jan 20 2001	20	Jan 1 2001	Jan 10 2001
Alex	Jan 1 2001	Jan 30 2001	30	Jan 1 2001	Jan 10 2001
Alex	Jan 1 2001	Feb 5 2001	36	Jan 1 2001	Jan 10 2001
Alex	Jan 1 2001	Feb 20 2001	51	Jan 1 2001	Jan 10 2001
Alex	Jan 1 2001	Jan 20 2001	20	Jan 11 2001	Jan 20 2001
Alex	Jan 1 2001	Jan 30 2001	30	Jan 11 2001	Jan 20 2001
Alex	Jan 1 2001	Feb 5 2001	36	Jan 11 2001	Jan 20 2001
Alex	Jan 1 2001	Feb 20 2001	51	Jan 11 2001	Jan 20 2001
Alex	Jan 1 2001	Jan 30 2001	30	Jan 21 2001	Jan 30 2001
Alex	Jan 1 2001	Feb 5 2001	36	Jan 21 2001	Jan 30 2001
Alex	Jan 1 2001	Feb 20 2001	51	Jan 21 2001	Jan 30 2001
Alex	Jan 1 2001	Feb 5 2001	36	Feb 1 2001	Feb 5 2001
Alex	Jan 1 2001	Feb 20 2001	51	Feb 1 2001	Feb 5 2001
Alex	Jan 1 2001	Feb 20 2001	51	Feb 11 2001	Feb 20 2001
Alex	Jan 11 2001	Jan 20 2001	10	Jan 11 2001	Jan 20 2001
Alex	Jan 11 2001	Jan 30 2001	20	Jan 11 2001	Jan 20 2001
Alex	Jan 11 2001	Feb 5 2001	26	Jan 11 2001	Jan 20 2001
Alex	Jan 11 2001	Feb 20 2001	41	Jan 11 2001	Jan 20 2001
Alex	Jan 11 2001	Jan 30 2001	20	Jan 21 2001	Jan 30 2001
Alex	Jan 11 2001	Feb 5 2001	26	Jan 21 2001	Jan 30 2001
Alex	Jan 11 2001	Feb 20 2001	41	Jan 21 2001	Jan 30 2001
Alex	Jan 11 2001	Feb 5 2001	26	Feb 1 2001	Feb 5 2001
Alex	Jan 11 2001	Feb 20 2001	41	Feb 1 2001	Feb 5 2001
Alex	Jan 11 2001	Feb 20 2001	41	Feb 11 2001	Feb 20 2001
Alex	Jan 21 2001	Jan 30 2001	10	Jan 21 2001	Jan 30 2001
Alex	Jan 21 2001	Feb 5 2001	16	Jan 21 2001	Jan 30 2001
Alex	Jan 21 2001	Feb 20 2001	31	Jan 21 2001	Jan 30 2001
Alex	Jan 21 2001	Feb 5 2001	16	Feb 1 2001	Feb 5 2001
Alex	Jan 21 2001	Feb 20 2001	31	Feb 1 2001	Feb 5 2001
Alex	Jan 21 2001	Feb 20 2001	31	Feb 11 2001	Feb 20 2001
Alex	Feb 1 2001	Feb 5 2001	5	Feb 1 2001	Feb 5 2001
Alex	Feb 1 2001	Feb 20 2001	20	Feb 1 2001	Feb 5 2001
Alex	Feb 1 2001	Feb 20 2001	20	Feb 11 2001	Feb 20 2001
Alex	Feb 11 2001	Feb 20 2001	10	Feb 11 2001	Feb 20 2001
Bob	Jan 5 2001	Jan 15 2001	11	Jan 5 2001	Jan 15 2001
Bob	Jan 5 2001	Feb 15 2001	42	Jan 5 2001	Jan 15 2001
Bob	Jan 5 2001	Feb 15 2001	42	Feb 5 2001	Feb 15 2001
Bob	Feb 5 2001	Feb 15 2001	11	Feb 5 2001	Feb 15 2001

(39 row(s) affected)

In this query, the c1 alias represents the first project in a series of projects. The c2 alias represents the last project in a series. The c3 alias represents a possible project in between c1 and c2 (see the seventh row of output). As it currently stands, this query simply generates a list of candidate periods. We need to eliminate periods that don't meet our criteria.

We can begin by eliminating any candidate periods that have neighbors. The SELECT statement in the following NOT EXISTS clause identifies candidates for which there is another project adjacent to the candidate end date (c2.JobEnd):

```
NOT EXISTS(
    SELECT * FROM ContractorsSchedules c4
    WHERE c4.ContractorId=c1.ContractorId AND
      c2.JobEnd+1 BETWEEN c4.JobStart AND c4.JobEnd)
```

Let's talk about this NOT EXISTS in detail. c2.JobEnd represents our candidate end date. We need to find out whether any other projects overlap that end date. Notice that we add one day to the end date. We do that because we wish to use the BETWEEN operator. If c2.JobEnd is one day prior to c4.JobStart, BETWEEN will return false. We add 1 to c2.JobEnd so that it overlaps any c4.JobStart date representing the next day. For example, if c2.JobEnd is January 10 and there exists another job for the period January 11–January 20, the addition of one day converts:

```
Jan 10 BETWEEN Jan 11 and Jan 20
```

to:

```
Jan 11 BETWEEN Jan 11 and Jan 20
```

This condition will be true, and the candidate period ending on January 11 will be eliminated because the period can obviously be extended through January 20.

But what about c4.JobEnd? If c2.JobEnd is January 20 and c4.JobEnd is also January 20, adding one day to the c2.JobEnd date will bring it out of range. For example:

```
Jan 20 BETWEEN Jan 11 and Jan 20
```

becomes:

```
Jan 21 BETWEEN Jan 11 and Jan 20
```

It's not a problem, because if two projects end on the same date, that end date is still a valid ending date for a series of projects. Later in the query, we'll use the GROUP BY clause to eliminate any possible duplicate rows that result from two projects ending (or beginning) on the same date.

Just as we eliminate candidates' date ranges that can be extended going forward, we also need to eliminate those candidates' date ranges that can be extended going backwards. The following logic is used to do this:

```
NOT EXISTS(
    SELECT * FROM ContractorsSchedules c5
    WHERE c5.ContractorId=c1.ContractorId AND
      c1.JobStart-1 BETWEEN c5.JobStart AND c5.JobEnd)
```

As you can see, this logic is similar to the previous NOT EXISTS clause. The difference is that we are working with c1.JobStart, and we subtract one day rather than add, because we are looking backwards this time.

The following version of the query shows the results of eliminating candidate periods that can be extended forwards or backwards:

```
SELECT
    c1.ContractorId ContractorId,
    CAST(c1.JobStart AS CHAR(12)) JobStart1,
    CAST(c2.JobEnd AS CHAR(12)) JobEnd2,
    DATEDIFF(d,c1.JobStart, c2.JobEnd)+1 Length,
    CAST(c3.JobStart as CHAR(12)) JobStart3,
    CAST(c3.JobEnd as CHAR(12)) JobEnd3
FROM
    ContractorsSchedules c1,
    ContractorsSchedules c2,
    ContractorsSchedules c3
WHERE
    c1.ContractorId=c2.ContractorId AND c1.JobStart <= c2.JobStart AND
    c1.ContractorId=c3.ContractorId AND
        c3.JobStart BETWEEN c1.JobStart AND c2.JobEnd AND
    NOT EXISTS(
        SELECT * FROM ContractorsSchedules c4
        WHERE c4.ContractorId=c1.ContractorId AND
            c2.JobEnd+1 BETWEEN c4.JobStart AND c4.JobEnd) AND
    NOT EXISTS(
        SELECT * FROM ContractorsSchedules c5
        WHERE c5.ContractorId=c1.ContractorId AND
            c1.JobStart-1 BETWEEN c5.JobStart AND c5.JobEnd)
```

ContractorId	JobStart1	JobEnd2	Length	JobStart3	JobEnd3
Alex	Jan 1 2001	Jan 30 2001	30	Jan 1 2001	Jan 10 2001
Alex	Jan 1 2001	Jan 30 2001	30	Jan 11 2001	Jan 20 2001
Alex	Jan 1 2001	Jan 30 2001	30	Jan 21 2001	Jan 30 2001
Alex	Jan 1 2001	Feb 5 2001	36	Jan 1 2001	Jan 10 2001
Alex	Jan 1 2001	Feb 5 2001	36	Jan 11 2001	Jan 20 2001
Alex	Jan 1 2001	Feb 5 2001	36	Jan 21 2001	Jan 30 2001
Alex	Jan 1 2001	Feb 5 2001	36	Feb 1 2001	Feb 5 2001
Alex	Feb 1 2001	Feb 5 2001	5	Feb 1 2001	Feb 5 2001
Alex	Jan 1 2001	Feb 20 2001	51	Jan 1 2001	Jan 10 2001
Alex	Jan 1 2001	Feb 20 2001	51	Jan 11 2001	Jan 20 2001
Alex	Jan 1 2001	Feb 20 2001	51	Jan 21 2001	Jan 30 2001
Alex	Jan 1 2001	Feb 20 2001	51	Feb 1 2001	Feb 5 2001
Alex	Jan 1 2001	Feb 20 2001	51	Feb 11 2001	Feb 20 2001
Alex	Feb 1 2001	Feb 20 2001	20	Feb 1 2001	Feb 5 2001
Alex	Feb 1 2001	Feb 20 2001	20	Feb 11 2001	Feb 20 2001
Alex	Feb 11 2001	Feb 20 2001	10	Feb 11 2001	Feb 20 2001
Bob	Jan 5 2001	Jan 15 2001	11	Jan 5 2001	Jan 15 2001
Bob	Jan 5 2001	Feb 15 2001	42	Jan 5 2001	Jan 15 2001
Bob	Jan 5 2001	Feb 15 2001	42	Feb 5 2001	Feb 15 2001
Bob	Feb 5 2001	Feb 15 2001	11	Feb 5 2001	Feb 15 2001

Our WHERE clause is now complete, and we are left with a much shorter list of possible candidate periods. We've eliminated candidate periods that can be extended and, thus, are too short. Now, we need to eliminate duplicate rows from the result set. We use the following GROUP BY clause:

```
GROUP BY c1.ContractorId, c1.JobStart, c2.JobEnd
```

If you've been following along with our examples so far, you'll realize that adding this GROUP BY clause forces us to change our SELECT list. You'll see that change in a moment, but first we need to eliminate one more set of unwanted candidate periods.

We haven't checked for gaps yet within our candidate periods. Each candidate period (c1.JobStart through c2.JobEnd) represents a sequence of one or more projects. If more than one project is involved, we need to ensure that there are no unassigned days within the candidate period. This is where the HAVING clause comes into play.

Remember the c3 alias? It represents all periods whose start dates lay within any of our candidate periods. To ensure that there are no gaps, we count the days between c1.JobStart and c2.JobEnd and compare that result to the sum of the days for all the intervening projects:

```
HAVING
    SUM(DATEDIFF(d,c3.JobStart,c3.JobEnd)) + COUNT(*)
    =
    DATEDIFF(d,c1.JobStart,c2.JobEnd) + 1
```

The SUM function sums the lengths of all included periods (within c3). The first expression adds one day for each included period (i.e., each c3 row). This is done because DATEDIFF returns the difference between two dates and not the number of days involved. For example: Jan 2–Jan 1 = 1 day, yet that period represents 2 days. We lose one day from each c3 period that we look at, so the expression adds one day for each such period, well, almost.

The second DATEDIFF function call returns the total number of days in the candidate period. Here, too, we have to add one day to the DATEDIFF result, to calculate the number of days from the date difference. If the number of days in the candidate period is the same as the number of days in all periods falling within the candidate period, we know that there are no unassigned days, or gaps, and that our candidate period truly represents a contiguous period of activity for the contractor in question. This gets us to our complete query:

```
SELECT
    c1.ContractorId ContractorId,
    CAST(c1.JobStart AS CHAR(12)) JobStart,
    CAST(c2.JobEnd AS CHAR(12)) JobEnd,
    DATEDIFF(d,c1.JobStart, c2.JobEnd)+1 Length
FROM
    ContractorsSchedules c1,
    ContractorsSchedules c2,
    ContractorsSchedules c3
```

```
WHERE
    c1.ContractorId=c2.ContractorId AND c1.JobStart <= c2.JobStart AND
    c1.ContractorId=c3.ContractorId AND
        c3.JobStart BETWEEN c1.JobStart AND c2.JobEnd AND
    NOT EXISTS(
        SELECT * FROM ContractorsSchedules c4
        WHERE c4.ContractorId=c1.ContractorId AND
            c2.JobEnd+1 BETWEEN c4.JobStart AND c4.JobEnd) AND
    NOT EXISTS(
        SELECT * FROM ContractorsSchedules c5
        WHERE c5.ContractorId=c1.ContractorId AND
            c1.JobStart-1 BETWEEN c5.JobStart AND c5.JobEnd)
GROUP BY c1.ContractorId, c1.JobStart, c2.JobEnd
HAVING
    SUM(DATEDIFF(d,c3.JobStart,c3.JobEnd)) + COUNT(*)
    =
    DATEDIFF(d,c1.JobStart,c2.JobEnd) + 1
ORDER BY ContractorId, c1.JobStart
```

The GROUP BY clause defines the groups over which the SUM function operates. Each candidate period becomes one group. The HAVING clause functions as we've just described. The ORDER BY clause simply sorts the results by JobStart date for each contractor.

Note that our proposed solution to this recipe is applicable only in situations where business rules prevent contractors from having overlapping assignments. We've done that to simplify the query. The idea of counting days in the HAVING clause flies out the window when projects can overlap, because, in such a case, the number of project days can exceed the number of calendar days. To make our solution valid for cases where assignments are allowed to overlap, rewrite the HAVING clause as follows:

```
HAVING NOT EXISTS(
    SELECT c1.JobStart+i
    FROM Pivot
    WHERE i <= DATEDIFF(day,c1.JobStart,c2.JobEnd) AND
    NOT EXISTS (SELECT * FROM ContractorsSchedules c6
                WHERE c1.JobStart+i BETWEEN c6.JobStart AND c6.JobEnd
                AND c6.ContractorId = c1.ContractorId))
```

In this HAVING clause, we have a subquery against the Pivot table that returns one row for each date in the candidate period. We have yet another subquery that filters out those rows that correspond to scheduled projects. If all dates in the candidate period are scheduled, the outer subquery will return no rows, and the candidate period will be accepted. Otherwise, the candidate period will be rejected. The use of the Pivot table and the nested subquery add to the complexity of this solution.

5.16   Using Calendar Information with Periods

Problem

You want to find dates on which at least one contractor is available; however, you are interested only in work days, not in weekends and holidays.

Solution

Use the query shown earlier for finding available periods, and exclude all Saturdays, Sundays, and holidays from the results:

```
SELECT
    CAST(DATEADD(day,i,'2001-1-1') AS CHAR(12)) Date
FROM Pivot, ContractorsSchedules c1
WHERE
    DATEADD(day,i,'2001-1-1') BETWEEN '2001-1-1' AND '2001-2-28' AND
    DATEPART(weekday,DATEADD(day,i,'2001-1-1')) BETWEEN 2 AND 6 AND
    NOT EXISTS(SELECT * FROM Holidays
        WHERE holiday=DATEADD(day,i,'2001-1-1'))
GROUP BY i
HAVING (
    SELECT COUNT(DISTINCT c2.ContractorId)
    FROM ContractorsSchedules c2
    WHERE DATEADD(day,i,'2001-1-1') BETWEEN c2.JobStart AND c2.JobEnd)
    <
    COUNT(DISTINCT c1.ContractorId)

Date
------------
Jan  3 2001
Jan  4 2001
Jan 16 2001
Jan 17 2001
Jan 18 2001
Jan 19 2001
Jan 22 2001
...
```

Note that January 20 and 21 are not listed in this output, because those dates represent a Saturday and a Sunday. Similarly, January 1 is excluded because it is a holiday.

Discussion

This query uses the Pivot table to generate all possible dates in the range of interest. The results are joined to the ContractorsSchedules table, so that all possible reserved periods are joined to each date. The WHERE clause conditions function as follows:

- Condition 1 of the WHERE clause uses the DATEADD function to restrict the results to only the time period in which we are interested. In this example, that period is January 1, 2001 through February 28, 2001.

- Condition 2 of the WHERE clause uses the DATEPART function to exclude Saturdays and Sundays from the results.

- Condition 3 of the WHERE clause uses a subquery to exclude holidays from the results.

After the WHERE clause evaluations take place, each remaining selection of candidate members is grouped via the GROUP BY clause. Each row that is summarized represents one contractor who is available on the date in question. The HAVING clause restricts query results to those dates on which the total number of contractors exceeds the number of assigned contractors.

5.17   Using Calendar Information with Durations

Problems

You want to find out which day was 15 working days after January 1, 2001 to correctly determine the end date for a 15-day project. You must not count weekends and holidays.

Solution

Combine the calendar code shown earlier in the "Excluding Recurrent Events" and "Excluding Nonrecurring Events" recipes with a date stream, count the working days from the date of interest, and report the one that is 15 days out:

```
SELECT TOP 1
    CAST(DATEADD(day,p2.i,'2001-1-1') AS CHAR(12)) Date
FROM Pivot p1, Pivot p2
WHERE
    p1.i<=p2.i AND
    DATEPART(weekday,
        DATEADD(day,p1.i,'2001-1-1')) BETWEEN 2 AND 6 AND
    NOT EXISTS(SELECT * FROM Holidays
        WHERE holiday=DATEADD(day,p1.i,'2001-1-1'))
GROUP BY p2.i
HAVING COUNT(*)=15
ORDER BY DATEADD(day,p2.i,'2001-1-1')

Date
------------
Jan 23 2001
```

In this example, the project plan assumes 15 working days for the project, which is scheduled to start on January 1, 2001, so the job ends on January 23, 2001.

Discussion

Because we have to count 15 working days from a given date, our query has to implement some sequencing function. Otherwise, it's not possible in Transact-SQL to retrieve the Nth row from a result set without using a cursor. The need for a sequence is at the root of the Pivot table's self-join.

The query joins two instances of the Pivot table, which are aliased as p1 and p2. p2 is used to generate a sequence of dates, while p1 is used to generate, for each p2 date, all the dates that are less than the p2 date. The results are then grouped by p2.i, making the COUNT(*) value for each group into our counter. Look, for example, at the output from a slightly modified version of the query that omits the GROUP BY and HAVING clauses. A word of caution: this query is very expensive, though instructive, so give it a little time to return the result:

```
SELECT
    CAST(DATEADD(day,p2.i,'2001-1-1') AS CHAR(12)) p2i,
    CAST(DATEADD(day,p1.i,'2001-1-1') AS CHAR(12)) p1i
FROM Pivot p1, Pivot p2
WHERE
    p1.i<=p2.i AND
    DATEPART(weekday,
        DATEADD(day,p1.i,'2001-1-1')) BETWEEN 2 AND 6 AND
    NOT EXISTS(SELECT * FROM Holidays
        WHERE holiday=DATEADD(day,p1.i,'2001-1-1'))
ORDER BY DATEADD(day,p2.i,'2001-1-1')


p2i          p1i
------------ ------------
Jan  2 2001  Jan  2 2001
Jan  3 2001  Jan  2 2001
Jan  3 2001  Jan  3 2001
Jan  4 2001  Jan  2 2001
Jan  4 2001  Jan  3 2001
Jan  4 2001  Jan  4 2001
...
```

As you can see, we get one row for January 2 (because that is one day past January 1), two rows for January 3 (because that is two days past January 1), three rows for January 4, and so forth. These are all working days. The clauses in the WHERE clause have already eliminated weekends and holidays using techniques you've seen in previous recipes. Group these results by p2i, the date in the first column, and you get the following:

```
SELECT
    CAST(DATEADD(day,p2.i,'2001-1-1') AS CHAR(12)) p2i,
    COUNT(*) days_past
FROM Pivot p1, Pivot p2
WHERE
    p1.i<=p2.i AND
    DATEPART(weekday,
        DATEADD(day,p1.i,'2001-1-1')) BETWEEN 2 AND 6 AND
    NOT EXISTS(SELECT * FROM Holidays
        WHERE holiday=DATEADD(day,p1.i,'2001-1-1'))
GROUP BY p2.i
ORDER BY p2.i
```

```
p2i            days_past
-----------    -----------
Jan  2 2001    1
Jan  3 2001    2
Jan  4 2001    3
...
```

Now, it's simply a matter of using a HAVING clause (`HAVING COUNT(*)=15`) to restrict the output to those days on which the days_past count is 15, and then using TOP 1 to return the first such date. Days on which days_past=15 are those that are 15 working days past January 1, 2000 (counting January 1, 2000 as one of the working days). Because of weekends and holidays, there can actually be more than one such date. Our query ensures that the first such date will be a working day, because only working days advance the counter; the ORDER BY clause sorts the results in date order.

CHAPTER 6
Audit Logging

A *log* is a record of activities or a record of changes to the data in an object, such as a table. Logs can be implemented and used for many purposes. SQL Server implements database logs that are used to maintain database integrity and consistency, improve performance, and help you identify problems. Examples of such logs are transactional logs, cache logs, and disk logs. Some of these logs are accessible, but none of them is really designed to be useful in an auditing situation.

If you have a critical database and you want to keep an accurate record of user activity against that database, you can implement a system of audit logs. That's what the recipes in this chapter address. An audit log allows you to track the changes that users make to a table. You can find out who did what and when. Audit logs also allow you to track other activity in a system. If implemented correctly, you can even use an audit log to view a snapshot of a table's data as of a specific point in time.

6.1   Audit Logs

In this chapter, we'll show you how to implement an audit log that can be used to track changes to the data in a table or that can be used to track a user's activities at a higher level. Before you begin, there are several things that you need to think about. These include:

- Your objectives for the log
- Whether you want to log row-level changes or higher-level activities
- Whether you want to implement the log as a database table or as an operating-system file
- The storage unit that you want to use
- Whether you want to implement a local or global log

By nature, logs are sequential. Whether you are using a table or a flat file to implement your log, you need to ensure that new log records are always appended onto the end of the log. That way, your log reflects a true journal of the activity that took place—one that shows events in their correct order. It's essential to prevent log records from being edited or deleted and to prevent log records from being inserted out of sequence.

In addition to recipes for implementing an audit log, this chapter also includes recipes demonstrating additional techniques that you can use to extend the functionality of the logs that you create. You will find recipes for improving performance where large log tables are involved, recipes for supporting multiple-languages, and recipes for simulating server push.

Your Objectives for an Audit Log

When you design an audit log, you need to think about your objectives. Generally, an audit log should include sufficient information to provide an accurate and timely reconstruction of past events. Specific goals for the data in a log often include the following:

- Reconstructing past events
- Tracking user activity
- Detecting damaging behavior
- Analyzing problems

Event reconstruction is one of the most important goals for an audit log. You need to be able to determine when any given change occurred. Without that basic capability, none of the other goals will fall into place. In addition to knowing what changes occurred and when, it's often useful to know who made them. Recording the source of the changes allows you to track user activity and to watch for potentially damaging behavior. Do you have a user who is browsing payroll records just for the fun of it? The right kind of audit log will help you detect that. Logs can also be used for problem analysis. Should data become damaged, you can look at the log to determine when the problem first occurred and what program or user was responsible.

For all these reasons, audit-log records usually have two main components:

- A snapshot of the data being inserted, updated, or deleted
- Control information such as the time of day, the user involved, possibly the specific user program involved, and so forth

Access to audit-log information needs to be easy and consistent. The tougher it is to get at your log data, the less likely you will be to use it, and, consequently, having the log will be less beneficial. You also need to be very careful when designing and implementing audit-log functionality. Test things to be sure they work. Audit logs are sometimes put into place in a rush, without being thought out. The result is that problems with audit-log implementations may be detected only when an attempt is made to use the logs to resolve a problem. By then, it's too late.

Row-Level Versus Activity Logging

There are two fundamentally different approaches that you can take to audit logging. You can audit at the row level, or you can audit at the activity level. What's the difference? Row-level logs contain records for Data Manipulation Language (DML) events such as inserts, updates, and deletes. These events have meaning to the database, but not necessarily to the users. Activity-level logs record information about events, such as the shipment of an order, that have meaning to a user.

Row-level logs contain a detailed record of every INSERT, UPDATE, or DELETE operation on a table. Each time a row is added, changed, or deleted, a copy of that row is placed in the log along with a timestamp and perhaps some other information. If a single user operation results in several SQL statements being executed, the log will contain a record for each of those statements, but it may not be possible to look at the statements and derive the specific user action that initiated them.

As an example, consider the procedure used to record the shipment of an order in a hypothetical database. Orders, of course, may contain several items. For each item in the order, you must update the inventory table to reflect the quantity shipped. You also need to update the order record to indicate that the shipment occurred. Finally, you need to generate a shipment register record for the shipment itself. Figure 6-1 shows the log entries that you might expect to see if row-level logging were used. As you can see, row-level logging generates detailed logs showing each SQL statement executed against a set of tables.

Ord#	Shipped		Table *Orders* Log		Seq	Oper	Ord#	Shipped
001	Yes				1	Ins	001	No
					2	Upd	001	Yes

Part#	Quan		Table *Inventory* Log		Seq	Oper	Part#	Quan
1001	100				1	Ins	1001	125
1002	150				2	Del	1001	25
1003	350				3	Ins	1002	50
					4	Ins	1002	100
					5	Ins	1003	400
					6	Del	1003	50

Ship#	Method		Table *Shipment* Log		Seq	Oper	Ship#	Method
90001	Truck				1	Ins	90001	Truck

Figure 6-1. Row-level logging

The advantage of row-level logging is that the level of detail is good enough to reconstruct a view of the data of any point in time that you desire. You can view the data the way it appeared yesterday or the way it appeared a week ago. One disadvantage is in the amount of log data that is generated. You have to somehow manage, and periodically purge, all that data. Another disadvantage is that it becomes difficult to get a high-level view of activities. What if all you wanted to do was to generate a report of shipments and receipts as they occurred throughout the day?

Let's look at the same example again, this time from the standpoint of logging activities, and not the details of each change to a database row. The user-level activity that we are talking about is the shipping of an order, so that's the event that we will log. Figure 6-2 shows the activity-level log entries that you might expect to see. Activity-level logging generates a log of activities, each of which may represent the execution of several DML statements.

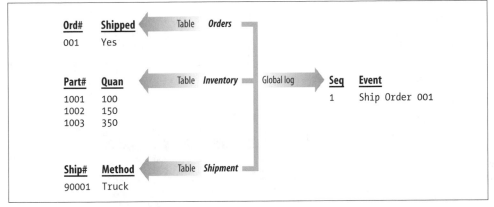

Figure 6-2. Activity-level logging

With activity-level logging, each shipped order results in just one log entry. Reading and understanding an activity-level log is much easier than reading and understanding a row-level log—at least as far as understanding high-level events is concerned—but activity-level logs are often more difficult to implement. Row-level logs can be implemented at the database level using triggers, while activity-level logs must be explicitly programmed into your application programs.

There is an important functional difference between row- and activity-level logs. Row-level logs contain all the information necessary to recreate past situations, whereas activity-level logs often contain little more than the names of the operations that were performed. If you need to reconstruct data as of some point in the past, then you need to implement row-level logs. If you need to know which operations occurred and when at a high level, you can use activity-level logs.

Database Tables Versus Operating System Files

Another consideration when designing an audit-log system is whether you want to store your log in an operating-system file or in a database table. External files are usually used for system logs and are often ASCII files that can be manipulated using tools such as grep and Perl. Operating-system files are not very useful when you're auditing for business purposes, because you can't query and manipulate the data in a file the way you can with the data in a table.

Audit logs for business purposes are most useful when they are implemented using standard database tables. You can query the logs and generate reports using any number of SQL-based query and reporting tools on the market. You can also easily write SQL SELECT statements to reconstruct snapshots of the data in a point in time or to retrieve particular records of interest. Since this is a SQL cookbook, the recipes in this chapter all deal with table-based audit logs.

Storage Units

The *storage unit* for an audit log is the record, and, for purposes of this book, a record represents a row in an audit table. Log records have two components: a body and a descriptor. These are illustrated in Figure 6-3.

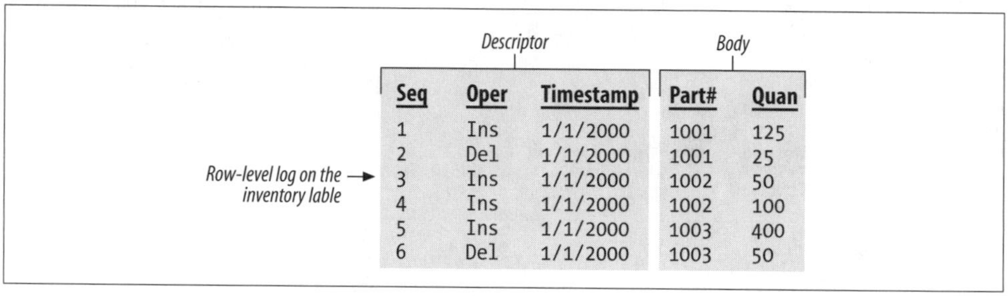

Seq	Oper	Timestamp	Part#	Quan
1	Ins	1/1/2000	1001	125
2	Del	1/1/2000	1001	25
3	Ins	1/1/2000	1002	50
4	Ins	1/1/2000	1002	100
5	Ins	1/1/2000	1003	400
6	Del	1/1/2000	1003	50

Figure 6-3. Log records

The *body* of the log record contains the operational data stored for auditing purposes. For row-level logs, the body consists of a copy of the row that was inserted, updated, or deleted. For activity-level logs, the body contains a description of the event that triggered the log entry.

The *descriptor* stores additional information that is necessary to reconstruct the sequence of events and interpret the log. This information includes such things as timestamps, sequential log numbers, usernames, process IDs, program names, DML operation names, and so forth. At the very least, a descriptor needs to include information, such as a timestamp or a sequence number, that can be used to place events in their proper order.

Global Versus Local Logs

A *global log* is one where all the log entries are funneled to one central table. A *local log* is one where each table being audited has a second log table associated with it. Row-level logs are almost always implemented as local logs. Typically, each table being audited has a different set of columns, making it difficult to record all changes in one table. A local log is used instead, and each local log ends up being an extended replicas of the main table. In other words, they contain all the columns from the main table, plus additional columns for the log's descriptor.

Activity-level logging, on the other hand, can easily be implemented with one global table. The key issue with activity-based logging is to record the events that take place and perhaps some key information about each. You also, of course, need to record descriptor information, such as a timestamp or a sequence number. To use a global table for an audit log, you need to develop a structure that will handle all event types. This usually ends up being a series of string-based columns that store user-friendly messages.

6.2   The Warehouse Example

You have a warehouse system that stores the current quantity on hand of each product in stock. Those values change in real time throughout the day as products are shipped in or out of the shop.

Your stock record, which has been simplified for this example, looks like this:

```
CREATE TABLE Stock(
    ProductId CHAR(40),
    Qty INTEGER
    PRIMARY KEY(ProductId)
)
```

Recipes in this chapter are based on this example.

6.3   Row-Level Logging

Problem

You must implement a row-level log for a database table. With respect to our example, you wish to log changes to data in the Stock table so that you can review such changes at a later date. You need an auditing system that will allow you to track all the changes on each product.

Solution

As a basis for implementing this row-level log, you'll create a log table that mirrors the structure of your Stock table. The name of this table will be StockLog. All of the columns that make up the Stock table will be replicated in the StockLog table and will make up the operational portion of the log record. In addition, the StockLog table will contain some additional columns to indicate the time and type of operation that occurred. These additional columns will make up the log record's descriptor. Triggers will then be used to automatically log activity occurring on the Stock table.

The following CREATE TABLE statement creates the StockLog table:

```
CREATE TABLE StockLog(
    ProductID CHAR(40),
    Qty INTEGER,
    Type CHAR(1) CHECK (type IN ('D','E','I','N')),
    UserId VARCHAR(40),
    EventTime DATETIME,
    LogId INTEGER IDENTITY,
    EventId UNIQUEIDENTIFIER
    PRIMARY KEY(LogId)
)
```

Each record contains a body and a descriptor. The body is usually a copy of the original record structure, and the descriptor holds additional information needed to identify specific events. Figure 6-4 highlights the structure of the StockLog record.

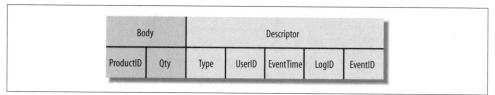

Figure 6-4. The StockLog Record

Once the StockLog table has been created, you can create the triggers that will record the activity on the Stock table. Three triggers are needed: one to record inserts in the log, one to record updates, and one to record deletes. You can use the following CREATE TRIGGER statements to create these triggers:

```
CREATE TRIGGER InsertStock
ON Stock
FOR INSERT
AS
BEGIN
    INSERT INTO StockLog
        (ProductId, Qty, Type, EventID, UserId, EventTime)
        SELECT i.ProductId, i.Qty, 'I', NEWID( ),
            CURRENT_USER, CURRENT_TIMESTAMP
        FROM inserted I
END
GO

CREATE TRIGGER DeleteStock
ON Stock
FOR DELETE
AS
BEGIN
    INSERT INTO StockLog
        (ProductId, Qty, Type, EventID, UserId, EventTime)
        SELECT d.ProductId, d.Qty, 'D',NEWID( ),
            CURRENT_USER, CURRENT_TIMESTAMP
        FROM deleted d
```

```
END
GO

CREATE TRIGGER UpdateStock
ON Stock
FOR UPDATE
AS
BEGIN

    DECLARE @ProductId CHAR(40)
    DECLARE @dQty INTEGER
    DECLARE @iQty INTEGER
    DECLARE @guid UNIQUEIDENTIFIER

    DECLARE UpdateStockLog CURSOR
        FOR SELECT d.ProductID,d.Qty,i.Qty
              FROM deleted d, inserted i
              WHERE d.ProductId=i.ProductId
    OPEN UpdateStockLog

    FETCH NEXT FROM UpdateStockLog
    INTO @ProductId, @dQty, @iQty

    WHILE (@@FETCH_STATUS=0) BEGIN
        SELECT @guid=NEWID( )
        INSERT INTO StockLog
            (ProductID, Qty, Type, EventID, UserID, EventTime)
            VALUES(@productID,@dQty,'E', @guid,
               CURRENT_USER,CURRENT_TIMESTAMP)
         INSERT INTO StockLog
            (ProductID, Qty, Type, EventID, UserID, EventTime)
            VALUES(@productID,@iQty,'N', @guid,
               CURRENT_USER,CURRENT_TIMESTAMP)

        FETCH NEXT FROM UpdateStockLog
        INTO @ProductId, @dQty, @iQty
    END

    CLOSE UpdateStockLog
    DEALLOCATE UpdateStockLog
END
GO
```

Discussion

This solution records activity in the Stock table by inserting records into the Stock-Log table. The idea is to include all the columns from the Stock table in the log, together with some additional columns to identify the user, the type of action taken, and the time the action was taken.

Some servers support mechanisms at the system level that are similar to the one shown here. These are sometimes referred to as journaling mechanisms. If these are available in your environment, you may want to use those native mechanisms instead of implementing an audit log using triggers. Either way, this example is useful because it will help you to understand the logic behind such mechanisms and the problems that might occur when using them.

Log table structure

The StockLog table contains five columns not in the original Stock table. These columns have the following purposes:

Type
> Records the type of operation. The type code will be one of the following:
>
> D   Marks a record that was deleted from the Stock table.
>
> I   Marks a new record that was inserted into the Stock table.
>
> E   Marks the before version of a Stock table record that was updated.
>
> N   Marks the after version of a Stock table record that was updated.

UserID
> Records the name of the user who performed the operation that was logged.

EventTime
> Records the time at which an operation occurred.

LogId
> Serves to identify each log record uniquely. Since this ID number is sequential, it also serves as a basis for correctly ordering the log records.

EventId
> Stores event identification. This is primarily used with update actions where two log records are used to represent one event. In such a case, both log entries will be given the same value for this column. Linking the before and after versions of an updated record facilitates future analysis of the log.

In the triggers created for this recipe, the CURRENT_TIMESTAMP and CURRENT_USER functions are used to populate the EventTime and UserId columns. Not all database servers use the same names for these functions, but all database servers implement this type of functionality. If you are using a database other than SQL Server, you may need to make minor changes to the example code for it to run in your environment.

The LogId column is incremented sequentially by virtue of its being declared using the IDENTITY keyword when the StockLog table was created. Again, different databases have different mechanisms for implementing sequentially increasing primary keys. Oracle, for example, requires that you use a stored sequence. Use a mechanism appropriate for your environment.

Log triggers

The three triggers used to maintain the log correspond to the three SQL statements—INSERT, DELETE, and UPDATE—that can be used to change the data in a table. For INSERT and DELETE statements, the triggers simply need to make a copy of the row being inserted or deleted and log it together with the user ID, timestamp, operation code, and log sequence number. For example, if you inserted two records and then deleted one, your log might look as follows:

```
ProductID  Qty  Type UserId  EventTime                LogId
---------- ---- ---- ------- ------------------------ ------
Bananas    100  I    Jenny   2000-06-27 22:41:41.150  1
Apples     40   I    Teena   2000-06-27 22:41:41.177  2
Apples     40   D    Teena   2000-06-27 22:41:41.183  3
```

The update trigger is a bit more complex than the other two, because it needs to deal with two versions of the row being updated—the original version and the modified version. One way to think of an update is as a combination of a delete followed by an insert. The deleted row represents the original version of the row, while the inserted row represents the new version. Our update trigger records the execution of an UPDATE statement in terms of those two steps. The deletion of the original row is marked using the type code E. That is immediately followed by an insert marked using the type code N. The codes E and N are used to differentiate update events from real delete and insert events. The following example shows the log records that would be generated as a result of a change in the quantity of bananas in the warehouse:

```
ProductID  Qty  Type UserId  EventTime                LogId
---------- ---- ---- ------- ------------------------ ------
Bananas    100  E    Jenny   2000-06-27 22:44:13.060  4
Bananas    200  N    Jenny   2000-06-27 22:44:13.060  5
```

With updates, two log entries are generated for one event. Special attention needs to be given to be sure that you can come back later and link up the two rows in question for any given update operation. In this recipe, we use the EventId column to record a unique identifier for each event. The EventId column was declared with the UNIQUEIDENTIFIER type—a special type reserved by SQL Server for system-generated unique identifiers. Each log trigger makes a call to the NEWID() function to retrieve a unique identifier for each event. This identifier is stored in the EventId column in all log records generated as a result of the event.

 While values in columns of type UNIQUEIDENTIFIER are guaranteed unique, they are not guaranteed to be sequential. To ensure the sequential nature of the log, an IDENTITY column (LogID in this case) must be used.

The update trigger joins are inserted and deleted on their respective ProductId values. The deleted table holds the before versions of all rows being updated, while the inserted table holds the after versions of those same rows. The join on ProductId serves to match each before row with its corresponding after row. This approach, while efficient, requires that updates to a row's primary key values (ProductId in this case) never occur.

In SQL Server, triggers are executed just once in response to a triggering statement. SQL, however, allows you to modify many rows with one statement. To generate a unique event ID for each row being updated by an UPDATE statement, the Update-Stock trigger uses a cursor to iterate through each of the affected rows. A new event ID is generated each time through the loop, and this event ID is recorded in the log entries for the row being processed.

With a log such as the StockLog table, it is possible to play back events in the order in which they occur. The table is essentially a journal of events created sequentially and classified by type. Thus, it is possible to restore the table to the way it was at any point in time, and it is also possible to track the activity of each individual user.

 While the solution shown in this recipe allows you to track, insert, update, and delete an activity, it does not allow you to track query an activity—triggers are not available on SELECT statements. If you need to record queries in an audit log, you can restrict table access to a stored procedure, force all database users to query through that procedure, and then have the stored procedure record those queries in a log.

6.4   Reporting Log Events

Problem

You need a human-readable report of the activity on the Stock table. You want the report to show activity in the correct order, and you want to see only one row on the report for each update operation. A row-level log table, such as the StockLog table from the previous recipe, records events in the order in which they occur. You can easily generate reports of these events.

Solution

Based on the Stock table, you can use the following query to generate a human readable report of the audit log in the StockLog table:

```
SELECT
    MAX(UserID) AS UserID,
    MAX(
        CASE
            WHEN Type='D' THEN 'Deleted'
            WHEN Type='I' THEN 'Inserted'
            ELSE 'Updated'  END) AS Type,
```

```
        MAX(ProductID) AS ProductID,
        MAX(CASE
                WHEN Type!='N' THEN Qty
                ELSE null END) AS Qty1,
        MAX(CASE
                WHEN Type='N' THEN Qty
                ELSE null END) AS Qty2,
        MAX(EventTime) EventTime
FROM StockLog
GROUP BY EventId
ORDER BY max(LogId)
```

When you execute this query, you may receive the following message: "Warning: Null value eliminated from aggregate." This is nothing to worry about. The message is informing you that some of the values summarized using MAX were NULL. This is, in fact, the intended use, since we are explicitly setting the qty values in some rows to NULL to ignore them.

As an example of how this query functions, let's assume that the following SQL statements had been executed against the stock table. Each INSERT and DELETE statement would have generated one log entry, while the UPDATE statement would have generated two.

```
INSERT INTO Stock(ProductID,Qty)
        VALUES('Banana',10)
INSERT INTO Stock(ProductID,Qty)
        VALUES('Apple',20)
INSERT INTO Stock(ProductID,Qty)
        VALUES('Orange',30)
UPDATE STOCK SET Qty=2
        WHERE ProductID='Banana'
DELETE FROM Stock
        WHERE ProductID='Banana'
```

Given the operations shown here, the query in this recipe will produce the following results:

UserID	Type	ProductID	Qty1	Qty2	EventTime
Max	Inserted	Banana	10	NULL	2000-06-27 22:51:30.017
Justin	Inserted	Apple	20	NULL	2000-06-27 22:51:30.023
Joshua	Inserted	Orange	30	NULL	2000-06-27 22:51:30.027
Ryan	Updated	Banana	10	2	2000-06-27 22:51:30.027
Gerard	Deleted	Banana	2	NULL	2000-06-27 22:51:30.030

This report is more readable than what you would get were you simply to query the raw data from the audit-log table, and it can be easily understood by users. Of course, the query shown in this recipe can easily be adapted to narrow down the results to just the data needed to answer specific questions. For example, you might want to report on the activity of a single user, or you might want to report on a single product.

Discussion

There are four key things to notice about the query in this recipe:

- The first CASE statement translates the type codes.
- CASE statements divide quantity values into two columns.
- The grouping functions combine updates into one row.
- The ORDER BY clause sorts the activity by LogId.

The CASE statements in this query translate the one-letter type codes to words that will have meaning to the person reading the report. Thus, D is translated to Deleted, I to Inserted, and so forth.

You'll notice that this query returns two quantity columns. This is done to report both the old and new quantities for an update operation. The first quantity column, named Qty1, will contain the quantities for any operation with a type code not equal to N. This includes insert and delete operations. It also includes the original quantity (type code E) from an update operation. The following CASE statement, embedded in the query, sets the value for this column:

```
MAX(CASE WHEN Type!='N' THEN Qty
        ELSE null END) AS qty1
```

If the type is not equal to N, the qty1 column returns the quantity; otherwise, it returns a NULL value. A similar CASE statement is used to place the quantity value into the Qty2 column whenever it is not placed in the Qty1 column. In other words, the second quantity column takes on the quantity from type N log records. These represent the updated values from update operations.

The effects of the CASE statements are fairly obvious. The use of grouping functions to convert two update-related log records into one output record is not so obvious, and it deserves some extra explanation. The following example illustrates the output that this query would generate were the grouping functions not used. The two records in the example are types N and E, which means they were generated as the result of an UPDATE statement.

```
UserID   Type      ProductID   Qty1   Qty2   EventTime
-------  --------  ----------  -----  -----  --------------------------
Ryan     Updated   Banana       10    NULL   2000-06-27 22:51:30.027
Ryan     Updated   Banana      NULL    2     2000-06-27 22:51:30.027
```

Notice that the CASE statement has translated the type codes N and E both to the word Updated. The result is that all columns in both rows are identical except for the Qty1 and Qty2 columns. You can combine these two rows by using the SQL GROUP BY clause. Group the two rows based on the EventID, and simply take the maximum value of each column. In the case of the UserID, Type, and ProductID columns, both vales are the same, so applying the MAX function returns just one occurrence of each value. In the case of Qty1 and Qty2, applying the MAX function returns the numbers, eliminating the NULLs. That's because numbers are always higher than NULLs. The resulting single row would be:

```
UserID  Type      ProductID  Qty1  Qty2  EventTime
-------  --------  ---------- ----- ----- ---------------------------
Ryan    Updated   Banana     10    2     2000-06-27 22:51:30.027
```

The use of grouping in this particular example to combine the two log entries from an update operation into one row on the report depends on two things. Each operation must have a unique EventId, and update operations must not have changed any values other than the quantity for a product. As long as each insert and delete operation has a unique EventId, the log entries for those operations will never be grouped with any others. Similarly, as long as each update record only represents a change in quantity, the other columns in the log entries will be identical, and the log entries will be successfully combined into one record for the report.

> The query used in this section to report on the log is designed under the assumption that updates do not change the primary key for a row—in this case, the ProductID. If changing the primary key is a possibility, you will need to treat the primary-key columns in the same manner as the Qty column was treated.

6.5   Generating Current Snapshots

Problem

You have an audit log from which you need to generate a current snapshot of the table on which the log is based. In other words, you want to generate the original table from the log.

Solution

The following query can be executed against the StockLog table to regenerate the data in the Stock table:

```
SELECT ProductID, Qty
FROM StockLog
WHERE LogId IN
   (SELECT
      (SELECT (CASE WHEN MAX(Type)!='D'
         THEN MAX(s.LogID)
         ELSE 0 END)
      FROM StockLog s1
      WHERE s.ProductID=s1.ProductID
         AND s1.LogID=MAX(s.LogID))
    FROM StockLog s
    GROUP BY ProductID)
```

The generated result is as follows:

```
ProductID   Qty
----------  ----
Apple       20
Orange      30
...
```

Discussion

Another use for a row-level audit-log table, such as the StockLog table, is to regenerate the data for the table being logged. For example, you might want to do this if you had accidentally deleted the main table.

The query shown in this recipe lists the ProductID and Qty columns for the most recent version of each row in the Stock table. Information for deleted records, where the log type code is a D, is not returned by the query. To explain the logic behind this query, it's best to look at the subquery separately. To begin with, the following pseudocode captures the essence of the function of the main query:

```
SELECT ProductID, Qty
FROM StockLog
WHERE LogID IN [most recent valid log entry
                for each product, excluding deleted rows]
```

In the query that returns the most recent log entries for each product, a subquery is used to return the LogID of the most recent log entry for each product that doesn't represent a delete operation. The code to exclude the deleted rows is highlighted in the following example:

```
SELECT ProductID, Qty
FROM StockLog
WHERE LogId IN
    (SELECT
        (SELECT (CASE WHEN MAX(Type)!='D'
           THEN MAX(s.LogID)
           ELSE 0 END)
        FROM StockLog s1
        WHERE s.ProductID=s1.ProductID
           AND s1.LogID=MAX(s.LogID))
    FROM StockLog s
    GROUP BY ProductID)
```

For each group—remember that each group represents one product—this subquery finds the most recent log entry. The most recent log entry is determined by looking at the LogID column. If the event is not a delete event, we include its LogID identifier in the result set. If the event is a delete event, a 0 is returned instead of the LogID value. When the StockLog table was first created, the LogID column was defined using the IDENTITY keyword. That means it begins with 1 and increments by 1. Since no log record has an ID of 0, our snapshot query will not return any data for log records representing deletes.

Since we are generating a snapshot, GROUP BY is used to find only the last event for each product. See the highlighted code in the following example. All those products that were deleted from the Stock table have their last events marked by a LogId of 0. Only the ones with valid, nonzero, LogIds are used to generate the snapshot:

```
SELECT ProductID, Qty
FROM StockLog
WHERE LogId IN
    (SELECT
        (SELECT (CASE WHEN MAX(Type)!='D'
            THEN MAX(s.LogID)
            ELSE 0 END)
        FROM StockLog s1
        WHERE s.ProductID=s1.ProductID
            AND s1.LogID=MAX(s.LogID))
    FROM StockLog s
    GROUP BY ProductID)
```

The list of LogId values generated by the subquery is used by the main query as a basis for selecting the most recent ProductID and Qty value for each product.

The query in this recipe is quite complex and may take a long time to execute. Because of that, it is not suitable for use in reports that run frequently. For occasional reporting, however, this can be quite useful.

6.6   Generating Time-Restricted Snapshots

Problem

You want to generate a snapshot of a table with the rows as they appeared at a specific point in time in the past.

Solution

A time-restricted snapshot is one that returns a view of the table as of a given moment in time. The StockLog audit log can be used to build a time-restricted snapshot of the Stock table.

This solution builds on the previous recipe for building a snapshot of the table as it currently exists. The difference is that we are now restricting the results based on the timestamp in the EventTime column. The @TIME variable in this recipe represents the point in time that you want the snapshot to represent.

```
SELECT ProductID, Qty
FROM StockLog
WHERE logID IN
    (SELECT
        (SELECT (CASE WHEN MAX(Type)!='D'
            THEN MAX(s.LogID)
            ELSE 0 END)
```

```
        FROM StockLog s1
        WHERE s.ProductID=s1.ProductID
            AND s1.LogID=MAX(s.LogID))
    FROM StockLog s
    WHERE s.EventTime <= @TIME
    GROUP BY ProductID)
```

Discussion

As you can see, this code is an extension of the current snapshot solution shown previously. That solution has been extended to include one additional restriction in the WHERE clause that limits the results to the most current data as of the date represented by the @TIME variable. Log records generated after the time in question are ignored. The resulting snapshot represents the data in the Stock table at the exact moment specified by @TIME.

 You need to set the @TIME variable to a valid date and time prior to executing this query. Alternatively, you can replace @TIME with a constant representing a valid date/time value.

The query in this recipe uses `s.EventTime <= @TIME` to capture all events up to and including the time in question. If you only want to consider events that occurred prior to the specified time, use the less than (<) operator.

6.7   Undoing Table Changes

Problem

You want to implement an undo mechanism for a table that allows you to undo the most recent action. You can use a row-level audit log as the basis for an undo mechanism.

Solution

The following stored procedure retrieves the most recent log record, which is the one with the highest LogID value, and reverses the action that caused that log record to be generated in the first place.

```
CREATE PROCEDURE UndoLog
AS
    DECLARE @ProductID CHAR(40)
    DECLARE @Qty INTEGER
    DECLARE @Type CHAR(1)
```

```
SELECT
    @ProductID=ProductID,
    @Qty=Qty,
    @Type=Type
FROM StockLog
WHERE LogId=(SELECT MAX(LogId)
    FROM StockLog) AND Type!='N'

IF @type='D'
    INSERT INTO Stock(ProductID,Qty)
        VALUES(@productID,@qty)

IF @type='I'
    DELETE FROM Stock WHERE ProductID=@productID

IF @type='E'
    UPDATE Stock SET Qty=@qty
        WHERE ProductID=@productID
```

Following is a snapshot of the log after the first three inserts:

```
ProductID    Qty
----------   ----
Banana       10
Apple        20
Orange       30
```

Discussion

The first thing this procedure does is to identify the most recent event recorded in the StockLog table. This is done by the SELECT query, which identifies the most recently generated log record, and then retrieves the stock data from that record. In the case of an update event, the type E record will be retrieved. Type N records are specifically excluded. The type E record can be used to undo the effects of an UPDATE statement, because it represents the before image of the stock record that was changed.

With the data retrieved, it is fairly simple to restore the original state of the row in question: execute a statement opposite to the one that was initially executed. For an INSERT statement, the opposite action is to execute a DELETE statement and vice versa. For an UPDATE statement, the opposite action is to update the row involved and set the columns back to their original values. To do this, use the before image contained in the type E log entry for an UPDATE statement.

The undo action resembles the use of the ROLLBACK statement to abort a transaction. The important differences, however, are that the action of the UndoLog procedure is, itself, logged in the audit log and that the action of the UndoLog procedure is more controllable. The undo procedure in this recipe only reverses the most recent event, but you have the ability to customize it to do more than that.

6.8   Minimizing Audit-Log Space Consumption

Problem

You are going to implement an audit log, but you need a way to minimize space consumption so that the resulting log uses disk space as efficiently as possible. It's still important to be able to construct an accurate snapshot of the base table as it appeared at any give point in time.

Solution

The log recipe shown earlier in this chapter implemented a log that contained a complete snapshot of a row for every operation performed on that row. While simple to implement and to query, the result is a log that contains a great deal of redundant information where update and delete operations are concerned. To minimize the space used by a row-level log, you can design it such that a column value is recorded only when it is changed. Thus, a change to one column in a row does not cause an entirely new copy of that row to be written to the log. Instead, only the before and after versions of the modified column are recorded in the log. Similarly, with deletes, only the delete action needs to be recorded.

For purposes of this recipe, assume that the Stock table to be audited can be created using the following statement:

```
CREATE TABLE Stock(
    ProductId CHAR(40),
    Qty INTEGER,
    Price INTEGER,
    PRIMARY KEY(ProductId)
)
```

Given this table, the solution requires that a log table is created and that triggers are created to record changes to the data in the Stock table's audit log.

Step 1: Create the audit table

Create an audit table that stores the audit data for the base table. The following statement creates a table named StockLog that can be used to log changes made to the table named Stock:

```
CREATE TABLE StockLog(
    ProductId CHAR(40) NOT NULL,
    Qty INTEGER NULL,
    Price INTEGER NULL,
    EventTime DATETIME NOT NULL,
    DeleteFlag CHAR(1) NULL,
    LogId INTEGER IDENTITY
)
```

As you can see, the audit table has a similar structure to the Stock table's, with the following exceptions:

- One additional column is included to store the timestamp (the date and time of the event).
- One column is included to represent DELETE events.
- LogId column is added to uniquely identify events and support sequencing order between them.
- All columns, except for the timestamp and primary-key columns, are explicitly allowed to be null.

Step 2: Implement the audit triggers

This set of triggers records all insert, update, and delete activity in the StockLog table, but the approach is slightly different from the previous audit-log recipe in this chapter. This time, column values are not recorded for deletes, and only modified columns are recorded with update log entries. Pay special attention to the CASE statements in the updateStock trigger as you read the code.

```
CREATE TRIGGER insertStock
ON Stock
FOR INSERT
AS
BEGIN
    INSERT INTO StockLog
        (ProductId, Qty, Price, DeleteFlag, EventTime)
        SELECT i.ProductId, i.Qty, i.Price, null, CURRENT_TIMESTAMP
        FROM inserted I
END
GO


CREATE TRIGGER deleteStock
ON Stock
FOR DELETE
AS
BEGIN
    INSERT INTO StockLog
        (ProductId, Qty, Price, DeleteFlag, EventTime)
        SELECT d.ProductId, null, null, 'D', CURRENT_TIMESTAMP
        FROM deleted d
END
GO


CREATE TRIGGER updateStock
ON Stock
FOR UPDATE
AS
BEGIN
        INSERT INTO stockLog
        (ProductId, Qty, Price, DeleteFlag, EventTime)
```

```
SELECT d.productId,
  (CASE WHEN d.Qty!=i.Qty THEN i.Qty ELSE NULL END),
  (CASE WHEN d.Price!=i.Price THEN i.Price ELSE NULL END),
  null, CURRENT_TIMESTAMP
FROM deleted d,inserted I
WHERE d.ProductId=i.ProductId


END
GO
```

Discussion

Space can often become an issue if all details are to be stored in a log. This technique demonstrates how to store the information with minimum space consumption.

The concept underlying the solution shown here is that column values are only recorded in the log table when they change. An INSERT operation is the only operation where the log record will contain a complete copy of a row. For UPDATE operations, the log will only contain the new values for the columns that were changed and the value of the row's primary key. All columns not changed by an UPDATE statement are left set to NULL in the log record to avoid storing data redundantly. In this way, space consumption is minimized. Deletes are a bit different. Each log record has a delete flag in its descriptor. When a row is deleted, the delete flag is set in the corresponding log's record.

Consider, for example, the following DML statements:

```
INSERT INTO Stock(ProductID, Qty, Price)
   VALUES ('Bananas', 10, 112)

INSERT INTO Stock(ProductID, Qty, Price)
   VALUES ('Apples', 20, 223)

UPDATE Stock
   SET Qty=25
   WHERE ProductID='Apples'

UPDATE Stock
   SET Qty=30
   WHERE ProductId='Apples'

DELETE FROM Stock
   WHERE ProductId='Bananas'
```

The audit-log entries generated by these statements would be as follows:

```
SELECT LogId, ProductId, Qty, Price, DeleteFlag, EventTime
FROM  stockLog

GO
```

```
LogId   ProductId   Qty   Price   DeleteFlag  EventTime
------  ----------  ----  ------  ----------  -------------------------
1       Bananas     10    112     NULL        2000-06-27 23:01:25.943
2       Apples      20    223     NULL        2000-06-27 23:01:25.950
3       Apples      25    NULL    NULL        2000-06-27 23:01:25.970
4       Apples      30    NULL    NULL        2000-06-27 23:01:25.970
5       Bananas     NULL  NULL    D           2000-06-27 23:01:25.993
```

The first two DML statements were INSERT statements, and, consequently, the log entries each contain a complete copy of the data being inserted. The next two DML statements, however, were UPDATE statements. Both of these updated only one column, and the log entries reflect that fact by setting the other columns to NULL. The final log entry represents a deletion of the Bananas record. The D in the DeleteFlag column indicates that the record was deleted. No other information need be recorded; consequently, both the Qty and Price columns have been set to NULL. Most database systems optimize the storage of NULLS such that the amount of space used for that purpose is negligible.

Snapshot generation

Generating a snapshot of the Stock table is more difficult when the log records changes to a single column than it is when each log record contains a complete copy of the row being changed. In the case of the audit log described in this recipe, you can use the following SELECT statement to generate a snapshot of the base table as of a specific time. The @TIME variable in the example represents the "as of" time used for the snapshot generation. For testing purposes, you can replace it with CURRENT_TIMESTAMP to return the current snapshot.

```
SELECT t.ProductId,
    Qty=(SELECT TOP 1 tQ.Qty FROM StockLog tQ
        WHERE tQ.Qty IS NOT NULL
            AND tQ.ProductId=t.ProductId
            AND tQ.EventTime <= @TIME
        ORDER BY tQ.LogId DESC),
    Price=(SELECT TOP 1 tP.Price FROM StockLog tP
        WHERE tP.Price IS NOT NULL
            AND tP.ProductId=t.ProductId
            AND tP.EventTime <= @TIME
        ORDER BY tP.LogId DESC)
FROM StockLog t
WHERE  t.EventTime<=@TIME
GROUP BY t.ProductId
HAVING NOT EXISTS(SELECT * FROM StockLog
    WHERE productID=t.productID
    AND logID=MAX(t.logID) AND DeleteFlag='D')
```

This SELECT statement contains a number of subqueries: one for each column in the Stock table to retrieve the most recent values for those columns and one at the end to eliminate all deleted rows from the report. Each subquery retrieves the most recent value of a column with respect to the date specified by the @TIME variable.

The one exception is that the primary key column does not require a subquery because we are assuming that the primary key does not change.

To get the most recent value for a column, we execute a subquery. The subquery ignores rows where the column is NULL. The subquery sorts the rows in descending order by LogId and returns the topmost value, which is the most recent value of the column. The subquery respects the time you pass (@TIME) and will ignore values set later than that time. The following example shows the subquery used to return the most recent value for column Qty:

```
SELECT TOP 1 tQ.Qty FROM StockLog tQ
WHERE tQ.Qty IS NOT NULL
    AND tQ.ProductId=t.ProductId
    AND tQ.EventTime <= @TIME
ORDER BY tQ.LogId DESC
```

This same subquery is used for each column in the table, except for the columns in the record descriptor.

The WHERE clause in the main query limits the scope of the selection to the rows that were inserted before or on the date and at the time represented by @TIME. The ProductId column is then used to group the result set. Grouping is done because we are interested only in one instance (a snapshot) of each row in the original table.

Deleted records

The HAVING clause in the query eliminates Stock records that have been deleted, so that they don't appear in the snapshot. The HAVING clause looks like this:

```
HAVING NOT EXISTS(SELECT * FROM StockLog
    WHERE productID=t.productID
    AND logID=MAX(t.logID) AND DeleteFlag='D')
```

The subquery in the HAVING clause checks to see if the most recent log entry for a Stock record represents a delete. If it does, then that Stock record is not returned as part of the snapshot.

Dealing with NULL values

If the Stock table includes some columns that are allowed to be NULL, the solution shown in this recipe will not work properly. That's because the query to generate a snapshot has no way to know whether a NULL value in a particular column represents a NULL column value or if it just means that there has been no change for that column.

One possible way to deal with NULL values is to use a second column as a flag to indicate whether the first is a null. This flag column can be a BIT type if the database implementation allows it, or it can be a character type such as a CHAR(1). A BIT type allows for TRUE and FALSE values. The StockLog table is extended with the columns representing the NULL values:

```
CREATE TABLE StockLog(
    ProductId char(40) NOT NULL,
    Qty INTEGER NULL,
    Price INTEGER NULL,
    IsEmptyPrice BIT,
    IsEmptyQty BIT,
    EventTime DATETIME NOT NULL,
    DeleteFlag CHAR(1) NULL,
    LogId INTEGER IDENTITY
)
```

Assuming that you implemented a flag column named IsEmptyQty and that you used 1 to represent a NULL value, and 0 otherwise, the subquery in the snapshot query would need to use a WHERE clause, such as the one shown here:

```
SELECT t.ProductId,
    Qty=(SELECT TOP 1 tQ.Qty FROM StockLog tQ
        WHERE tQ.IsEmptyQty=0
            AND tQ.ProductId=t.ProductId
            AND tQ.EventTime <= @TIME
        ORDER BY tQ.LogId DESC ),
    Price=(SELECT TOP 1 tP.Price FROM StockLog tP
        WHERE tP.IsEmptyPrice=0
            AND tP.ProductId=t.ProductId
            AND tP.EventTime <= @TIME
        ORDER BY tp.LogId DESC)
FROM StockLog t
WHERE  EventTime<=@TIME
GROUP BY t.ProductId
HAVING NOT EXISTS(SELECT * FROM StockLog
    WHERE productID=t.productID
    AND logID=MAX(t.logID) AND DeleteFlag='D')
```

This solution requires only minimal changes to the SELECT statement used to generate snapshots. It also doesn't consume much space in an implementation where the DBMS supports the BIT datatype. Sybase and MS SQL Server both support BIT types. The storage of such BIT types is optimized by combining all the BIT columns in a row together into as few bytes as possible. If there are 8 bit columns, they will consume just 1 byte per row.

6.9   Online Account Balancing

Problem

You need to create an account-balancing solution, where accounts can be debited or credited with different products. Each credit or debit will be recorded in a history table. Your system then needs to generate the current position, or balance, of an account based on its debit/credit history.

Solution

The code shown in this recipe is actually a part of an online portfolio tracking system for a brokerage application. The idea is to use the accounting principle of credits and debits to record each event affecting an account. These credits and debits can then be summarized to list the portfolio. The portfolio is the list of products in an account.

The following table, named StockRecord, can be used to store events in the system. Each account can have multiple products in its portfolio. An important column in this table is the ValidDate column. Each event has a validity date that states the date from which the position is valid. For example, if a trade is made with a settlement period of five days, it means that even if we bought the product today, it will not be available and shown in the portfolio until five days from now. All such events should be taken into consideration when building an account balance for a particular date.

```
CREATE TABLE StockRecord (
    RecordId INTEGER IDENTITY,
    AccountId INTEGER NOT NULL,
    ProductId VARCHAR(40),
    Qty NUMERIC(20,4) NULL,
    Type CHAR(1) NOT NULL
        CHECK(Type in ('C','D','O','L','B')),
    ValidDate DATETIME,
    PRIMARY KEY(RecordID)
)
```

The type column contains a type code indicating the type of transaction that occurred. Table 6-1 describes the meaning of the various type codes used in this application.

Table 6-1. Transaction type codes

Code	Type	Description
C	Credit	Signifies that a quantity of product was added to an account.
D	Debit	Signifies that a quantity of product was removed from the account.
O	Opening position	Records an account's opening position for a specific product. All events for the product recorded prior to this event are no longer valid for the purpose of calculating the current position.
L	Credit-line limit	Records the amount of a product that can be borrowed and is available for trading.
B	Blocked	Records the quantity of a product that is blocked and not available for trading.

The following is a representative example of the data that you would see in the StockRecord table:

```
RecordId  AccountId  ProductId  Qty      Type  ValidDate
--------- ---------- ---------- -------- ----- ---------------------------
1         3          IBM        20.0000  O     2000-07-02 07:30:09.000
2         3          CFT        40.0000  O     2000-07-03 07:30:21.000
3         3          MSFT       10.0000  C     2000-07-02 10:30:39.000
```

```
4          3          MSFT     10.0000   D     2000-07-02 10:45:54.000
5          3          MSFT     25.0000   C     2000-07-02 12:11:15.000
6          3          MSFT     15.0000   C     2000-07-02 12:41:22.000
7          3          MSFT     10.0000   B     2000-07-03 09:00:00.000
8          3          USD    1000.0000   L     2000-07-03 09:00:00.000
...
```

These results could be interpreted as follows: at 7:30 the account was opened, and 20 shares of IBM and 40 shares of CFT were put in as the opening balance. The client then bought, and later sold, MSFT stock at 10:30 and 10:45, respectively. At 12:11, the client bought 25 shares of MSFT. After half an hour, the client bought additional shares of MSFT. During the day, the client arranged a line of credit, which will be available on the following day. 10 shares of MSFT were used as a collateral.

With the StockRecord table created, and with the codes in Table 6-1 being used to record transactions, you can use the following query to generate the current portfolio for the accounts in the system:

```
SELECT
    AccountID,
    ProductID,
    (SUM(CASE WHEN Type='C' OR Type='L' OR Type='O'
            THEN Qty ELSE 0 END)-
      SUM(CASE WHEN Type='D' OR Type='B'
            THEN Qty ELSE 0 END)) Total,
     SUM(CASE WHEN Type='B'
            THEN Qty ELSE 0 END) Blocked,
    MAX(s.ValidDate) ValidDate
FROM StockRecord s
WHERE s.ValidDate BETWEEN
        ISNULL((SELECT MAX(st.ValidDate)
                FROM StockRecord st
                WHERE st.AccountID=s.AccountID AND
                      st.ProductID=s.ProductID AND
                      st.Type='O'),'1900-1-1')
                AND CURRENT_TIMESTAMP
    GROUP BY s.AccountID, s.ProductID
```

Given the StockRecord rows displayed in the example, you would obtain the following position report when you executed the current position query:

```
AccountID   ProductID   Total      Blocked   ValidDate
----------  ----------  ---------- --------  --------------------------
3           CFT         40.0000    .0000     2000-07-02 07:30:21.000
3           IBM         20.0000    .0000     2000-07-03 07:30:09.000
3           MSFT        40.0000    10.0000   2000-07-02 09:00:00.000
3           USD       1000.0000    .0000     2000-07-03 09:00:00.000
...
```

This position report includes all changes to the account up until the time of the query. It excludes all changes that become valid subsequent to the time at which the query was executed. Since the line of credit doesn't become valid until tomorrow, it is not reflected in the current position. Likewise, the blockage of 10 shares of Microsoft stock to be used as collateral is not reflected in the current position.

Discussion

This recipe illustrates one way to extend the basic concepts of an auditing mechanism to give your systems some additional flexibility. It allows users to have access to their history of transactions, and it also allows them to generate their current portfolios based on that history. The biggest advantage of such a system is that you have a direct relationship between the event-based views and the cumulative views of an account's portfolio. Every change in the stock record is immediately reflected in the portfolio view of an account.

The logic behind this solution is actually derived from audit-logging mechanisms explained earlier in this chapter. The query groups the current portfolio's events by the ProductID and AccountID columns. This is logical since we want to report on each product in each account. The following GROUP BY clause accomplishes this:

```
GROUP BY s.accountID, s.productID
```

The query also limits the scope of the event records that it looks at to those that fall between the date of a product's opening position and the current date. If there is no opening position available for a product, the query defaults the opening-position date to January 1, 1900.

> The default opening-position date needs to be set early enough to ensure that all transactions for a product are captured. If you expect to enter transactions for dates prior to January 1, 1900, then use an earlier date as your default.

The WHERE clause highlighted in the following example shows the logic that restricts event records to those that fall between the opening position date and the current date:

```
WHERE s.ValidDate BETWEEN
      ISNULL((SELECT MAX(st.ValidDate)
             FROM StockRecord st
             WHERE st.AccountID=s.AccountID AND
                   st.ProductID=s.ProductID AND
                   st.Type='0'),'1900-1-1')
             AND CURRENT_TIMESTAMP
```

Once the date limits are set and the correct records have been returned, the query sums all events that add quantities to the balance for a product and deducts from that the sum of all events that remove quantities from a product's balance. The result is the amount of each product in an account that is currently available for trading. The following code performs these computations:

```
(SUM(CASE WHEN Type='C' OR Type='L' OR Type='O'
        THEN Qty ELSE 0 END)-
    SUM(CASE WHEN Type='D' OR Type='B'
        THEN Qty ELSE 0 END)) Total,
  SUM(CASE WHEN Type='B'
    THEN Qty ELSE 0 END) Blocked
```

As you can see, blocking entries (Type='B') remove product from an account. Line of credit entries (Type='L'), on the other hand, as well as opening position entries (Type='O'), add product to an account.

Just for fun now, consider the following query. Unlike the previous query to display the current account positions, the following query returns the transaction history together with running totals for each of the products involved. This is a great tool for a trader to investigate scenarios and to anticipate when an account will have the funds or product to close a trade.

```
SELECT
    AccountID,
    ProductID,
    (SELECT SUM(CASE WHEN Type='C' OR Type='L' OR
            Type='O' THEN Qty ELSE 0 END)-
        SUM(CASE WHEN Type='D' OR Type='M' OR Type='B'
            THEN Qty ELSE 0 END)
    FROM StockRecord s1
    WHERE  s1.ValidDate >=
        isnull((SELECT MAX(st.ValidDate)
        FROM StockRecord st
        WHERE st.AccountID=s.AccountID AND
            st.ProductID=s.ProductID AND
            st.Type='O'),'1900-1-1') AND
            s1.ValidDate<=MAX(s.ValidDate)AND
            s1.AccountID=s.AccountID AND
            s1.ProductID=s.ProductID) Available,
        CONVERT(CHAR(10),s.ValidDate,102) ValidDate
    FROM StockRecord s
    GROUP BY s.accountID, s.productID,
        CONVERT(CHAR(10),s.ValidDate,102)
    HAVING MAX(s.validDate) >=
        ISNULL((SELECT MAX(st.validDate)
            FROM StockRecord st WHERE
            st.accountID=s.accountID AND
            st.productID=s.productID AND
            st.type='O'),'1900-1-1')
```

Although at first glance this query looks a bit scary, it works very similarly to the current portfolio query given earlier in the recipe. You could obtain a similar result by running the current portfolio query against the StockRecord table for each date on which a position changed. With this query, however, you can obtain a complete historical record in one step.

Finally, you could report the transaction history with a running total for each product using the second query shown in this recipe. The output from that query would look like this:

```
AccountID  ProductID  Available  ValidDate
---------- ---------- ---------- ----------
3          CFT        40         2000.07.02
3          IBM        20         2000.07.02
3          MSFT       40         2000.07.02
3          MSFT       30         2000.07.03
3          USD        1000       2000.07.03
```

From this result, you can see that on the July 2, there was a change in the balance of shares for CFT, IBM, and MSFT. Changes planned for the next day affect MSFT and the line of credit. The amount of available MSFT stock drops to 30 because 10 shares are being used as collateral and the line of credit increases to $1,000.

6.10   Activity-Level Logging

Problem

You want to implement a global logging mechanism that can be used by an application to record arbitrary events. Instead of each event representing a change to a specific database row, each of these events will represent some high-level action taken by a user.

Solution

To create a global logging mechanism for use in tracking high-level activities, perform the following steps:

1. Create a global log table to log the events.
2. Create an event master table to define events and to associate each of them with a severity level.
3. Create a global severity-limit variable to hold the current severity-limit setting.
4. Create a procedure that can be used to log an event.

Step 1: Create a global log table

The first step is to create a global log table to record events as they occur. The log table should not be linked to any one base table. Instead, it should be flexible enough to record events involving any table, or set of tables, in the database. The following table shows one possible implementation of a log table for recording activities:

```
CREATE TABLE EventLog (
    EventId INTEGER IDENTITY,
    CodeId INTEGER NOT NULL,
    IdPointer VARCHAR(40) NULL,
    IdPointerType CHAR(1) NULL,
    EventMessage VARCHAR(255) NULL,
    PRIMARY KEY(EventId)
)
```

The EventLog table's IdPointer and IdPointerType columns are used to generically point to an important row in a table being modified by the activity being logged. The IdPointer column is used to record primary key values, while the IdPointerType column identifies the table containing the row corresponding to the given primary key. For example, if you want an event-log entry to point to an order record, you would insert the order ID value into the IdPointer column and an 'O' into the IdPointerType column. On the other hand, if you want to associate an event with an invoice, you would store the invoice ID into the IdPointer column and an 'I' into the IdPointerType column.

Step 2: Create an event master table

The next step is create an event master table that defines all possible events that can be logged. The EventLogMaster table shown in the following example represents one possible implementation that you can use:

```
CREATE TABLE EventLogMaster (
    CodeID INTEGER NOT NULL,
    MessageText VARCHAR(255),
    Severity INTEGER,
    LangId CHAR(1),
    PRIMARY KEY(codeID,langID)
)
```

This particular event master table allows you to define event messages in more than one language. The LangId column identifies the language used for the message text and it forms part of the table's primary key. The Severity column stores the security level associated with an event. As you'll see later, the code in this recipe allows you to limit the recording of events by severity level.

Step 3: Create a global severity-limit variable

Your next task is to implement a mechanism allowing you to globally define the minimum severity level that you are interested in logging. Only events with a severity level equal to or higher than the one you define will be logged to the EventLog table.

If your database system supports global variables, use them. Declare a global variable, and set it to whatever severity level you wish. By adjusting this severity level up and down, you can dynamically control the level of detail recorded in your EventLog table. This can be an invaluable debugging aid. If your database system doesn't support global variables, you can use a small table to record the current severity-limit setting. This is the solution used in the code for this particular recipe. For example:

```
CREATE TABLE GlobalVariables(
    VarName VARCHAR(10),
    VarValue INT)

INSERT INTO GlobalVariables (VarName, VarValue) VALUES ('Severity',3)
```

This table contains rows that you can think of as corresponding to global variables. The VarName column identifies a global variable name, and the VarValue column contains the value for that variable. In this case, the global variable name is "Severity," and the value has been set to 3.

Step 4: Create a stored procedure to log events

Finally, you need to create a stored procedure that you can use to log an event. Call the procedure whenever you want to record an event. The procedure created by this recipe is named EventMessage. It allows you to pass several values as parameters. Values that you can pass to the procedure include: the error-message identifier, a pointer to a database row together with a code identifying the type of row, and an arbitrary event message. The @EventMessage parameter stores the event message, which is a generic ASCII string you build that contains data specific to a particular event. Here is the code for the EventMessage procedure:

```
CREATE PROCEDURE EventMessage
    @CodeID INTEGER,
    @IdPointer VARCHAR(40)=null,
    @IdPointerType VARCHAR(1)=null,
    @EventMessage VARCHAR(255) = null

AS
    DECLARE @Severity INTEGER
    DECLARE @SevPerm INTEGER

    SELECT
        @Severity=MAX(Severity)
    FROM EventLogMaster
    WHERE CodeID=@CodeID

    SELECT
        @SevPerm=VarValue
    FROM GlobalVariables
    WHERE VarName='Severity'

    IF @Severity>=@SevPerm
        INSERT INTO EventLog(CodeId, IdPointer,
            IdPointerType, EventMessage)
        VALUES(@CodeID, @IdPointer, @IdPointerType,
            @EventMessage)
```

Once you create the EventMessage procedure, you can invoke it from key locations in your application code. Events will then be logged as allowed by the current severity-level setting.

Discussion

The solution in this recipe uses a global list of possible event messages that are identified by an ID number. This ID number corresponds to the CodeID column in the EventLogMaster table. Each message has a severity level indicating its importance. When an error or important event is detected, your code can call the EventMessage procedure and pass in the appropriate CodeID value. The event will then be logged, as long as the severity level permits it.

If the event relates to a row in a table, that row can be identified by passing in the row's primary key using the @IdPointer variable. You would also need to identify the table by passing in an appropriate table code via the @IdPointerType parameter. This general framework allows you to reference different tables from the same log.

You also have the option of recording a specific message for each event. This message is passed to the procedure via the @EventMessage parameter and will be stored in the EventMessage column of the EventLog table. You can build the message using string concatenation to hold whatever values you believe are relevant for each particular event.

The EventLogMaster and EventLog tables can easily be extended to include system information such as a timestamp, the CURRENT_USER, or a detailed explanation of the cause for an event. The basic framework shown here provides you with a great deal of flexibility.

Defining severity levels

The current severity level is checked in the EventMessage procedure every time it is called. If the severity limit for a message is less than the current global severity level, this indicates that the message should be logged, and the EventMessage procedure will then record the event in the EventLog table. Messages with severity limits above the current global security level are not logged. This is useful for debugging purposes, because you can enable or disable the logging of certain events just by changing the global severity level. You could, for example, set the global severity level to a high value for normal operations. This would prevent any events from being logged. Then, if a user reported problems, you could decrease the global severity level, thereby dynamically enabling logging of the events needed to resolve the user's problem.

The number and type of severity levels can vary for each system that you design. Some systems use eight or more severity levels, some use fewer. Table 6-2 shows one possible severity-level classification scheme that you might use.

Table 6-2. Possible severity-level classifactions

Severity	Level	Description
0	Debug	An event logged only for debugging purposes.
1	Regular	A regular event.
2	Notice	A regular, but significant event.
3	Warning	A warning event, indicating a possible problem.
4	Error	An error event representing an error that the system is designed to handle gracefully.
5	Critical	An error event that the system is not designed to handle and that, therefore, represents a critical error.

In a development environment, you may want to have the debug level enabled, so that you can get the maximum amount of detail for use in resolving bugs. In a production environment, on the other hand, you may want to log only warning or higher events.

Extending error messages

With support of the string-manipulation functions, it is possible to create generic event messages that combine several values in a user-friendly manner. For example, assume that you have defined a message that records the purchase of a product. The generic message text in the EventLogMaster table might be "Purchase of product" or something similar. To record a purchase, and to record along with it the number and type of objects purchased, you could invoke the EventMessage procedure as follows:

```
EventMessage 456,'T357','0','Bananas 10'
```

In this example, the procedure was called for message number 456, which indicates that product was purchased. The next two parameters identify order #T357 as the record affected by this event. The last parameter indicates that order #T357 was for the purchase of 10 bananas.

Reporting

To report on the activity log described in this recipe, you need to join the EventLog and EventLogMaster tables together. The EventLog table records the specific events that occurred, while the EventLogMaster table records the text messages corresponding to those events. Remember that the language ID needs to be part of your query. For example:

```
SELECT EventId, MessageText, EventMessage
FROM EventLog l JOIN EventLogMaster m
ON l.CodeId=m.CodeID
WHERE LangId='E'
```

A possible extension of this activity-logging technique is changing the message-text format to allow inline message expansion. Instead of "Purchase of product," the message text for event ID 3 could be defined as: 'Purchase of %2 %1'. If your server supports regular-expression evaluation, or even simple search and replace, you can substitute the name and quantity of the product purchased for the %2 and %1 placeholders.

An activity log, such as the one described here, cannot easily be used to reconstruct a snapshot of a table as of a specific point in time, because it does not record each and every SQL statement that modifies the data in the table.

Another possible query that you might want to implement for a log like this is one that scans for important messages with high severity levels. By running such a query periodically, you can identify important events that might otherwise remain unnoticed, allowing you to correct problems before they become critical.

6.11   Partitioning Large Log Tables

Problem

Log tables are usually very large in that they contain a large number of rows. However, only the most recent events are usually accessed on a frequent basis. You want to create a structure that will take advantage of this fact, allowing the more recent records to be queried in an efficient manner.

Solution

Divide your log table into two tables. They should both have the same structure. One table will hold the most recent events—for example, the current month's data, and the other table will hold everything else. The table with the most recent data can be referred to as the current log, while the other table is referred to as the archive log. You can then combine the data from the two tables into one row set using the following query:

```
SELECT p1, p2, p3 ... pn FROM log_work
UNION
SELECT p1,p2,p3 ... pn FROM  log_archive
```

Discussion

With this kind of a structure, the current log will always be relatively short compared to the archive log. This is good for insert operations, especially if you choose not to index the table. New log entries are always written to the current log table, and the fewer the indices to maintain, the better your performance will be. Because it's relatively small, you may still be able to get decent query performance from the current log table even without an index. The archive log table, on the other hand, should be indexed since it's relatively large.

This combined structure is very efficient for many types of operations, but it requires additional work on the part of your programmers, who must develop regular batch procedures that periodically move older log records from the current log table to the archive table. Still, when performance is the critical goal, this solution can be very beneficial.

The UNION query can be nicely encapsulated into a UNION view. Then you have a view that behaves as a single table even though the underlying implementation uses two tables. Unfortunately, not all database vendors implement UNION views. If you are not using MS SQL Server, you'll have to check your database server's documentation to see if the UNION view option is available to you.

 The solution shown in this recipe doesn't apply only to log tables. It can be applied to any type of large table, where only a small fraction of the rows in that table are used consistently and the rest are used infrequently.

6.12   Server Push

Problem

You want to implement a code-based server-push replication mechanism with your SQL database server to notify client applications that an event has occurred. For example, you may wish to update a help-desk supervisor's screen each time a new help-desk call arrives. Your goal is to have an external system notified of significant activities or events as they occur.

Solution

This solution shows you how to simulate a server-push mechanism by repeatedly polling from the client at regular intervals. To start with, you need to have a table on the server to which you can log the activities that you want pushed. The following Event table will be used in this recipe:

```
CREATE TABLE Event (
    EventId INTEGER IDENTITY,
    Code INTEGER,
    EventTime DATETIME,
    PRIMARY KEY(EventId)
)
```

This Event table logs events that are generated within the system. Different event codes would be used for different types of events. For each logged event, a timestamp is also recorded in the Event table. The event-log entries are generated by the software operating on the database, perhaps through the use of a stored procedure. See the "Activity-Level Logging" recipe for an example.

The idea in this recipe is to simulate server push with a client-pull mechanism. To do this, you have to create an external program that repeats one query indefinitely. This query repeatedly polls the database for new log entries, and the client program can then initiate appropriate actions in response to those entries. The following pseudocode illustrates the process that must occur in the client software:

```
init @mark
REPEAT
    SELECT Code,EventId FROM event
        WHERE @mark < EventId
        ORDER BY EventId
    store read rows into internal structure
    FOR EACH row in the structure
        initiate the action for the event
        @mark:=id
    END FOR
UNTIL forever
```

The variable @mark in this example is an internal client variable that holds the ID of the log entry most recently read from the event table. Each time a log record is read, the @mark variable is updated. The polling query uses @mark to ensure that only new log entries are retrieved. Only log entries with ID numbers greater than @mark are retrieved.

Discussion

The solution opens up a wide variety of possibilities and allows programmers to give an active role to their database systems. Rather than being limited to serving requests as they come in from clients, the database can now be the initiator of an event or of a process.

Newer database systems have built-in support for both push and pull replication mechanisms; however, these mechanisms are usually not portable across vendor platforms. The solution presented here is portable and provides the flexibility of integrating SQL-based systems with external systems. A stored database procedure can now initiate an action in a system external to the database. You may, for example, use a stored procedure to trigger pager notification to the DBA or system operator when a significant event occurs.

Ticketing

Here *ticketing* refers to the practice of assigning unique identifiers to each request made by the user of a system. A help-desk system, for example, might create a trouble ticket each time a user calls with a problem, and each trouble ticket would have a unique number to identify it.

Proper use of the @mark variable is critical when implementing polling code such as that shown in this recipe. First, you need to make sure that @mark is properly initialized. You need to decide what records you want the client to pull after it is started. Do you want the client to pull all log records that are available? Do you want to pull only those records logged after the client starts? Do you want the client to catch up with any records that might have been missed when the client was not running?

Initializing @mark to 0 each time you start the client will result in the client reading all existing log records each time it starts. It's unlikely that you'll want that behavior. A more reasonable approach is to have the client poll for new events that occur after the client starts. You can do that by using a query to grab the highest log ID number from the event table, such as the following:

```
SELECT @mark=MAX(EventId)
FROM Event
```

By initializing @mark like this each time you start your client, you ensure that you will see only new log entries. That's because those new entries will have IDs greater than the maximum value at the time the client starts.

If it is important that your client program processes all event records, even those posted during periods when the client wasn't running, you can add a column to the event table that allows you to flag rows that have been processed. Then, you can poll for those rows that haven't yet been processed.

In such cases, you have to initialize @mark variable to the smallest Id that still hasn't been sent:

```
SELECT @mark=MIN(EventId)
FROM Event
WHERE Sent=FALSE
```

Assuming that your flag column is named Sent, and that it is a Boolean column, the following pseudocode illustrates the process to follow:

```
init @mark
REPEAT
    SELECT Code,EventId FROM Event
        WHERE @mark < EventId and Sent=FALSE
        ORDER BY EventId
    store read rows into internal structure
    FOR EACH row in the structure
        BEGIN TRAN
            initiate the action for the event
            UPDATE Event SET Sent=TRUE
                WHERE Id=@id
                @mark:=@id
        END TRAN
    END FOR
UNTIL forever
```

Newly inserted rows will have the Sent column set to FALSE because they have not yet been processed by the client. Your client query can key off that to ensure that it only brings back unprocessed rows. You can also use the sent column to your advantage when you initialize the @mark variable. You just set @mark to the ID number of the earliest log record that hasn't yet been processed. For example:

```
SELECT @mark=MIN(EventId)
FROM Event
WHERE Sent=FALSE
```

The solution shown here ensures that each event is pushed only once. However, it does require additional UPDATE statements, which result in the use of server-side processing capacity. As with anything else, you have to look at the tradeoffs and decide if the technique makes sense for a given situation.

Polling as an alternative to triggers

This solution can also be viewed as an alternative to database triggers. Many database systems support triggers, but when built-in triggers are used, an action is initiated every time a row is added, deleted, or modified. Depending on what the trigger does, this can place a significant burden on the server, especially in times of peak activity. The time required for trigger execution can also add significantly to the time needed to execute a DDL statement.

Rather than use triggers, a client program can be configured to poll the server once per second (or some other acceptable time period) for a list of changes that have occurred since the previous poll. The client can then initiate appropriate actions. This results in a slight delay between the time a change is made and the proper events are triggered, but it also moves much of the work into the background where it won't affect the performance of the DML statements making the change.

Let's say that we have a small ticketing server, which stores quotes from a stock exchange. We want to use a server-push mechanism to send quotes to the user's screen, but if we use internal triggering, every new quote will end up being sent to, and displayed on, the user's screen. If activity peaks, and the volume of quotes reaches into the hundreds per second, the user will be overwhelmed with information. A better solution might be to have the client polled once per second and only retrieve the most recent quote for each ticker symbol. A query, such as the following, might be used for this purpose:

```
SELECT Symbol,
       MAX(CASE WHEN EventId=MAX(EventId)
           THEN Quote ELSE
           NULL END) quote
FROM Quote
WHERE @mark<EventId
GROUP BY Symbol
```

The query returns the last known quote for each symbol so long as that quote has been logged with an ID greater than that held in the @mark variable. The use of @mark saves us from having to retrieve the same quote more than once. Only new quotes since the previous poll need be retrieved.

Client stability

The polling solution described in this recipe brings additional flexibility to the table, but it also carries with it some potential reliability problems. When you separate the triggering mechanism from the server, you introduce another potential point of failure. If the client software fails, or if the connection between the client and the server is lost, you lose the whole push mechanism.

Think carefully about whether it pays off to introduce such a solution or not. Sometimes there is no other choice, and sometimes it is simply handier than other possible solutions. We can not overstress the importance of having proper error checking embedded in the code of the client. You may also want to implement a secondary service that periodically pings the client to check on performance and availability.

Support for multiple tables

All the code in this recipe has dealt with polling only one event table. You can easily add support for multiple tables by extending the same logic to those tables. You do not even need to add additional clients to poll more tables. One client can be written that periodically executes several SELECT queries against several different event tables. You do, however, need to guard against asking one client to handle too much work.

CHAPTER 7

Importing and Transforming Data

Transact-SQL-based systems often interact with much older, legacy systems. Data that is imported from such sources is often inefficiently structured and poorly organized. Usually after importing such data, you want to transform it into a structure that can be handled efficiently and that will easily support a wide variety of queries.

This chapter introduces concepts and recipes useful for working with imported data tables and their transformations. We show data normalization and other techniques for transforming badly structured data into a form more acceptable for SQL processing. Denormalized data is usually found when importing from nonrelational systems or from files designed for human use. In general, the more human-readable the data is, the less efficiently it can be manipulated using SQL statements.

Data rows can be inserted into SQL tables by using either the INSERT statement or an embedded import mechanism, such as the BULK INSERT statement. Once the rows are in SQL Server, they can be manipulated using standard SQL commands.

In this chapter, we try to find a balance between the readability and efficiency of data tables. We discuss general techniques of folding and pivoting that can be used to transform human-readable data into SQL-friendly tables and back again. We show some techniques that you can use to ensure smooth linking between legacy data systems and SQL Server–based systems. We suggest some steps that you can follow to ensure that external data is imported safely, and we offer ways to provide efficient error handling for failed imports.

7.1   Considerations When Importing Data

Most database systems available today have their own proprietary import mechanisms. Some of these, such as Microsoft's Data Transformation Services (DTS) or the Bulk Copy Program (BCP) are implemented as external programs where you specify the format (usually ASCII) of the files to be imported and the table into which the data should be inserted. Though DTS is more user-friendly because of its graphical user interface, its performance (in general) is not as good as that of the BCP.

Another popular way to import data is to use the BULK INSERT statement—an extension of the SQL dialect that is accessible from the console or other interactive interfaces. Using BULK INSERT, you specify the file to load from and the table in the database that you want to receive the data. The BULK INSERT statement is useful for quick imports of ASCII files.

There are two major problem areas that you will encounter when importing data: error handling and performance. You can request that a load be aborted if an error occurs during the load process, or you can allow a certain number of errors to occur before the import operation is aborted. By default, SQL Server allows 10 errors before aborting a load. Often, though, you will want more flexibility in how the load process treats bad records. Rather than just having bad records rejected, you may want them to be loaded anyway and flagged as errors. That way, you can more easily go in later and correct the problems.

With respect to performance, SQL tables are usually associated with a number of indices, foreign-key references, and other constraints that are designed to improve access efficiency and to preserve data integrity. However, when rows are loaded one-by-one, updating indices and checking constraints for each row can place quite a burden on the server. As a query language, SQL is optimized more for querying than for inserting. If you can manage it, and you are loading a large amount of data, it's often beneficial to drop indices and constraints prior to the load and recreate them afterwards. Index checking and constraint validation are thereby batched into one large operation instead of many small ones.

Bulk Importing

When you insert rows one-by-one, the normal operation of your database server is to trigger the updating of indices on the table after each insert. Bulk importing, through the use of the BULK INSERT statement or the BCP utility, inserts rows of data much faster than conventional methods, because indexing is temporarily suspended. You can further improve the performance of an import operation by using the TABLOCK hint to request table locks. Then the server locks the table exclusively, inserts all the new rows in one step, and rebuilds the table's indices at the end of the load. The performance improvement from doing this can be significant, and the result is usually a very fast load.

 A bulk import is not exactly the same as manually disabling indices, loading the data, and manually recreating indices again. On the surface, the two approaches appear equivalent, but there are other efficiencies built into SQL Server's bulk-import mechanism. During a bulk operation, the optimizer uses the existing index structure to insert rows more efficiently and as a basis for rebuilding the indices more quickly after the import is complete.

In general, bulk importing is useful in an environment where the database does not need to be available 100% of the time. In such cases, we recommend that you use table locking to improve performance. To do a bulk import with the table locked, you need a time window during which you can be sure that no users will need to access the table or tables that you are loading. In a 24×7 environment, where you can't afford the downtime or risk other inconveniences from bulk inserts, you have to be innovative and use more sophisticated techniques. Alternatively, you can settle for the lower performance provided by tools that perform row-level importing.

Normalized Data

Data normalization is an important subject with respect to relational databases. Normalization refers to the technique of finding functional dependencies between attributes and of resolving those dependencies so that data is stored in an efficient and useful manner. Efficient and useful for the database, that is. Normalized data is seldom efficient from a human viewpoint. SQL, however, has been specifically designed to work best with normalized data.

Normalized tables have no groups of repeating, data nor do they have attributes that are dependant on one another. Redundancy and other anomalies in data are avoided. For example, look at the following comparative balance-sheet report covering the three years from 2000 to 2002:

```
CompanyId   Company     Category     2000     2001     2002
---------   ---------   ---------    -------  -------  --------
12445       ABC, Inc    Assets       36,755   37,472   38,973
12445       ABC, Inc    Liability    22,252   22,924   24,476
12445       ABC, Inc    Equity       14,230   14,548   14,497
```

The data in this report is presented in a non-normalized form. The CompanyId and Company columns are dependent on each other—each company ID number represents a specific company name, and there are three balance values in each row. Although this report is easy for a human to read, if you stored the data this way in your database, adding an additional year would be an expensive and quite complicated task. You would need to add and initialize an additional column for each year that you were adding, and that task would require each and every row to be read, expanded, and written back again. Not only does that present a problem with respect to I/O, but expanding a row to a larger size can lead to storage inefficiencies. Storing data, such as a company name, more than once is a waste of space.

Eliminate repeating columns

Restructuring the table into a more computer-friendly form makes processing much easier for SQL Server. The following table can store the data shown in the previous report, but in a more efficient manner:

```
CREATE TABLE BalanceSheets(
    CompanyId INTEGER,
    Company CHAR(200),
```

```
    Category CHAR(20),
    Year INTEGER,
    Dollars DECIMAL(12,2)
)
```

This table design results in one row for each company, category, and year combination. Adding more years, or more categories, is simply a matter of inserting new rows—existing rows do not need to be touched. The data for the report, as stored in the BalanceSheets table, looks like this:

```
CompanyId   Company   Category    Year   Dollars
-----------  ---------  ----------  ------  ---------
12445       ABC, Inc  Assets      2000   36,755
12445       ABC, Inc  Liability   2000   22,252
12445       ABC, Inc  Equity      2000   14,230
12445       ABC, Inc  Assets      2001   37,472
12445       ABC, Inc  Liability   2001   22,924
12445       ABC, Inc  Equity      2001   14,548
12445       ABC, Inc  Assets      2002   38,973
12445       ABC, Inc  Liability   2002   24,476
12445       ABC, Inc  Equity      2002   14,497
```

Good as it is, this table is still not normalized. The Company column is dependent on the CompanyId column (or vice versa, if you prefer). For any given company ID, the associated company name is always the same. You can gain efficiencies in both storage space and manageability by further normalizing this table design to factor out the company name.

Factor out dependent columns

The last step in normalizing the balance-sheet data is to factor out the company name so that it is not repeated in each row of data. You can further gain some storage efficiencies by representing the category as a code rather than as a text string. The final design for the table holding the balance-sheet data looks like this:

```
CREATE TABLE BalanceSheets2 (
    CompanyId INTEGER,
    CategoryId CHAR(1),
    Year INTEGER,
    Dollars DECIMAL(12,2)
)
```

The BalanceSheet2 table shown here can be referred to as a detail table, because it contains the detailed balance-sheet data. As you can see, some supporting master tables are needed to resolve company and category ID numbers into human-readable text strings. Those tables can be defined as follows:

```
CREATE TABLE CompanyMaster(
    CompanyId INTEGER,
    CompanyName CHAR(200),
    PRIMARY KEY(CompanyId)
)
```

```
CREATE TABLE CategoryMaster(
    CategoryId CHAR(1),
    CategoryName CHAR(20),
    PRIMARY KEY(CategoryId)
)
```

The data in the detail table looks like this:

```
CompanyId   CategoryId Year   Dollars
----------- ---------- ------ ---------
12445       A          2000   36,755
12445       L          2000   22,252
12445       E          2000   14,230
12445       A          2001   37,472
12445       L          2001   22,924
12445       E          2001   14,548
12445       A          2002   38,973
12445       L          2002   24,476
12445       E          2002   14,497
```

The data is now normalized. There are no more functional dependencies or repeating groups of data. Removing any additional data columns would result in a loss of information from the system.

Note that, while it is normalized, the readability of the data is reduced. A simple query to the BalanceSheets2 detail table produces results that are not nearly as readable as those shown earlier on the original balance-sheet report. However, the normalized data can easily be manipulated using SQL, and simple joins can be used to associate company and category names with their respective ID and code values. For example:

```
SELECT b.CompanyId, o.CompanyName, a.CategoryName,
    b.Year, b.Dollars
FROM
    BalanceSheets2 b
    JOIN CategoryMaster a ON b.CompanyId=o.CompanyId
    JOIN CompanyMaster o ON b.CategoryId=a.CategoryId
```

This query returns one row for each company, category, and year combination. Using the Pivot table technique shown later in this chapter, you can write a SQL query that will return the data in the same form used in the report that you saw at the beginning of this section.

Reduced memory requirements

A normalized data structure not only is efficient for the database engine, it also saves memory and disk space. The first table, named BalanceSheets, uses approximately 240 bytes per row (CompanyId 4, Company 200, Category 20, Year 4, Dollars 12). The second table, named BalanceSheets2, is normalized and only requires 21 bytes per row (CompanyId 4, CategoryId 1, Year 4, Dollars 12). In our case, the 21 bytes required for each normalized row is only 9% of that required by the non-normalized data.

Think of the impact of normalization on memory pages[*] and the resulting I/O needed to query the table. Assume that your server stores 8KB of data per memory page (the default for SQL Server). In the case of the non-normalized table, each page can store about 33 records (leaving some space for overhead). If each balance sheet requires 3 records (for assets, liabilities, and equities), then each page will store 11 yearly balance sheets. When the data is normalized, however, each memory page can hold more than 350 records (again, leaving some space for overhead), which is equal to about 115 yearly balance sheets.

 Space requirements for master tables are usually insignificant compared to those required by detail tables. With only three categories, all the CategoryMaster rows will fit on one 8KB page.

If you have 10,000 balance sheets and you run a query to generate a statistical survey of that data, using the non-normalized approach will result in 900 page reads. Using the normalized approach will result in only around 86 reads for the data, plus a couple more to pull in the small amount of data from the CompanyMaster and CategoryMaster tables. This is a significant performance improvement in terms of I/O and is a result of efficiently structuring the data.

 When you design your systems, try not to force users to think in normalized data structures. That is your job. Users should have a simple and friendly interface, with all sorts of available views. On the system level, however, data should be as clear and simplified as possible for it to be manipulated efficiently using SQL.

Master/Detail Framework

Most of today's database solutions use a master/detail framework. The concept is a natural one for relational systems since it comes directly from table normalization. The whole idea is to take columns with values that are repeated many times and replace them with a reference to a record in another table where each distinct value is stored only once. Such a table is referred to as a master table. The table containing the references is referred to as a detail table.

The master/detail table structure provides several advantages when it is implemented in a relational database. One advantage is the space that you save when you replace long character strings that are repeated in numerous rows with a short reference to master record. Another important advantage, this time related to manageability, is the ability to change the values in the master table easily. It's a lot easier and faster to change a company name if it is only stored once in a master table than if it is stored many times in a detail table.

---

[*] A memory page is the smallest unit that can be saved internally in the database servers' memory. Usually, they are the smallest chunks read or written to the disk. Therefore, it is not important how big the tables rows are, but how many rows can be stored in one memory page.

Duplicates

A *duplicate* is a row that is repeated at least twice with the same values in the same columns. You will encounter duplicates often when importing data. This is especially true for imports involving a mix of both old and new data. Duplicates are often a product of inconsistencies, or of bad data conversions, and are sometimes the only way of detecting that something went wrong during the import.

There are two types of duplicates: full and partial. *Full duplicates* are rows that have the same values for all columns. *Partial duplicates* are rows with duplication only in a specific subset of columns.

A duplicate has an occurrence count that represents the number of times it occurs in a given table. You might, for example, have the same row duplicated 5 times. In that case, the duplicate count would be 5. Sometimes this occurrence count is referred to as a degree of duplication. All nonduplicated rows have an occurrence count of 1.

The process of eliminating duplicate values is called reduction, and the mechanism for it is built into standard SQL as the DISTINCT clause of the SELECT statement. A SELECT DISTINCT eliminates duplicate results from the result set. If two rows have the same column values, that set of values will only appear once in the final result.

Counting duplicates

The duplicate occurrence count can be useful when business rules specify, or limit, the number of occurrences of a row or of a given value. A typical, and simple, example of such a business rule is a general accounting principle that each credit must have a corresponding debit. For each item your company buys, there should be two accounting entries; however, they still reflect only one event.[*] Each event has its own ID. Consequently, each ID is associated with two entries: a debit and a credit. It is very easy to test whether your accounting records comply with the dual-entry rule or not. You just have to check if any row has an occurrence count other than 2. For example:

```
SELECT EventId FROM Balances
GROUP BY EventId
HAVING count(*)<>2
```

As you move on to more complex cases, the code obviously gets more complicated, but the principle remains the same. You can use the vocabulary defined in this section to define duplication requirements for a table. In the accounting example, a table recording book entries must have an occurrence count of 2 on the column identifying events.

---

[*] This is not entirely true, but this is a book on SQL, not accounting, so ignore the details for a moment.

7.2　Working Examples

To demonstrate our recipes, we'll use a simplified university system with tables for a student register, a teacher register, a campus bookstore, student grades, and so forth.

Bookstore

You have a 24×7 online sales support system for a campus bookstore. The bookstore has a warehouse that runs a standalone warehouse system. The warehouse is run by an external partner, and the warehouse system comes from a third-party vendor. The warehouse system calculates the exact stock inventory several times a day and needs to update the central database used by your sales support system with that information. The central database is your database, which is your responsibility.

Assume that your sales support system implements the following table to keep track of the quantities of books that are available:

```
CREATE TABLE Bookstore(
    BookId INTEGER UNIQUE,
    Name CHAR(40),
    Quantity INTEGER,
    Price DECIMAL(10,2),
    Type CHAR(20)
)
```

For demonstration purposes, let's fill the table with some data:

BookId	Name	Quantity	Price	Type
1	Software Engineering	5	15.00	Manual
2	Modern Operating Systems	7	20.00	Reference
3	Learn SQL	15	18.00	Textbook
4	Learn Advanced SQL	1	8.00	Textbook
5	JavaScript Tutorial	5	10.00	Textbook
6	Modern Operating Systems	7	20.00	Reference
7	Learn SQL	15	18.00	Textbook

This table stores information on every book that is available in your warehouse. Several times a day, the warehouse transmits new inventory positions that need to be validated and loaded into this table.

Rankings

Each year, the student-aid office calculates the average ranking of students eligible for a university scholarship. The office holds ranking information in a large spreadsheet that looks as follows:

Id	Name	Y2000	Y2001	Y2002
1	Joe	7	8	9
2	Anna	1	2	3
3	Billy	4	5	6
...				

Workers at the student-aid office know how to export their spreadsheet into an ASCII table, which you will ultimately load into the following SQL table:

```
CREATE TABLE StudentRankings(
    Id INTEGER,
    Name CHAR(10),
    Y2000 INTEGER,
    Y2001 INTEGER,
    Y2002 INTEGER
)
```

Scores

The Academic Director of the university's School of Accounting stores the scores of students in a SQL table named StudentScores. The table structure is as follows:

```
CREATE TABLE StudentScores (
    CourseId CHAR(20),
    StudentName CHAR(40),
    Score DECIMAL(5,2)
)
```

The data that you have to work with in the Scores table looks like this:

```
CourseId StudentName Score
-------- ----------- -----
Accn101  Mike        78.3
Bkn1002  Mike        56.5
Tax1232  Mike        89.8
Accn101  Hannah      76.4
Bkn1002  Hannah      67.6
Tax1232  Hannah      78.8
Accn101  Andrew      45.3
Bkn1002  Andrew      45.5
Tax1232  Andrew      68.5
```

Dissertations

You have a table named StudentThesis that holds information on Ph.D. student dissertations and that lists the members of the dissertation committee in front of which each student defended his thesis:

```
CREATE TABLE StudentThesis (
    StudentId INTEGER,
    Member1 INTEGER,
    Member2 INTEGER,
    Member3 INTEGER,
    Grade CHAR(2)
)
```

The data in the Thesis table looks like this:

```
StudentId  Member1  Member2  Member3  Grade
---------- -------- -------- -------- ------
1            234      322      456     A
2            456      322      344     B
3            456      455      344     A
4            322      123      455     C
```

The three Member columns identify the professors by their identification numbers. These numbers can be used in a query against the Professors table (a master table) to get each professor's name. Here is a sample of the data in the Professors table:

```
Id   Name
---- -----
123  Smith, John
456  Newton, Isaac
455  Einstein, Albert
344  Base, Samuel
322  Anderson, Terry
234  Baird, Frances
```

Similar master records exist for the students in a Student table:

```
StudentId    StudentName
-----------  --------------------
1            Bob One
2            Mark Twain
3            Brent Thrice
4            Joe Forth
```

7.3   Importing External Data

Problem

You want to import data from an external text file. The import can be done in a batch process, because users do not need access to the destination table while the import takes place.

Solution

Use one of SQL Server's built-in import mechanisms, such as the BULK INSERT statement, to import the data from the ASCII file. Be careful with respect to validation and error handling. Follow these steps:

1. Make sure that the data to be imported is in an ASCII file.

2. Filter the data for obvious inconsistencies.

3. Import the data into your database using the BCP utility or BULK INSERT statement.

4. Check for errors.

Step 1: Make sure that the data to be imported is in an ASCII file

Almost all import mechanisms today support importing from ASCII text files. This is good, because text files are the easiest to deal with when something goes wrong. You can use any text editor to inspect and debug the data. If your external data source is another database, you can export data from that database into a text file and then load from that text file into your target database.

Step 2: Filter the data for obvious inconsistencies

Use Perl, awk, or VBScript to filter and preprocess the data to be loaded. Keep in mind the datatypes of the columns that you are loading. Each datatype has its own set of common problems. Table 7-1 lists some of the common problems that you will encounter when loading data from an external source.

Table 7-1. Common data-import problems

Datatype	Possible problems
NUMERICAL	Check the decimal and digit-grouping symbols. European and U.S. standards are exactly opposite of each other. Make sure that your systems understand the decimal symbol that you use in the ASCII files. It's best to omit or discard digit-grouping symbols if possible. They add no value to the import process.
CHAR	Check the quote symbol and its interpretation by the database server. By default, SQL Server imports all characters between field delimiters.
DATE	There are many possible problems with the way dates are formatted, so it's best to transform dates into the universal YYYY-MM-DD HH:MM format. This format is recognized as a standard by the ANSI committee and is the default format for SQL Server.
INTEGER	Be cognizant of the size of an INTEGER in your database server. Most servers use 4 bytes to store INTEGER datatypes. If the numeric values that you are importing exceed the range of an INTEGER type (−2,147,483,648 through 2,147,483,647), you should import them as NUMERICAL. You can also use an extended INTEGER if that type is available on your system.

Other possible issues include how fields are separated in the data file and the characters used to mark the end of a row and the end of a file. However, these types of issues are easy to detect, and you can usually deal with them early in the development process.

Step 3: Import the data into your database

Import the data using one of SQL Server's import mechanisms. One of the easiest ways to import data from a text file is to use the BULK INSERT statement as shown in the following example:

```
BULK INSERT Northwind.dbo.Orders
    FROM 'C:\orders\orders.txt'
    WITH (FIELDTERMINATOR='|',TABLOCK)
```

Step 4: Check for errors

Checking for errors, and then dealing with them, is the hardest part of any import process. If your import system returns any error codes or other information that can be used to detect problems, be sure to take advantage of those features.

A quick trick that you can use to determine if a load was successful or not is also to take an initial count of the rows in the table being loaded. Do this before loading any data. Also count the lines in the ASCII file that you are loading. Import the data and count the rows in the table again. Calculate the difference between the row counts before and after the import. If the difference in row counts is the same as the line count from the ASCII file, you can assume that all rows have been inserted and that no rows have been rejected. Be careful with this technique. It's only valid when you can be certain no other users are modifying the data in the table that you are loading.

Discussion

The SQL language itself does not accommodate the importing of data into a database. In general, there are two approaches to the problem of doing an import. One approach is to use an external program that connects to the server as a client, reads the data from the ASCII file, and stores it into the database using INSERT statements. The other approach is for the database vendor to implement proprietary commands for importing or exporting data. SQL Server's BULK INSERT statement is an example of such a command. Proprietary commands such as these usually follow the general form of SQL statements, but they are not standardized across vendor platforms.

7.4   Importing Data into a Live System

Problem

You need to import data from an external source, and your users need to have full access to the target tables even while the import is taking place. Furthermore, you need a mechanism for validating the imported data before it is stored in the production tables.

Solution

To avoid contaminating the operational system with bad data, we will design our import process around the use of a buffer table. This buffer table will have a structure similar to the system's operational table, but with extra columns to support error handling and the import process. Data will be loaded into the buffer table. A stored procedure will then be invoked to validate each row in the buffer table. Rows that pass validation tests will be loaded into the operational table. Rows that fail validation will be flagged as errors so that they can be corrected later.

Step 1: Create buffer tables

Create a buffer table for the table that is being loaded by the import process. The following BookstoreBuffer table is the buffer table for the Bookstore table in the Bookstore application that we will be loading in this recipe:

```
CREATE TABLE BookstoreBuffer (
    Id UNIQUEIDENTIFIER DEFAULT NEWID( ),
    BookId INTEGER,
    Name CHAR(40),
    Quantity INTEGER,
    Price DECIMAL(10,2),
    Type CHAR(20),
    Status CHAR(1) DEFAULT 'I'
)
```

The Status column is used to hold the status of imported rows. The Id column forms the primary key, providing a unique identifier for each row that can later be used with the validation procedure. Table 7-2 lists the values that will be used for the Status column.

Table 7-2. Buffer table status values

Value	Status	Description
I	Imported	The row has been imported into the buffer table, but has not yet been validated and loaded into the operational table.
A	Added	The row has been validated, and the new information has been added to the operational table.
R	Rejected	The row has failed validation and has, consequently, been rejected.

All newly inserted rows should be marked with an 'I' to indicate that they have been imported, but not yet validated and added to the operational table. This can be done either through triggers or by the code that loads the data. The next section shows the procedure to validate and add the newly imported data to the Stock table.

Step 2: Build validation procedures

Create a stored procedure for the table being loaded that validates each newly imported row in the associated buffer table. Rows that pass validation should be used to update the operational table. Rows that fail validation should be flagged as rejections. The following ImportRow procedure reads from the BookstoreBuffer table and updates the Bookstore table:

```
CREATE PROCEDURE ImportRow @RowId UNIQUEIDENTIFIER
AS BEGIN
    DECLARE @BookId INTEGER
    DECLARE @Name CHAR(40)
    DECLARE @Quantity INTEGER
    DECLARE @Price DECIMAL(10,2)
    DECLARE @Type CHAR(20)
```

```
DECLARE @checkFlag integer

SELECT @BookId=BookId,
       @Name=Name,
       @Quantity=Quantity,
       @Price=Price,
       @Type=Type
   FROM BookstoreBuffer
   WHERE Id=@RowId

/* Place validation code here. Set @checkFlag to 0
for good records, and set it to 1 for bad records.
*/
IF @quantity < 0
   SELECT @checkFlag=1
ELSE
   SELECT @checkFlag=0

/* If the row passed validation, update the operational table.
*/
IF @checkFlag=0 BEGIN
   UPDATE Bookstore
      SET
         Name=@Name,
         Quantity=@Quantity,
         Price=@Price,
         Type=@Type
      WHERE bookID=@bookId
   IF @@rowcount=0
      INSERT INTO Bookstore(BookId, Name, Quantity, Price, Type)
         VALUES(@BookId, @Name, @Quantity, @Price, @Type)
   UPDATE BookstoreBuffer SET Status='A' WHERE Id=@rowID
END ELSE
   UPDATE BookstoreBuffer SET Status='R' WHERE Id=@rowID
END
```

Steps 1 and 2 obviously only need to be performed once. Steps 3 and 4 should be used whenever new data needs to be imported.

Step 3: Insert rows

Insert the rows to be imported into the buffer table. Do this using a custom program or use a generic import utility. Please note that the procedure shown in this recipe is designed to validate and update a single row at the time. The programmer writing the load program needs to generate a new row ID for each row using the NEWID( ) function, insert that row into the buffer table, and then run the validation procedure.

 A simple extension of this technique is to write a validation procedure that processes all newly imported rows in the buffer table. You'll see an example of such a procedure in the next recipe.

Step 4: Check for rejected data

Check the buffer tables for rows that have a status value of R. These are rejected rows that could not be inserted into the system. Use a query such as the following:

```
SELECT * FROM BookstoreBuffer WHERE status='R'
```

This query returns all the rows from the BookstoreBuffer table that were not successfully inserted into the Bookstore table. Once you've identified the problem data, you can correct it, rerun the ImportRow procedure for those rows, and check for errors again.

Discussion

The buffer-table framework shown in this recipe can be used to import any type of data from an external system. A significant advantage is that you can delegate the actual import into the database to outside programmers, and yet, you retain control over the data that ends up being inserted into the operational tables. The key to that, of course, is to give the outside programmers access only to the buffer table while you retain control over the procedure used to move data from the buffer table to the operational table.

Because the validation procedure, ImportRow in this recipe, only loads valid data into the operational table, you can run the import process without restricting user access to the target table. If there are referential integrity issues to deal with, you can code the validation procedure to deal with those as well.

A key issue to think about when implementing this type of solution is how you want to deal with rows that have been imported, validated, and loaded into the production table. The procedure shown in this recipe keeps those rows around, but marks them with a status of A to show that they were accepted. The advantage to doing this is that you end up with a complete history of imported data in the Bookstore table. The disadvantage is that that history will end up consuming a large amount of disk space over time.

If you don't need to keep a history of accepted rows, you can delete each one after it is processed. With respect to the ImportRow procedure, the following code could be used:

```
IF @checkFlag=0
    DELETE BookstoreBuffer WHERE Id=@id
```

Deleting each row one-by-one may result in poor performance. DELETE statements are usually more expensive than UPDATES. Because of that, we recommend that you do one mass delete of all accepted rows after the entire load process has been completed.

7.5   Importing with a Single Procedure

Problem

The previous recipe requires a call to the import procedure after each row is inserted into the buffer table. You have a large number of rows that you need to insert simultaneously. You would like to load all your data into the buffer table and then make just one procedure call to move that data into your live table.

Solution

The solution is to design a stored procedure that opens a cursor on the buffer table to retrieve and process all the newly imported rows. As in the previous recipe, newly imported rows are marked with a status value of `'I'`.

The following procedure is named ImportFull. It continues with the Bookstore example introduced in the previous recipe. All newly imported rows are fetched via the cursor named BufferCursor. Each of these rows is validated. Rows that pass the validation tests are loaded into the live production table. Rows that fail validation are rejected and their status is changed to R.

```
CREATE PROCEDURE ImportFull
AS BEGIN
    DECLARE @id UNIQUEIDENTIFIER

    DECLARE @BookId INTEGER
    DECLARE @Name CHAR(40)
    DECLARE @Quantity INTEGER
    DECLARE @Price DECIMAL(10,2)
    DECLARE @Type CHAR(20)

    DECLARE @CheckFlag INTEGER

    DECLARE BufferCursor CURSOR FOR
        SELECT Id, BookId, Name, Quantity, Price, Type
        FROM BookstoreBuffer WHERE Status='I'

    OPEN BufferCursor

    FETCH NEXT FROM BufferCursor
        INTO @Id, @BookId, @Name, @Quantity, @Price, @Type

    WHILE @@FETCH_STATUS=0
    BEGIN
        /* Place validation code here. Set @checkFlag to 0
           for good records, and set it to 1 for bad records.
        */
        IF @Quantity < 0
            SELECT @CheckFlag=1
        ELSE
            SELECT @CheckFlag=0
```

```
    /* If the row passed validation, update the operational table.
    */
    IF @checkFlag=0 BEGIN
      UPDATE Bookstore
      SET
        Name=@Name,
        Quantity=@Quantity,
        Price=@Price,
        Type=@Type
      WHERE bookID=@bookId
      IF @@ROWCOUNT=0
        INSERT INTO Bookstore(BookId, Name, Quantity, Price, Type)
          VALUES(@BookId, @Name, @Quantity, @Price, @Type)
      UPDATE BookstoreBuffer SET Status='A' WHERE Id=@Id
    END ELSE
      UPDATE BookstoreBuffer SET Status='R' WHERE Id=@Id

    FETCH NEXT FROM BufferCursor
      INTO @Id, @BookId, @Name, @Quantity, @Price, @Type
  END

  CLOSE BufferCursor
  DEALLOCATE BufferCursor
END
```

Discussion

The ImportFull procedure shown here uses a procedural code and a cursor to step through the rows of the buffer table. This is efficient, and it gives you a chance to look at each row separately. Good rows are inserted into the production table. Bad rows are marked as rejects so that they can be identified and fixed at a later time.

7.6 Hiding the Import Procedure

Problem

You are using the buffer-table framework for importing data, but you want to hide the import procedure from the user. You want users to load new data into a buffer table, but, from that point on, you want the rows to be processed automatically. You don't want the user to have to worry about initiating the validation procedure.

Solution

The solution here is to use a trigger to drive the validation process. As rows are loaded into the buffer table, an insert trigger will automatically validate those rows, and load them into the live production table. The following trigger will process new rows loaded into the BookstoreBuffer table:

```
CREATE TRIGGER UpdateBookstoreBuffer
ON BookstoreBuffer
FOR INSERT
AS BEGIN
   DECLARE @id UNIQUEIDENTIFIER

   DECLARE @BookId INTEGER
   DECLARE @Name CHAR(40)
   DECLARE @Quantity INTEGER
   DECLARE @Price DECIMAL(10,2)
   DECLARE @Type CHAR(20)

   DECLARE @CheckFlag INTEGER

   DECLARE BufferCursor CURSOR FOR
      SELECT Id, BookId, Name, Quantity, Price, Type
      FROM BookstoreBuffer WHERE Status='I'

   OPEN BufferCursor

   FETCH NEXT FROM BufferCursor
      INTO @Id, @BookId, @Name, @Quantity, @Price, @Type

   WHILE @@FETCH_STATUS=0
   BEGIN
      /* Place validation code here. Set @checkFlag to 0
         for good records, and set it to 1 for bad records.
      */
      IF @quantity < 0
         SELECT @checkFlag=1
      ELSE
         SELECT @checkFlag=0

      /* If the row passed validation, update the operational table.
      */
      IF @CheckFlag=0 BEGIN
         UPDATE Bookstore
         SET
            Name=@Name,
            Quantity=@Quantity,
            Price=@Price,
            Type=@Type
         WHERE bookID=@bookId

         IF @@ROWCOUNT=0
            INSERT INTO Bookstore(BookId, Name, Quantity, Price, Type)
               VALUES(@BookId, @Name, @Quantity, @Price, @Type)
         UPDATE BookstoreBuffer SET Status='A' WHERE Id=@Id
      END ELSE
         UPDATE BookstoreBuffer SET Status='R' WHERE Id=@Id
```

```
        FETCH NEXT FROM BufferCursor
            INTO @Id, @BookId, @Name, @Quantity, @Price, @Type
    END

    CLOSE BufferCursor
    DEALLOCATE BufferCursor
END
```

The code in this trigger still expects the status flag of all newly inserted rows to be set to 'I'. You can see that the SELECT statement for the cursor named BufferCursor is restricted to those rows. New rows with a status of other than 'I' will still be inserted, but they will be ignored by this trigger. Remove the WHERE clause from the cursor's SELECT statement if you prefer not to worry about setting the status on newly inserted rows.

Discussion

Using a trigger as shown in this recipe is advantageous in terms of usability, because the user loading the data has one less thing to think about. When a procedure is used, as in the previous recipe, the load process looks like this:

1. Load data into buffer table

2. Invoke stored procedure to process the newly loaded data

3. Check for rejected records

This process isn't too bad, but if someone performs steps 1 and 3, skipping step 2, he might be misled into thinking that all their data had been successfully loaded when, in fact, it hadn't. Using a trigger to automatically process each row loaded into the buffer table leads to a two-step process that looks like this:

1. Load data into buffer table

2. Check for rejected records

For the user doing the load, this is conceptually easier to deal with. Unfortunately, there is a potential performance penalty that may offset this gain in usability. When you use a stored procedure to validate newly loaded data, you control when that stored procedure is executed, and you can schedule it for a time during which the performance impact will be minimal. You also gain some advantages from processing data in bulk. When a trigger is used, each row must be validated at the moment it is inserted. If you are loading a large amount of data, this validation could impact the performance of your production system.

All in all, triggers improve usability; however, you have to carefully consider the possible performance consequences of a trigger-based solution. If performance is an issue and you want control over when data is moved from the buffer table to the production table, then use stored procedures. If your load volumes are low, and you don't expect performance to be an issue, then you may find using triggers to be more convenient.

7.7 Folding Tables

Problem

You imported a wide, non-normalized table with columns organized in an array-like manner. You need to convert the data in that table to a more normalized form. For each non-normalized row in the original table, you need to generate several rows of normalized output. Taking the ranking spreadsheet from the student's office, you would prefer to have a list-like report, where the rank for each student in a year would represent one row, so the columns named Y2000, Y2001, and Y2002 are the ones that need to be flattened. Given the data shown earlier in this chapter for the ranking spreadsheet, you want to see output like this:

```
Name        Year Rank
----------  ---- -----------
Anna        2000 1
Anna        2001 2
Anna        2002 3
Billy       2000 4
Billy       2001 5
Billy       2002 6
Joe         2000 7
Joe         2001 8
Joe         2002 9
...
```

Solution

The act of taking a row in table and converting it into two or more narrower rows in an output table is referred to as *folding*. There are at least three approaches that you can take to fold data. An easy-to-understand approach is to use a union query. In some cases, you may be able to fold the data by joining the table to itself. A more general approach is to fold the data using a Pivot table.

Using a union query to fold data

A very easy-to-understand approach to folding data is to write one SELECT statement for each column that you want to fold and then union all those statements together. With respect to the bookstore example being used for this recipe, you could use the following query to fold the three columns:

```
SELECT Name, '2000' Year, Y2000 Rank FROM StudentRankings
UNION
SELECT Name, '2001', Y2001 FROM StudentRankings
UNION
SELECT Name, '2002', Y2002 FROM StudentRankings
```

The first SELECT statement returns the data for the year 2000, the second returns data for the year 2001, and the third returns data for the year 2002. The column alias Rank is used in the first SELECT statement to provide a name for the column containing the ranking data.

This appears to be a simple and straightforward solution, so why worry about any other approach? There are two reasons, actually, why you might not want to use a UNION query like the one shown here. One reason is that older versions of SQL servers didn't allow a UNION query to be encapsulated into a view. The other reason is performance. In the example shown here, three SELECT statements are being executed, requiring the server to make three passes through the table. For a small table, that might not present a problem, but as the amount of data in the table increases, so will the performance hit that you take by doing this.

Using a self-join to fold data

You can use a self-join to fold the data if the following statements are true:

- You have at least as many rows in the table as you have columns to fold
- You have a numerical column, such as an Id column
- The values in the numerical column begin with 1 and are guaranteed to be sequential

We are folding three columns (Y2000, Y2001, and Y2002), and our Student-Rankings table has three rows, so the first point is covered. The row Id number is sequential, starts with 1, and has no gaps, so the second two points are also covered.

The following query, then, can be used to fold the three volume columns into one:

```
SELECT t1.Name Name,
    (CASE WHEN t2.Id=1 THEN '2000'
        WHEN t2.Id=2 THEN '2001'
        WHEN t2.Id=3 THEN '2002' END) Year,
    (CASE WHEN t2.Id=1 THEN t1.Y2000
        WHEN t2.Id=2 THEN t1.Y2001
        WHEN t2.Id=3 THEN t1.Y2002 END) Volume
FROM StudentRankings t1, StudentRankings t2
WHERE t2.Id BETWEEN 1 AND 3
ORDER BY Name, Year
```

If you've never seen a query like this before, you may need to stare at it for a while before it begins to make sense. All the data comes back from the occurrence of the StudentRankings table that has the alias name t1. The WHERE clause restricts the t2 table so that only three rows are returned. These three rows have Id numbers 1, 2, and 3 and are used to control the results returned by the CASE statements. The discussion section for this recipe explains how this works in more detail.

Using the Pivot table to fold data

If you can't do a self-join with your data, you can use a more general approach to folding data that involves a Pivot table.

You need to have at least as many rows in the Pivot table as columns that you are folding. Just be sure that your Pivot table is large enough. Once the Pivot table has been created and populated, you can use it to fold the data by joining it to your data table. The following query, for example, folds the data in the StudentRankings table:

```
SELECT Name Name,
   (CASE WHEN i=1 THEN '2000'
      WHEN i=2 THEN '2001'
      WHEN i=3 THEN '2002' END) Year,
   (CASE WHEN i=1 THEN Y2000
      WHEN i=2 THEN Y2001
      WHEN i=3 THEN Y2002 END) Volume
FROM StudentRankings, Pivot
WHERE i BETWEEN 1 AND 3
ORDER BY Name, Year
```

This query is essentially the same as the one shown earlier in the section on self-joins. The only difference is that the t2 table, in this case, is the Pivot table and not another instance of the StudentRankings table.

Discussion

The table-folding techniques shown here can be quite useful when working with data from legacy systems. These systems often have tables or other data structures containing repeating data elements, such as the three rank columns in our example. By folding the tables containing data from such systems, you can restructure the data into a more normalized form. The normalized data is then more easily used in relational operations, such as a table-join or a group-by summarization.

Typically, table folding is done in batch procedures when data from an external system is imported into a SQL database. Folding is fairly efficient, since it can be done in one query. To implement the same process in a classical programming language, at least two nested loops would be needed. The first loop would need to step through the entire table, while the second would need to iterate through the columns in each row and generate a flattened result.

The self-join shown in this recipe is very similar to the join used with the Pivot table. With the self-join solution, the second occurrence of the table was limited to only the first three rows. It effectively functioned as the Pivot table. Why, then, do we show both solutions? The self-join is shown here partly for artistic reasons. Some programmers simply do not like to have more tables than absolutely necessary. It's also easier to write one query than it is to create a Pivot table, populate it with data, and then write a query. From a performance point of view, however, the Pivot table query is better. If you are writing a batch procedure that is going to be used often, the Pivot table solution is the one to go with.

The logic behind the two join queries is quite simple. They both use two tables. The information is taken from the first table. The second table helps in folding the first. In general, if you join a table with N rows and a table with M rows, the result has N * M rows. Each row from the first table is matched with each row from the second one. This behavior is exactly what we need to fold data. The second table is used as a guiding table that extracts M (in our case, three) columns from the first one.

The following data represents the intermediate result set produced by the join operation in the queries:

Name	Y2000	Y2001	Y2002	i
1	1	2	3	1
1	1	2	3	2
1	1	2	3	3
2	4	5	6	1
2	4	5	6	2
2	4	5	6	3
3	7	8	9	1
3	7	8	9	2
3	7	8	9	3

As you can see, each data row is repeated three times. This gives us one row for each of the three columns that we need to fold. The i column (which was t2.id in the self-join) distinguishes between the three, otherwise duplicate, rows. The i column can then be used within a CASE statement to return the rank column of a student for each year.

There are actually two CASE statements in the query, and they are almost the same. The first CASE statement uses the i value as a basis for returning a year. The second uses the i value as a basis for returning the student's rank value for that year.

7.8 Pivoting Tables

Problem

You want to produce a report in grid format. The rows in the table first have to be grouped, and then the values of interest from each group must be printed horizontally across one row of the report. A pivot report is the opposite of data folding. You could think of it as unfolding the data.

Taking the BalanceSheet2 table from the introduction to this chapter, you want create a human-readable report of balance sheets. The report should look like this:

CompanyId	Year	Assets	Liabilities	Equity
12445	2000	36759.00	22252.00	14230.00
12445	2001	37472.00	22924.00	14548.00
12445	2002	38973.00	24476.00	14497.00

You can readily see that the problem here is to unfold the normalized data and present it in a format that contains three score values in each row.

Solution

The solution is a three-step process. First, identify some key items such as the column that you want to use as a row label. Second, write a query based on the key items that you identified in Step 1. Finally, execute that query.

Step 1: Identifying key items

To generate a pivot report, you need to identify the following key items:

- The column(s) containing the value to use as a row label. In our example, this will be CompanyId and Year columns, because we want each business year to be listed on a separate row.

- The column labels. In our example, we are interested in three courses, so the course codes Assets, Liabilities, and Equity will be our column labels.

- A database column to correlate values to columns in the final report. In our case, we will use the CategoryId column.

- The values to report. In our example, we are reporting the year's results in a simplified balance sheet structure. Category results come from the Dollars column.

Once you've identified these values, you can plug them into the template shown next.

Step 2: Writing the query

To write the query to produce a pivot report, start with the following template, and plug in the key items that you identified in the previous section.

```
SELECT rowlabel_column,
    MAX(CASE WHEN columnlabel_column=value1
            THEN reportedvalue END) AS columnlabel1,
    MAX(CASE WHEN columnlabel_column=value2
            THEN reportedvalue END) AS columnlabel2,
    MAX(CASE WHEN columnlabel_column=value3
            THEN reportedvalue END) AS columnlabel3,
    . . .
FROM table
GROUP BY rowlabel_column
```

rowlabel_column
> The column containing the row label.

columnlabel_column
> The column that drives the value of the column label.

value, value2, value3 . . .
> Values corresponding to column labels. Each column in the final report corresponds to a different value.

reportedvalue
> The value to report.

columnlabel1, columnlable2, columnlabel3 . . .

The values to use as column labels. In our example, these correspond to the values in the columnlabel_column.

table

The table containing the data on which the report is based.

When the key items in our example are applied to the template, the following code is produced:

```
SELECT CompanyId, Year,
    MAX(CASE WHEN CategoryId='A'
            THEN Dollars END) AS Assets,
    MAX(CASE WHEN CategoryId='L'
            THEN Dollars END) AS Liabilities,
    MAX(CASE WHEN CategoryId='E'
            THEN Dollars END) AS Equity
FROM BalanceSheets2
GROUP BY CompanyId, Year
```

In our example, the column headings are exactly the same as the values in the database column that is used to sort values into various columns on the report. Values for the category 'A', for example, are reported under a column titled Assets.

Step 3: Run the query

The third and final step is to execute the query to generate the report. The results from executing the query shown in Step 2 are as follows:

```
CompanyId   Year        Assets          Liabilities     Equity
----------- ----------- --------------- --------------- --------------

12445       2000        36759.00        22252.00        14230.00
12445       2001        37472.00        22924.00        14548.00
12445       2002        38973.00        24476.00        14497.00
```

As you can see, these results are in the desired format: one row per business year and three categories per row.

Discussion

Pivoting a table is a powerful reporting technique that is widely used in SQL programming. It is fast and efficient, and only one pass through the table is needed to generate the final result. You do need to use a set of pivot values to differentiate the data in one column from that in another. Once the proper pivot values are known, you can use them as the basis for positioning the value that you want to report on in the appropriate column in the final report.

When SQL-92 introduced the CASE statement, the pivoting techniques shown here became much more popular than before. Prior to having the CASE statement available, programmers had to use embedded characteristic functions, which were often vendor-specific. The expressions used to position values in the correct column on the report also frequently included calls to functions such as SIGN and ABS. Those implementations were very unreadable, but they did the same thing—they implemented conditional logic in SQL queries.

The code shown in this recipe steps through each row in the table. The CASE statements for each result column filter out all rows that do not correspond to the particular pivot values of interest. The CASE statements also position category values in their correct columns. The intermediate result table is the same length as BalanceSheets2, but with more columns—one for each pivot value. In any given row, only one of the pivot value columns is NOT NULL.

To create the final report, the resulting rows are grouped as a result of using the GROUP BY clause. All the rows for each business year are combined into one. Since we know that there is only one value per business year in each pivot column, any aggregate function may be used to return that value. In this recipe, the MAX function was used.

 If it were possible for one business year to have two or more values for the same course, additional logic would need to be added to the query to decide which of those values should be reported.

The role of the aggregate function can be extended beyond that shown in this example. Say that you are reporting quarterly results rather than yearly scores and that you want to report a business year's result as the sum of all quarters for that year. Your BalanceSheets2 table in this case might look like this:

```
CREATE TABLE QuarterlyBalanceSheets (
    CompanyId INTEGER,
    CategoryId CHAR(1),
    Year INTEGER,
    Quarter INTEGER,
    Dollars DECIMAL(12,2)
)
```

The following data shows how the table stores quarterly results of the company:

CompanyId	CategoryId	Year	Quarter	Dollars
12445	A	2002	1	1579.00
12445	L	2002	1	345.00
12445	E	2002	1	1579.00
12445	A	2002	2	2666.00
12445	L	2002	2	324.00
12445	E	2002	2	2342.00
12445	A	2002	3	1909.00
12445	L	2002	3	453.00
12445	E	2002	3	1456.00
12445	A	2002	4	6245.00
12445	L	2002	4	567.00
12445	E	2002	4	5678.00

Because there are now multiple scores for each company/year combination, it is no longer valid to use a function such as MAX to return just one score. We can, however, use other aggregate functions such as AVG or SUM. For example:

```
SELECT CompanyId, Year,
    SUM(CASE WHEN CategoryId='A'
            THEN Dollars END) AS Assets,
    SUM(CASE WHEN CategoryId='L'
            THEN Dollars END) AS Liabilities,
    SUM(CASE WHEN CategoryId='E'
            THEN Dollars END) AS Equity
FROM BalanceSheets2
GROUP BY CompanyId, Year
```

In this case, the result reported for each year will be the sum of all quarter results for that year:

```
CompanyId   Year  Assets     Liabilities  Equity
----------- ----- ---------  ------------ ---------
12445       2000  36759.00   22252.00     14230.00
12445       2001  37472.00   22924.00     14548.00
12445       2002  38973.00   24476.00     14497.00
```

7.9   Joining Arrays with Tables

Problem

You want to join non-normalized data that has been imported and stored in an array-like format with data from one or more normalized tables. You want the results of the join to be normalized, so, in essence, this is a recipe for folding a table and doing a join at the same time.

Your task is to produce a report listing from the StudentThesis table, listing each student together with the three members of his dissertation committee.

Solution

To produce this report, you need to combine the techniques of folding and joining data. Since the query does not need to return professor-specific information from the Thesis table, you can use the following query:

```
SELECT t.StudentId,p.Name
FROM StudentThesis t JOIN Professors p
ON
    t.Member1=p.Id OR
    t.Member2=p.Id OR
    t.Member3=p.Id
```

This query works because for any given combination of rows from the StudentThesis and Professor tables, a maximum of only one member Id from the StudentThesis table will be relevant. Each StudentThesis row will end up being joined with three different Professor rows. The first few lines of output from this query look like this:

```
StudentId    Name
------------ -----
1            Baird, Frances
1            Anderson, Terry
1            Newton, Isaac
2            Newton, Isaac
```

Once you've come this far, it's trivial to extend this query to also return the student names from the Students master table. Since the current query result and the master student records are both normalized, you just need to add some additional code to join the Students table to the previous results. For example:

```
SELECT t.StudentId, s.StudentName, p.Name
FROM StudentThesis t JOIN Professors p
    ON(t.Member1=p.Id OR
       t.Member2=p.Id OR
       t.Member3=p.Id)
    JOIN Students s
    ON t.StudentId=s.StudentId
```

Discussion

The first query shown in this recipe transforms the non-normalized StudentThesis table into a normalized result set and, at the same time, joins the StudentThesis data to the Professor table to retrieve the professors' names. The same result could be achieved by using the earlier recipe in this chapter as a basis for a subquery to fold the data, and then by joining that subquery with the Professor table to get the names. Such a query would look like this:

```
SELECT m.StudentId, p.Name
FROM
(SELECT t.StudentId StudentId,
        (CASE WHEN f.i=1 THEN t.Member1
              WHEN f.i=2 THEN t.Member2
              WHEN f.i=3 THEN t.Member3 END) Member
FROM StudentThesis t JOIN Pivot f
     ON f.i BETWEEN 1 AND 3) m
    JOIN Professors p
       ON m.Member = p.Id
```

This query, however, requires two SELECT statements to be executed, while the solution proposed in this recipe requires only one.

We do not recommend the use of this recipe's solution for anything other than batch procedures and infrequently generated reports. If you require real-time performance, you should restructure your data so that it is normalized.

7.10 Joining Arrays with Master Tables

Problem

You want to join a non-normalized array-like data table with a normalized master record. The results should still be non-normalized, but instead of showing coded values from the detail table, you want them to show the corresponding values from the master table.

Taking both the StudentThesis table and the Professors table, you want to join them to replace the member codes with the corresponding professor names. You want to do it so that the structure of the result corresponds to the structure of the Student-Thesis table—you want the resulting rows to have one student ID, three professor names, and one grade.

Solution

The following SELECT statement reproduces the structure from the non-normalized table (StudentThesis), but replaces the professors ID numbers with their corresponding professor names. Each line of the report will list a student ID together with the names of the three dissertation committee members for that student.

```
SELECT t.StudentId,
    MAX(CASE WHEN t.Member1=p.id
            THEN p.Name
            ELSE NULL END) Member1,
    MAX(CASE WHEN t.Member2=p.id
            THEN p.Name
            ELSE NULL END) Member2,
    MAX(CASE WHEN t.Member3=p.id
            THEN p.Name
            ELSE NULL END) Member3
FROM StudentThesis t, Professors p
GROUP BY t.StudentId
```

The results from executing this query will look like these:

```
StudentId  Member1          Member2         Member3
---------- ---------------- --------- ---- ----------------
1          Baird, Frances   Anderson, Terry Newton, Isaac
2          Newton, Isaac    Anderson, Terry Smith, John
3          Newton, Isaac    Einstein, Albert Base, Samuel
4          Anderson, Terry  Smith, John     Einstein, Albert
```

Discussion

The query shown in this recipe is driven by the StudentThesis table, and it uses aggregation combined with conditional logic to link each member Id number with its corresponding master record in the Professors table. You may well wonder about the need for aggregation. To explain that, let's start by looking at the following, simpler query:

```
SELECT t.StudentId, p1.Name, p2.Name, P3.Name, t.Grade
FROM
    StudentThesis t JOIN Professors p1 ON t.Member1 = p1.Id
    JOIN Professors p2 ON t.Member2 = p2.Id
    JOIN Professors p3 ON t.Member3 = p3.Id
```

This query also returns professor names in place of their Id numbers, but it does so by joining one instance of the Professors table for each member Id column in the StudentThesis table. The large number of table joins, three in this case, will reduce the efficiency of the query. To understand how aggregation can help us, let's take a look at the Cartesian product that you get when you join the StudentThesis and Professor tables together. Here's an excerpt that shows the Cartesian product for one student record:

```
StudentId Member1 Member2 Member3 Grade Id  Name
--------- ------- ------- ------- ----- --- --------------------
1         234     322     456     A     123 Smith, John
1         234     322     456     A     456 Newton, Isaac
1         234     322     456     A     455 Einstein, Albert
1         234     322     456     A     344 Base, Samuel
1         234     322     456     A     322 Anderson, Terry
1         234     322     456     A     234 Baird, Frances
```

Because you have all possible combinations of all rows, you are ensured that for any given member Id column from the StudentThesis table, you will have at least one row with the corresponding professor's name from the Professors table. The following CASE expression, which happens to be for the member1 column, takes advantage of that fact to return the appropriate professor name when the Id in the member1 column matches the Id column of the Professors table:

```
CASE WHEN t.Member1=p.Id
    THEN p.Name
    ELSE NULL END
```

When there's a match between the two Id values, the professor name is returned by the CASE expression. Otherwise, when there's no match, a NULL is returned. The result is that the Cartesian product now looks like this:

```
studentid member1   member2   member3   grade  id   name
--------- --------- --------- --------- ------ ---- -----------------
1         NULL      NULL      NULL      A      123  Smith, John
1         NULL      NULL      Newto...  A      456  Newton, Isaac
1         NULL      NULL      NULL      A      455  Einstein, Albert
1         NULL      NULL      NULL      A      344  Base, Samuel
1         NULL      Ander...  NULL      A      322  Anderson, Terry
1         Baird...  NULL      NULL      A      234  Baird, Frances
```

This is fine, but we really want one row to be returned for each student, not six rows as shown here. We can use aggregation to collapse these six rows into one. The recipe query uses GROUP BY t.StudentId to accomplish that. The name and id columns from the professor table aren't needed, so they aren't included in the select list. The MAX function is used to extract the one relevant value from each member column. Each column has only one non-NULL value. Since aggregate functions ignore NULLs, that one value is the one returned by MAX.

While the query using aggregation is more complex than the simple query shown earlier, it's more efficient because only one table-join is needed instead of three. A further advantage is that the number of joins does not increase as the number of member columns increases.

7.11   Joining Arrays with Multiple Master Records

Problem

You want to join a non-normalized table with multiple master records. With respect to our example, you want to write a query that returns results that match the structure of the StudentThesis table, but you want the member Id codes to be replaced by professor names and you want the student Id numbers to be replaced by student names as well. The problem is very similar to that in the previous recipe, but this time you are joining two tables instead of one.

Solution

Here is the query to create a report in which student IDs and member codes are replaced by their student and member names:

```
SELECT s.studentName,
    MAX(CASE WHEN t.Member1=p.id
            THEN p.Name
            ELSE NULL END) Member1,
    MAX(CASE WHEN t.Member2=p.id
            THEN p.Name
            ELSE NULL END) Member2,
    MAX(CASE WHEN t.Member3=p.id
            THEN p.Name
            ELSE NULL END) Member3
FROM Professors p,
    StudentThesis t JOIN Students s ON t.StudentId=s.StudentID
GROUP BY s.studentName
```

The results of executing this query will look like this:

```
StudentName        Member1         Member2          Member3
------------------ --------------- ---------------- ----------------
Bohdan Khmelnytsky Newton, Isaac   Einstein, Albert Base, Samuel
Ivan Mazepa        Anderson, Terry Smith, John      Einstein, Albert
Jenny Gennick      Baird, Frances  Anderson, Terry  Newton, Isaac
Teena Corlis       Newton, Isaac   Anderson, Terry  Base, Samuel
```

Discussion

The code is a clear example that joins on non-normalized data sets do not interfere with other operations. We can add additional joins to additional master records without any significant effect on the code or on the result. (Of course, adding a join always has an impact on performance.)

It's worth noting that aggregation was not needed on the s.StudentName column because that column replaced the StudentId column in the GROUP BY clause as the basis for grouping the rows together. The grouping is enough to ensure that we only see one occurrence of each student's name.

The solution shown in this recipe, and in the previous one, can be quite useful when manipulating legacy data sets to prepare quick, ad hoc reports.

7.12 Extracting Master Records from Tables

Problem

You have a wide, non-normalized table with string columns that are repeated several times in a row. You want to restructure the table into a narrower form, replacing the strings with key values that point to rows in a master table that contain the longer string values. You not only need to restructure your table, you need to create a new master table with the necessary string values.

Let's say that the dean's office is maintaining a list of Ph.D. students; however, the list is currently in a spreadsheet format like this:

```
CREATE TABLE ThesisOld (
    StudentId INTEGER,
    Member1 CHAR(255),
    Member2 CHAR(255),
    Member3 CHAR(255),
    Grade CHAR(2)
)
```

The spreadsheet is filled with repeated names of professors:

```
StudentId  Member1          Member2           Member3
---------- ---------------- ----------------- ----------------
1          Baird, Frances   Anderson, Terry   Newton, Isaac
2          Newton, Isaac    Anderson, Terry   Smith, John
3          Newton, Isaac    Einstein, Albert  Base, Samuel
4          Anderson, Terry  Smith, John       Einstein, Albert
```

Your job is to normalize the ThesisOld data and automatically copy it into tables ThesisData and ProfessorMaster.

Solution

The process of creating and populating a new master table, and of restructuring the fact table, consists of these four steps:

1. Create a new master table.
2. Extract master record values from the current fact table, and use them to populate the new master table.
3. Create a new fact table.
4. Populate the foreign keys in the new fact table with pointers to the appropriate master records.

The following sections describe each step in detail.

Step 1: Creating the new master table

Create the new master table, which will be named ProfessorMaster, as follows:

```
CREATE TABLE ProfessorMaster(
    ProfessorId INTEGER IDENTITY,
    ProfessorName CHAR(255) UNIQUE
)
```

The two key items to note about this new master table is that it contains one column for the professor name and one integer primary key column. The value in the Id columns will eventually be used in the new fact table as a foreign key into this table. Since we want the data to be normalized, there will be one master record for each professor.

Step 2: Extracting master record values

A SELECT query can retrieve the names from the ThesisOld table. Each row in the ThesisOld table contains three professors' names so a table-folding technique must be used to get all three names into one column. The following UNION query represents one approach:

```
SELECT Member1 FROM ThesisOld
UNION
SELECT Member2 FROM ThesisOld
UNION
SELECT Member3 FROM ThesisOld
```

Since professors may have sit on more than one thesis defense each, something needs to be done to ensure that only one instance of each professor name is returned. Because the query shown here is a UNION query, duplicate elimination is taken care of for us. By definition, a UNION query eliminates duplicate rows from the result set.

For this recipe, we will use a UNION query to fold together the three professors' names from each row in the ThesisOld table. To get the results into the new ProfessorMaster table, we can use the following INSERT ... SELECT ... FROM statement:

```
INSERT INTO ProfessorMaster(ProfessorName)
SELECT Member1 FROM ThesisOld
UNION
SELECT Member2 FROM ThesisOld
UNION
SELECT Member3 FROM ThesisOld
```

After this statement is executed, the ProfessorMaster table will contain one row for each distinct professor name.

Step 3: Creating the new fact table

The ThesisOld table contains three professor name columns. The new fact table must contain three references to ProfessorMaster records. The primary key of the ProfessorMaster table is an integer, so the three pointers must be integers. The new fact table, which will be named ThesisData, can be created as follows:

```
CREATE TABLE ThesisData(
    StudentId INTEGER,
    Member1 INTEGER,
    Member2 INTEGER,
    Member3 INTEGER,
    Grade CHAR(2)
)
```

Step 4: Populating the new fact table

The final step in the process is to populate the new fact table. Data must not only be taken from the old fact table, it also must be joined with the appropriate rows from the new master table. The following statement pulls all the data together and inserts it into the new fact table:

```
INSERT INTO ThesisData(StudentId, Member1, Member2, Member3, Grade )
    SELECT StudentId,

    (SELECT m.ProfessorId
        FROM ProfessorMaster m
        WHERE t.Member1 = m.ProfessorId),
    (SELECT m.ProfessorId
        FROM ProfessorMaster m
        WHERE t.Member2 = m.ProfessorName),
    (SELECT m.ProfessorId
        FROM ProfessorMaster m
        WHERE t.Member3 = m.ProfessorName),
    Grade
FROM ThesisOld AS t
```

This query may look complicated, but it's not as bad as it seems. The first column in the select list is the StudentId value from the ThesisOld table. This goes into the new table unchanged. The second, third, and fourth columns in the select list retrieve the ProfessorId from the ProfessorMaster record for the professor named in the Thesis-Old table. This ProfessorId is stored as a foreign key in the new ThesisData table. The rest of the columns are simply copied.

Discussion

The procedure described in this recipe can be used when normalizing data imported from external sources. The human-readable spelling of names consumes a great deal of space, which makes changing those names difficult. The new structure centralizes the used strings into one master table.The integrity of the procedure described in this recipe depends on the assumption that no data in the ThesisOld table is being changed while the procedure is underway. If data in the ThesisOld table is being changed, then there is the possibility that some names may not get captured and stored in the new master table. This, in turn, will prevent the proper foreign-key references from being recorded in the new ThesisData table. The ultimate result is that data will be lost.

You can use the following query to verify that all professors names in the Member1 column of the ThesisOld table have been properly recorded in the new Professor-Master table:

```
SELECT DISTINCT StudentId, ProfessorName
FROM ThesisOld AS t
WHERE NOT EXISTS (
    SELECT * FROM ProfessorMaster AS m
    WHERE m.ProfessorName=t.Member1)
```

Similar queries can be used to check other columns. If any results are returned, the Id values in the result set will identify those records that have been inserted during the time that the steps in this recipe were being performed. You can either drop all the data and repeat the procedure from scratch or manually fix the problems that each query identifies.

Once you are certain that all the data in the new master table and ThesisData table is correct and consistent, you can create a foreign-key constraint from the ThesisData table to the master tables. While not absolutely necessary, such a constraint will protect data integrity as future changes are made to the data in those tables.

7.13   Generating Master Records Online

Problem

Your users are accustomed to entering non-normalized data into a table through a spreadsheet interface. However, you want to have the data internally represented using a master/detail structure, replacing character-string values that the users enter with IDs that reference those same values in the master tables.

For example, your users are accustomed to working with spreadsheets like Thesis-Old from the previous recipe, but you want the data stored in normalized tables like the ThesisData and ProfessorMaster table.

Solution

Allow the users to enter their data into the non-normalized table as they are currently doing. Write a trigger that takes all newly inserted data into that table and distributes it between a separate set of master/detail tables. To make the solution more robust, you can create a VIEW that takes data from the master/detail tables and returns it in the non-normalized format. You can also write a stored procedure to support updates.

The steps to implement this solution are described as follows. The code shown in this recipe is based on the same ThesisOld and ProfessorMaster tables that were used in the previous recipe.

Step 1: Setting up the tables

This recipe is based on the three tables shown in the previous recipe. Their structures are as follows:

```
CREATE TABLE ThesisData(
    StudentId INTEGER,
    Member1 INTEGER,
    Member2 INTEGER,
    Member3 INTEGER,
    Grade CHAR(2)
)

CREATE TABLE ThesisOld (
    StudentId INTEGER,
    Member1 CHAR(255),
    Member2 CHAR(255),
    Member3 CHAR(255),
    Grade CHAR(2)
)

CREATE TABLE ProfessorMaster(
    ProfessorId INTEGER IDENTITY,
    ProfessorName CHAR(255) UNIQUE
)
```

The ThesisOld table will be used as the non-normalized table into which new records are inserted. The ProfessorMaster table will represent the master table in the master/detail relationship, while the ThesisData table will represent the detail table.

Step 2: Creating the INSERT substitute

For every record inserted into the ThesisOld table, there must be a corresponding insert into the ThesisData table. The ThesisData table contains the StudentId and the Ids of the three members of the commitee. Whenever a new professor name is inserted into the ThesisOld table, that name must be used to create a corresponding master record in the ProfessorMaster table. To do all this, create a trigger that takes inserted records from the ThesisOld table and distributes their data appropriately to both the master table and the detail table. Use the following code:

```
CREATE TRIGGER ThesisOldIns
ON ThesisOld
FOR INSERT
AS BEGIN

    DECLARE @StudentId INTEGER
    DECLARE @Grade CHAR(2)
    DECLARE @Member1 INTEGER
    DECLARE @Member2 INTEGER
    DECLARE @Member3 INTEGER
    DECLARE @Name1 CHAR(255)
    DECLARE @Name2 CHAR(255)
    DECLARE @Name3 CHAR(255)

    DECLARE ThesisOld CURSOR
        FOR SELECT StudentId, Member1, Member2, Member3, Grade
                FROM inserted
    OPEN ThesisOld

    FETCH NEXT FROM ThesisOld
        INTO @StudentId, @Name1, @Name2, @Name3, @Grade

    WHILE (@@FETCH_STATUS=0) BEGIN

        SELECT @Member1=ProfessorId FROM ProfessorMaster WHERE ProfessorName=@Name1
        IF @@ROWCOUNT=0 BEGIN
            INSERT INTO ProfessorMaster(ProfessorName) VALUES(@Name1)
            SELECT @Member1=ProfessorId FROM ProfessorMaster WHERE ProfessorName=@Name1
        END

        SELECT @Member2=ProfessorId FROM ProfessorMaster WHERE ProfessorName=@Name2
        IF @@ROWCOUNT=0 BEGIN
            INSERT INTO ProfessorMaster(ProfessorName) VALUES(@Name2)
            SELECT @Member2=ProfessorId FROM ProfessorMaster WHERE ProfessorName=@Name2
        END

        SELECT @Member3=ProfessorId FROM ProfessorMaster WHERE ProfessorName=@Name3
        IF @@ROWCOUNT=0 BEGIN
            INSERT INTO ProfessorMaster(ProfessorName) VALUES(@Name3)
            SELECT @Member3=ProfessorId FROM ProfessorMaster WHERE ProfessorName=@Name3
        END

        INSERT INTO ThesisData(StudentId,Member1,Member2,Member3,Grade)
            VALUES(@StudentId,@Member1,@Member2,@Member3, @Grade)
```

```
    FETCH NEXT FROM ThesisOld
        INTO @StudentId, @Name1, @Name2, @Name3, @Grade

    END

    CLOSE ThesisOld
    DEALLOCATE ThesisOld
END
```

Step 3: Supporting the SELECT statement

To support SELECT statements, create a view on the data and master tables that returns a combined view of the data that matches the data provided by the ThesisOld table. The view for our example would be:

```
CREATE VIEW ThesisDataView AS
    SELECT d.StudentId, m1.ProfessorName Member1,
        m2.ProfessorName Member2, m3.ProfessorName Member3, d.Grade
    FROM ThesisData d JOIN ProfessorMaster m1 ON d.Member1=m1.ProfessorId
        JOIN ProfessorMaster m2 ON d.Member2=m2.ProfessorId
        JOIN ProfessorMaster m3 ON d.Member3=m3.ProfessorId
```

Step 4: Supporting the UPDATE statement

For UPDATE, the values can be updated in master tables directly (if the UPDATE is related to values that are stored in master tables). You might want to embed this into a trigger, so the mechanism is hidden from the user. For example, the following trigger would handle online updates to the ThesisOld table, which has three member columns. Changes to member names are propagated to the ThesisData table in the form of new Member Id numbers.

```
CREATE TRIGGER ThesisOldUpd
ON ThesisOld
FOR Update
AS BEGIN

    DECLARE @StudentId integer
    DECLARE @ProfessorIdI integer
    DECLARE @Name1D CHAR(255)
    DECLARE @Name2D CHAR(255)
    DECLARE @Name3D CHAR(255)
    DECLARE @Name1I CHAR(255)
    DECLARE @Name2I CHAR(255)
    DECLARE @Name3I CHAR(255)

    DECLARE ThesisOld CURSOR
        FOR SELECT i.StudentId, i.Member1, i.Member2, i.Member3, d.Member1,
                d.Member2, d.Member3
                FROM inserted i, deleted d
                WHERE i.StudentId=d.StudentId
    OPEN ThesisOld

    FETCH NEXT FROM ThesisOld
        INTO @StudentId, @Name1I, @Name2I, @Name3I, @Name1D, @Name2D, @Name3D
```

```
WHILE (@@FETCH_STATUS=0) BEGIN

    IF @Name1D<>@Name1I BEGIN
        SELECT @ProfessorIdI=ProfessorId FROM ProfessorMaster
            WHERE ProfessorName=@Name1I
        IF @@ROWCOUNT=0 BEGIN
            INSERT INTO ProfessorMaster(ProfessorName) VALUES(@Name1I)
            SELECT @ProfessorIdI=ProfessorId FROM ProfessorMaster
                WHERE ProfessorName=@Name1I
        END
        UPDATE ThesisData SET Member1=@ProfessorIdI WHERE StudentId=@StudentId
    END

    IF @Name2D<>@Name2I BEGIN
        SELECT @ProfessorIdI=ProfessorId FROM ProfessorMaster
            WHERE ProfessorName=@Name2I
        IF @@ROWCOUNT=0 BEGIN
            INSERT INTO ProfessorMaster(ProfessorName) VALUES(@Name2I)
            SELECT @ProfessorIdI=ProfessorId FROM ProfessorMaster
                WHERE ProfessorName=@Name2I
        END
        UPDATE ThesisData SET Member2=@ProfessorIdI WHERE StudentId=@StudentId
    END

    IF @Name3D<>@Name3I BEGIN
        SELECT @ProfessorIdI=ProfessorId FROM ProfessorMaster
            WHERE ProfessorName=@Name3I
        IF @@ROWCOUNT=0 BEGIN
            INSERT INTO ProfessorMaster(ProfessorName) VALUES(@Name3I)
            SELECT @ProfessorIdI=ProfessorId FROM ProfessorMaster
                WHERE ProfessorName=@Name3I
        END
        UPDATE ThesisData SET Member3=@ProfessorIdI WHERE StudentId=@StudentId
    END


    FETCH NEXT FROM ThesisOld
        INTO @StudentId, @Name1I, @Name2I, @Name3I, @Name1D, @Name2D, @Name3D
    END

    CLOSE ThesisOld
    DEALLOCATE ThesisOld
END
```

Step 5: Supporting the DELETE statement

For the DELETE statement, it is enough to delete just the data-table record. In that
case, you leave the master record entries for possible further use:

```
CREATE TRIGGER ThesisOldDel
ON ThesisOld
FOR Delete
AS BEGIN
    DELETE FROM ThesisData WHERE StudentId IN (SELECT StudentId FROM deleted)
END
```

Of course, if you are sure that you will not need them anymore, you can also delete them from the master records.

Discussion

The concept described earlier can be applied for online use to implement online distribution of base records to both master and data tables. Most systems are designed with the master/detail table concept in mind. However, most also require users to maintain consistency of the tables manually. If a user wants to add a new row into the system, with no master records for a value in the row, he has to add a master record to the master tables first. Only then the data record can be inserted into the system. That is a two step process.

We can combine these two steps into one, but at the expense of complexity. To do this, use the procedure described earlier to provide functionality of the INSERT, SELECT, UPDATE, and DELETE statements. With that, you provide support for data/master record distribution without the hassle of having the user maintaining master records manually.

The INSERT trigger

The INSERT trigger uses a cursor to go through all inserted rows. For each row a series of statements is executed to ensure that each member name is associated with a member ID. If a member name is new, then a new record is created in the ProfessorMaster table. That crucial part of the code is repeated for every column and looks like this:

```
SELECT @Member1=ProfessorId FROM ProfessorMaster
WHERE ProfessorName=@Name1
IF @@ROWCOUNT=0 BEGIN
   INSERT INTO ProfessorMaster(ProfessorName) VALUES(@Name1)
   SELECT @Member1=ProfessorId FROM ProfessorMaster
      WHERE ProfessorName=@Name1
END
```

The first SELECT checks to see if the member's name is already in the master table. If it is not, the @@ROWCOUNT variable will return 0 and the INSERT statement will be invoked. That INSERT statement creates a new record in the ProfessorMaster table for the new member name. Another SELECT statement is then executed to retrieve the member Id number for the new record, and that Id number is stored in the @Member1 variable.

After all professor name columns are processed, the trigger inserts a row into the ThesisData table using the professor ID values. The following INSERT is used:

```
INSERT INTO ThesisData(StudentId,Member1,Member2,Member3,Grade)
   VALUES(@StudentId,@Member1,@Member2,@Member3, @Grade)
```

In this way, ThesisOld records containing three member names are converted into ThesisData records containing three member Id numbers.

The UPDATE trigger

The UPDATE trigger is similar to the INSERT trigger, but with a few extensions to handle the complexities of changing data. The important differences are in the code that handles each member column. That code looks like this:

```
IF @Name1D<>@Name1I BEGIN
    SELECT @ProfessorIdI=ProfessorId FROM ProfessorMaster
        WHERE ProfessorName=@Name1I
        IF @@ROWCOUNT=0 BEGIN
            INSERT INTO ProfessorMaster(ProfessorName) VALUES(@Name1I)
            SELECT @ProfessorIdI=ProfessorId FROM ProfessorMaster
                WHERE ProfessorName=@Name1I
        END
        UPDATE ThesisData SET Member1=@ProfessorIdI WHERE StudentId=@StudentId
    END
```

Here, the code first checks to see if the old and the new values of the column differ. If they are equal, the change in the row has taken place on a different column, and the rest of the processing for this column can be skipped. If the values are different, an UPDATE has been performed on the original table that changes this column, so we have to update our master and detail tables accordingly.

The first SELECT, together with the subsequent IF statement, retrieves a member Id value corresponding to the new value for the member name and places it into the @ProfessorIdI variable. If necessary, a new row is created in the ProfessorMember table. Finally, the UPDATE statement modifies the member Id reference in the ThesisData table so that it corresponds with the new name recorded in the Thesis-Old table.

7.14   Working with Duplicates

Problem

You've just imported a new set of rows into your buffer tables. However, you forgot to delete the previous import. Now you have a table with some duplicate rows. You need a set of tools to eliminate these duplicates and to prevent them from occurring in the future.

Let's say that you uploaded some data from your sales agent to the Bookstore table; however, due to a mistake in the code, the upload doubled some rows:

BookId	Name	Quantity	Price	Type
1	Software Engineering	5	15.00	Manual
2	Modern Operating Systems	7	20.00	Reference
3	Learn SQL	15	18.00	Textbook
4	Learn Advanced SQL	1	8.00	Textbook
5	JavaScript Tutorial	5	10.00	Textbook
6	Modern Operating Systems	7	20.00	Reference
7	Learn SQL	15	18.00	Textbook

Solution

We'll demonstrate a technique for dealing with duplicates on the Bookstore table. Please note that the BookId column is always unique and that it is used for identifying otherwise duplicated rows. This will be useful when only one representative of a duplicated set needs to be singled out.

The queries in this recipe show different ways to count duplicate rows, report on duplicate rows, extract nonduplicated rows, and eliminate duplicate rows.

Reduction

The term *reduction* refers to the elimination of duplicate rows. The following query returns all nonduplicate rows from the Bookstore table:

```
SELECT DISTINCT * FROM Bookstore
```

Because the DISTINCT keyword was used, any two rows containing the same set of values will be combined into one row in the query's result set. Because this query includes the primary-key column BookId, it's of no practical use in our particular case; some books still appear twice.

Selective reduction

Selective reduction is reduction that is performed only on a subset of the columns in a table. The following query retrieves each unique combination of name, price, and color from the Stock table:

```
SELECT DISTINCT Name, Type, Price FROM Bookstore
```

The table stores five different books:

```
Name                                     Type                  Price
---------------------------------------- --------------------- ---------
JavaScript Tutorial                      Textbook              10.00
Learn Advanced SQL                       Textbook              8.00
Learn SQL                                Textbook              18.00
Modern Operating Systems                 Reference             20.00
Software Engineering                     Manual                15.00
```

This time, because we did not include the always unique primary key, each book is listed only once.

Selecting duplicates

The following query shows how you can find duplicate name, price, and color combinations:

```
SELECT Name, Type, Price
FROM Bookstore
GROUP BY Name, Type, Price
HAVING count(*) > 1
```

The HAVING clause in this query ensures that if a given name, price, and color combination is only represented once, it will not be listed in the results from this query. Any such combinations that occur more than once will be listed:

Name	Type	Price
Learn SQL	Textbook	18.00
Modern Operating Systems	Reference	20.00

Counting occurrences

The following query produces a report showing the number of occurrences of each combination of values in a given set of columns. The results are sorted in order of highest occurrence.

```
SELECT Name, Type, Price, count(*) Count
FROM Bookstore
GROUP BY Name, Type, Price
ORDER BY count(*) DESC
```

The query lists all combinations of name, price, and type. It also lists the number of times each combination occurs. Combinations with the greatest number of occurrences will be listed first:

Name	Type	Price	Count
Learn SQL	Textbook	18.00	2
Modern Operating Systems	Reference	20.00	2
JavaScript Tutorial	Textbook	10.00	1
Learn Advanced SQL	Textbook	8.00	1
Software Engineering	Manual	15.00	1

To see the same information, but only for cases where the occurrence count is greater than 1, use the following variation on the query:

```
SELECT Name, Type, Price, count(*) Count
FROM Bookstore
GROUP BY Name, Type, Price
HAVING count(*) > 1
ORDER BY count(*) DESC
```

This second version of the query uses a HAVING clause to restrict the results to only those combinations of name, price, and type that occur multiple times:

Name	Type	Price	Count
Learn SQL	Textbook	18.00	2
Modern Operating Systems	Reference	20.00	2

Selecting by number of occurrences

The following query selects duplicates over a subset of columns where the occurrence count is at least 3:

```
SELECT Name, Type, Price, count(*) Count
FROM Bookstore
GROUP BY Name, Type, Price
HAVING count(*) >= 3
```

You can replace the constant 3 in this query with any other occurrence count threshold of interest.

Selecting nonduplicates

The following query selects nonduplicated rows over a subset of columns, ignoring the ones that are duplicated:

```
SELECT Name, Type, Price
FROM Bookstore
GROUP BY Name, Type, Price
HAVING count(*)= 1
```

In this example, rows representing id, name, and qty combinations that occur more than once will not be returned in the result set:

```
Name                     Type                   Price
------------------------ ---------------------- ------------
JavaScript Tutorial      Textbook               10.00
Learn Advanced SQL       Textbook               8.00
Software Engineering     Manual                 15.00
```

Selecting duplicates with an odd occurrence count

If you're interested in duplicates where the occurrence count is an odd number other than 1, use a query such as this:

```
SELECT Name, Type, Price, count(*) Count
FROM Bookstore
GROUP BY Name, Type, Price
HAVING count(*) % 2 = 1 AND count(*)>1
```

Since 1 is considered an odd number, but does not imply duplication, the WHERE clause specifically excludes rows with an occurrence count of 1.

Selecting duplicates with an even occurrence count

A similar query can be used to retrieve duplicates where the occurrence count is an even number:

```
SELECT Name, Type, Price, count(*) Count
FROM Bookstore
GROUP BY Name, Type, Price
HAVING count(*) % 2 = 0
```

Note that there is no need to specifically exclude rows with an occurrence count of 1, because 1 is not an even number.

Deleting duplicate rows

You may find yourself faced with a situation where you want to arbitrarily delete duplicate data from a table. Data like this is often the result of running an import procedure twice. As long as you have at least one unique value, such as a primary key value, to identify each row, you can arbitrarily delete duplicates using a single DELETE statement. The statement in the following example deletes duplicate rows, arbitrarily retaining one record for each fruit and color combination:

```
DELETE
FROM Warehouse
WHERE BookId NOT IN (
    SELECT MAX(BookId)
    FROM Bookstore
    GROUP BY Name, Type
    HAVING COUNT(*) > 1)
```

The subquery in this example identifies the highest ID number value for each name and color combination. This identifies the row that we are arbitrarily going to keep. All other rows with that name and color combination are deleted. The key here is that the ID is unique for all rows in a name and type combination.

Preventing duplicates

To ensure that no duplicates can be inserted into a table, create a unique index using the UNIQUE INDEX clause, or create a UNIQUE constraint while creating a table. For example, the following statement creates an index named BookstoreInd that does not allow any two rows in the Bookstore table to have the same combination of values for the Name, Type, and Price columns:

```
CREATE UNIQUE INDEX BookstoreInd on Bookstore
    (Name, Type, Price)
```

Discussion

SQL has built-in support for enforcing an occurrence count of 1 on a table. This support can be in the form of a UNIQUE constraint or a unique index on the table. To enforce an occurrence count other than 1, you'll need to use triggers.

When using the SELECT DISTINCT clause in a SELECT statement, you should be very careful about performance. At first glance, SELECT DISTINCT may seem like a good tool to use; in reality, such a statement can be very expensive to execute. Using the DISTINCT keyword in a SELECT statement causes a sorting operation to occur when such query is run. The only way that SQL Server can identify distinct values is to first sort all the results enough to group duplicates together. Then only one value, the *distinct* value, is returned from each set of duplicates. Because of the performance impact of the sort, you should avoid the use of DISTINCT unless it is absolutely necessary. The following query shows a typical example of the DISTINCT keyword being used unnecessarily. The query uses a subquery within an EXISTS predicate to check for rows in table B that correspond to those in table A:

```
SELECT * FROM A
WHERE EXISTS(
    SELECT DISTINCT *
    FROM B
    WHERE B.id=A.id)
```

This code returns the correct results, but the use of DISTINCT in the subquery hurts performance. This is because DISTINCT forces a sort to occur for each execution of the subquery. Since the subquery is a correlated subquery—executed for each row—the result is a lot of sort activity.

The purpose of the EXISTS predicate is to test for the existence of at least one row by executing a subquery. Since only one row is needed to cause a TRUE result to be returned, there's no point in using DISTINCT. It doesn't matter if more than one row satisfies the subquery: one is enough. By omitting DISTINCT, you allow the optimizer to stop when that one row is found.

CHAPTER 8

Statistics in SQL

The recipes in this chapter show you how to effectively use SQL for common statistical operations. While SQL was never designed to be a statistics package, the language is quite versatile and holds a lot of hidden potential when it comes to calculating the following types of statistics:

- Means, modes, and medians
- Standard deviations
- Variances
- Standard errors
- Confidence intervals
- Correlations
- Moving averages
- Weighted moving averages

In spite of the fact that you can use SQL to generate statistics, it is not our intention to promote SQL as the best language for that purpose. As in any other situation, a strong dose of common sense is necessary. If you need a fast, easy-to-use tool for quick analysis of an existing data set, then the concepts presented in this chapter may prove quite helpful. However, if you need to perform a broad and thorough statistical analysis, you may be better off loading an extract of your database data into a specialized statistics package such as SPSS or GNU R.

 Statistical calculations often yield values with many digits to the right of the decimal point. In this chapter, we've *rounded* all such values to two decimal digits. Thus, we will show a result of 672.98888888893032 as 672.99.

8.1   Statistical Concepts

Statistics is an interesting branch of mathematics that is becoming more important in the business world. To fully understand the recipes in this chapter, you'll need to have some grasp of statistics. You also need to understand the language of statistics. In this section, we'll provide a brief introduction to some of the statistical terms that you'll see throughout this chapter. Then we'll explain—in non-SQL terms—the math behind the statistics generated by this chapter's recipes.

Learn More About Statistics

If you would like to learn more about statistics than we can cover in this chapter, or you would like to see formal mathematical definitions for the types of statistics that we generate, you should consult a good book on the subject. There are many good titles out there, but we have found the following to be particularly useful:

Hanke, John and Arthur Reitsch. *Business Forecasting,* 6th Edition. Prentice Hall, 1998.

Huff, Darrell and Irving Geis. *How to Lie with Statistics*. W. W. Norton and Company, Inc., 1954.

There are two types of data that can be manipulated with statistical tools: cross-sectional data and time-series data. *Cross-sectional data* is a snapshot that is collected at a single point in time. It has no time dimension. A typical example of cross-sectional data would be a set of height measurements of children of different ages. Computing the average of all the measurements for a given age gives you the average height of a child of that age. The specific date and time on which any given measurement was taken is irrelevant. All that matters is the height of each child and the child's age when that height was measured.

The second type of data that you'll encounter is time-series data. With *time-series data*, every measurement has a time dimension associated with it. For example, you can look at stock-market prices over some period of time, and you'll find that the share price for any given company differs from day to day. And, not only from day to day, but also typically from hour to hour and minute to minute. A share price by itself means nothing. It's the share price coupled with the time at which that price was effective that is meaningful. A list of such prices and times over a given period is referred to as a time series.

We need to define five more terms before proceeding into the sections that describe the calculations behind the various statistics discussed in this chapter. These terms are population, sample, sample size, case, and value.

Consider the problem of having a large box of oranges for which you need to determine the sweetness level so that you can sell the box at the best possible price. That box of oranges represents your *population*. Now you could taste each orange in the box to check the sweetness level, but then you wouldn't have any oranges left to sell. Instead, you might choose to test only a few oranges—say, three. Those oranges that you test represent a *sample*, and the number of oranges in the sample represents the *sample size*. From a statistical point of view, you are testing a representative sample and then extrapolating the results to the oranges remaining in the box.

Continuing with our example, each orange in a sample represents a specific *case*. For each case—or orange—you must test the sweetness level. The result of each test will be a *value*—usually a number—indicating how sweet the orange really is. Throughout this chapter, we use the term *case* to refer to a specific measurement in the sample. We use the term *value* to refer to a distinct numeric result. A value may occur more than once in a sample. For example, three oranges (three cases) may all have the same sweetness value.

Now that you have a good grasp of the statistical terms used in this chapter, you can proceed to the following sections describing various statistical measurements and calculations. The calculations described in these upcoming sections form the basis for the recipes shown later in the chapter.

Mean

A *mean* is a type of average, often referred to as an *arithmetic average*. Given a sample set of values, you calculate the mean by summing all the values and dividing the result by the sample size. Consider the following set of height values for seven kids in a hypothetical fifth-grade class:

    100 cm
    100 cm
    100 cm
    110 cm
    115 cm
    120 cm
    180 cm

Given these values, you compute the mean height by summing the values and dividing by the sample size of seven. For example:

```
100+100+100+110+115+120+180 = 825 cm
825 cm / 7 = 117.86 cm
```

In this case, the mean height is 117.86 cm. As you can see, the mean height may not correspond to any student's actual height.

Mode

A *mode* is another type of statistic that refers to the most frequently occurring value in a sample set. Look again at the numbers in the previous section on means. You'll see that the number of occurrences is as follows:

100 cm three
110 cm one
115 cm one
120 cm one
180 cm one

It's obvious that the most frequently occurring value is 100 cm. That value represents the mode for this sample set.

Median

A *median* is yet another type of statistic that you could loosely say refers to the middle value in a sample set. To be more precise, the median is the value in a sample set that has the same number of cases below it as above it. Consider again the following height data, which is repeated from the earlier section on means:

100 cm
100 cm
100 cm
110 cm
115 cm
120 cm
180 cm

There are seven cases total. Look at the 110 cm value. There are three cases with values above 110 cm and three cases with values below 110 cm. The median height, therefore, is 110 cm.

Computing a median with an odd number of cases is relatively straightforward. Having an even number of cases, though, makes the task of computing a median more complex. With an even number of cases, you simply can't pick just one value that has an equal number of cases above and below it. The following sample amply illustrates this point:

100 cm
100 cm
100 cm
110 cm
115 cm
120 cm
125 cm
180 cm

There is no "middle" value in this sample. 110 cm won't work because there are four cases having higher values and only three having lower values. 115 cm won't work for the opposite reason—there are three cases having values above and four cases having values below. In a situation like this, there are two approaches you can take. One solution is to take the lower of the two middle values as the median value. In this case, it would be 110 cm, and it would be referred to as a *statistical median*. Another solution is to take the mean of the two middle values. In this case, it would be 112.5 cm [(115 cm+110 cm)/2]. A median value computed by taking the mean of the two middle cases is often referred to as a *financial median*.

It is actually possible to find an example where there is a median with an even number of cases. Such an example is: 1,2,3,3,4,5. There is an even number of cases in the sample; however, 3 has an equal number of cases above and below it, so that is the median. This example is exceptional, though, because the two middle cases have the same value. You can't depend on that occurring all the time.

Standard Deviation and Variance

Standard deviations and variance are very closely related. A *standard deviation* will tell you how evenly the values in a sample are distributed around the mean. The smaller the standard deviation, the more closely the values are condensed around the mean. The greater the standard deviation, the more values you will find at a distance from the mean. Consider again, the following values:

100 cm
100 cm
100 cm
110 cm
115 cm
120 cm
180 cm

The standard deviation for the sample is calculated as follows:

$$\sqrt{\frac{\sum (X - \bar{x})^2}{n - 1}}$$

Where:

X Is the value for a specific case in the sample.

$\bar{x}$ Is the mean value for all the cases in the sample.

n Is the number of cases in the sample.

Take the formula shown here for standard deviation, expand the summation for each of the cases in our sample, and you have the following calculation:

$$\sqrt{\frac{\begin{matrix}(100-117.86)^2 + (100-117.86)^2 + (100-117.86)^2 + (100-117.86)^2 \\ + (115-117.86)^2 + (120-117.86)^2 + (180-117.86)^2\end{matrix}}{7-1}}$$

Work through the math, and you'll find that the calculation returns 28.56 as the sample's standard deviation.

A *variance* is nothing more than the square of the standard deviation. In our example, the standard deviation is 28.56, so the variance is calculated as follows:

```
28.56 * 28.56 = 815.6736
```

If you look more closely at the formula for calculating standard deviation, you'll see that the variance is really an intermediate result in that calculation.

What Are These Strange Symbols?

In this chapter, we use some mathematical symbols that you may not have seen used since you were in college. In this sidebar, we present a short review of these symbols to help you better understand our recipes.

The Σ symbol is the summation operator. It's used as a shorthand way of telling you to add up all the values in a sample set. When you see ΣX in a formula, you know that you should sum all the values in the sample set labeled X. Some formulas are more complex than that. For example, you might see ΣXY in a formula. The X and Y refer to two sample sets, and this notation is telling you to multiply corresponding elements of each set together and sum the results. So, multiply the first case in X by the first case in Y. Then, add to that the result of multiplying the second case in X by the second case in Y. Continue this pattern for all cases in the samples.

Whenever you see two elements run together, you should multiply. Thus, XY means to multiply the values X and Y together. $n\Sigma XY$ means to multiple the value n by the value of ΣXY.

The $\sqrt{}$ symbol is the square-root operator. When you see $\sqrt{n}$, you need to find the value that, when multiplied by itself, yields n. For example, $\sqrt{9}$ is 3, because 3 * 3 = 9. Most calculators allow you to easily compute square roots. Another way to express 3 * 3, by the way, is to write it as 3^2. The small, raised 2 indicates that you should multiply the value by itself.

Finally, in our notation, we use a horizontal bar over a value to indicate the mean of a sample. For example: $\bar{x}$ indicates that you should compute the mean of the values for all cases in the sample labeled X.

Standard Error

A *standard error* is a measurement of a statistical projection's accuracy based on the sample size used to obtain that projection. Suppose that you were trying to calculate the average height of students in the fifth grade. You could randomly select seven children and calculate their average height. You could then use that average height as an approximation of the average height for the entire population of fifth graders. If you select a different set of seven children, your results will probably be slightly different. If you increase your sample size, the variation between samples should decrease, and your approximations should become more accurate. In general, the greater your sample size, the more accurate your approximation will be.

You can use the sample size and the standard deviation to estimate the error of approximation in a statistical projection by computing the *standard error of the mean*. The formula to use is:

$$\frac{s}{\sqrt{n}}$$

where:

s Is the standard deviation in the sample.

n Is the number of cases in the sample.

We can use the data shown in the previous section on standard deviation in an example here showing how to compute the standard error. Recall that the sample size was seven elements and that the standard deviation was 28.56. The standard error, then, is calculated as follows:

$$\frac{28.56}{\sqrt{7}} = \frac{28.56}{2.65} = 10.78$$

Double the sample size to 14 elements, and you have the following:

$$\frac{28.56}{\sqrt{14}} = \frac{28.56}{3.74} = 7.64$$

A standard-error value by itself doesn't mean much. It only has meaning relative to other standard-error values computed for different sample sizes for the same population. In the examples shown here, the standard error is 10.78 for a sample size of 7 and 7.64 for a sample size of 14. A sample size of 14, then, yields a more accurate approximation than a sample size of 7.

Confidence Intervals

A *confidence interval* is an interval within which the mean of a population probably lies. As you've seen previously, every sample from the same population is likely to produce a slightly different mean. However, most of those means will lie in the vicinity of the population's mean. If you've computed a mean for a sample, you can compute a confidence interval based on the probability that your mean is also applicable to the population as a whole.

Creating the t-distribution table

Confidence intervals are a tool to estimate the range in which it is probable to find the mean of a population, relative to the mean of a current sample. Usually, in business, a 95% probability is all that is required. That's what we'll use for all the examples in this chapter.

To compute confidence intervals in this chapter, we make use of a table called T_distribution. This is just a table that tells us how much we can "expand" the standard deviation around the mean to calculate the desired confidence interval. The amount by which the standard deviation can be expanded depends on the number of degrees of freedom in your sample. Our table, which you can create by executing the following SQL statements, contains the necessary t-distribution values for computing confidence intervals with a 95% probability:

```
CREATE TABLE T_distribution(
    p DECIMAL(5,3),
    df INT
)

INSERT INTO T_distribution VALUES(12.706,1)
INSERT INTO T_distribution VALUES(4.303,2)
INSERT INTO T_distribution VALUES(3.182,3)
INSERT INTO T_distribution VALUES(2.776,4)
INSERT INTO T_distribution VALUES(2.571,5)
INSERT INTO T_distribution VALUES(2.447,6)
INSERT INTO T_distribution VALUES(2.365,7)
INSERT INTO T_distribution VALUES(2.306,8)
INSERT INTO T_distribution VALUES(2.262,9)
INSERT INTO T_distribution VALUES(2.228,10)
INSERT INTO T_distribution VALUES(2.201,11)
INSERT INTO T_distribution VALUES(2.179,12)
INSERT INTO T_distribution VALUES(2.160,13)
INSERT INTO T_distribution VALUES(2.145,14)
INSERT INTO T_distribution VALUES(2.131,15)
INSERT INTO T_distribution VALUES(2.120,16)
INSERT INTO T_distribution VALUES(2.110,17)
INSERT INTO T_distribution VALUES(2.101,18)
INSERT INTO T_distribution VALUES(2.093,19)
INSERT INTO T_distribution VALUES(2.086,20)
INSERT INTO T_distribution VALUES(2.080,21)
```

```
INSERT INTO T_distribution VALUES(2.074,22)
INSERT INTO T_distribution VALUES(2.069,23)
INSERT INTO T_distribution VALUES(2.064,24)
INSERT INTO T_distribution VALUES(2.060,25)
INSERT INTO T_distribution VALUES(2.056,26)
INSERT INTO T_distribution VALUES(2.052,27)
INSERT INTO T_distribution VALUES(2.048,28)
INSERT INTO T_distribution VALUES(2.045,29)
INSERT INTO T_distribution VALUES(2.042,30)
INSERT INTO T_distribution VALUES(1.960,-1)
```

The df column in the table represents a degrees of freedom value. The term *degrees of freedom* refers to a set of data items that can not be derived from each other. You need a value for degrees of freedom to select the appropriate p value from the table. The p column contains a coefficient that corrects the standard error around the mean according to the size of a sample. For calculating confidence intervals, use the number of cases decreased by 1 as your degrees of freedom.

Calculating the confidence interval

To calculate the confidence interval for a sample, you first need to decide on a required probability. This will be the probability that the mean of the entire population falls within the confidence interval that you compute based on the mean of your sample. You also need to know the mean of your sample and the standard deviation from that sample. Once you have that information, calculate your confidence interval using the following formula:

$$\overline{X} \pm \frac{s}{\sqrt{n}} * P_{n-1}$$

where:

$\overline{X}$ Is the sample mean.

s Is the standard deviation in the sample.

n Is the number of values in the sample.

P Returns the t-distribution value from the T_distribution table for the required probability and the available degrees of freedom.

For example, consider the following data, which you also saw earlier in this chapter:

100 cm
100 cm
100 cm
110 cm
115 cm
120 cm
180 cm

The mean of this data is 117.86, and the standard deviation is 28.56. There are 7 values in the sample, which gives 6 degrees of freedom. The following query, then, yields the corresponding t-distribution value:

```
SELECT p
FROM T_distribution
WHERE df=6


p
-------
2.447
```

The value for *P*, which is our t-distribution value, is 2.447. The confidence interval, then, is derived as follows:

$$117.86 \pm \frac{28.56}{\sqrt{7}} * 2.447$$

$$117.86 - \frac{28.56}{\sqrt{7}} * 2.447 \text{ through } 117.86 + \frac{28.56}{\sqrt{7}} * 2.447$$

$$117.86 - \frac{28.56}{2.65} * 2.447 \text{ through } 117.86 + \frac{28.56}{2.65} * 2.447$$

$$117.86 - 10.78 * 2.447 \text{ through } 117.86 + 10.78 * 2.447$$

$$91.4813 \text{ through } 144.2387$$

Correlation

A *correlation coefficient* is a measure of the linear relationship between two samples. It is expressed as a number between −1 to 1, and it tells you the degree to which the two samples are related. A correlation coefficient of zero means that the two samples are not related at all. A correlation coefficient of 1 means that the two samples are fully correlated—every change in the first sample is reflected in the second sample as well. If the correlation coefficient is −1, it means that for every change in the first sample, you can observe the exact opposite change in the second sample. Values in between these extremes indicate varying degrees of correlation. A coefficient of 0.5, for example, indicates a weaker relationship between samples than does a coefficient of 1.0.

The correlation coefficient for two samples can be calculated using the following formula:

$$\frac{n\sum XY - \sum X \sum Y}{\sqrt{n\sum X^2 - (\sum X)^2} \sqrt{n\sum Y^2 - (\sum Y)^2}}$$

where:

X Are the values of the first sample.

Y Are the values of the second sample.

n Is the number of values in each sample.

Consider the two samples shown in Table 8-1. The first sample represents daily closing stock prices for a particular stock. The second sample represents the value of the corresponding stock-market index over the same set of days. An investor looking at this data might wonder how closely the index tracks the stock price. If the index goes up on any given day, is the stock price likely to go up as well? The correlation coefficient can be used to answer that question.

Table 8-1. Stock prices and index values

Day	Stock price	Index value
1	10	31
2	18	34
3	12	35
4	20	45
5	10	37
6	9	39
7	19	41
8	13	45
9	18	47
10	15	55

To compute the correlation coefficient of the stock price with respect to the index value, you can take the values shown in Table 8-1 and plug them into the formula shown earlier in this section. It doesn't matter which is X and which is Y. For this example, let X represent the stock price, and Y will represent the index value. The resulting calculation is as follows:

$$\frac{n\sum XY - \sum X \sum Y}{\sqrt{n\sum X^2 - (\sum X)^2}\sqrt{n\sum Y^2 - (\sum Y)^2}}$$

$$\frac{n(x_1 y_1 + \ldots + x_{10} y_{10}) - (x_1 + \ldots + x_{10})(y_1 + \ldots + y_{10})}{\sqrt{n(x_1^2 + \ldots + x_{10}^2) - (x_1 + \ldots + x_{10})^2}\sqrt{n(y_1^2 + \ldots + y_{10}^2) - (y_1 + \ldots + y_{10})^2}}$$

$$\frac{10 * (10 * 31 + \ldots + 15 * 55) - (10 + \ldots + 15) * (31 + \ldots + 55)}{\sqrt{10 * (10^2 + \ldots + 15^2) - (10 + \ldots + 15)^2} * \sqrt{10 * (31^2 + \ldots + 55^2) - (31 + \ldots + 55)^2}}$$

If you put the numbers into the formula, where stock prices represent the *X* series, index numbers represent the *Y* series, and number of samples is 10, you get the correlation coefficient of 0.40. The result tells us that the stock price is weakly correlated with the market index.

The formula shown here looks scary at first, and it does take a lot of tedious work to compute a correlation by hand; however, you'll see that its implementation in SQL is quite straightforward.

Autocorrelation

Autocorrelation is an interesting concept and is very useful in attempting to observe patterns in time-series data. The idea is to calculate a number of correlations between an observed time series and the same time series lagged by one or more steps. Each lag results in a different correlation. The end result is a list of correlations (usually around fifteen), which can be analyzed to see whether the time series has a pattern in it.

Table 8-2 contains the index values that you saw earlier in Table 8-1. It also shows the autocorrelation values that result from a lag of 1, 2, and 3 days. When calculating the first correlation coefficient, the original set of index values is correlated to the same set of values lagged by one day. For the second coefficient, the original set of index values is correlated to the index values lagged by 2 days. The third coefficient is the result of correlating the original set of index values with a 3-day lag.

Table 8-2. Autocorrelation

	Index values	Lag 1	Lag 2	Lag 3
1	31			
2	34	31		
3	35	34	31	
4	45	35	34	31
5	37	45	35	34
6	39	37	45	35
7	41	39	37	45
8	45	41	39	37
9	47	45	41	39
9	55	47	45	41
10		55	47	45
11			55	47
12				55
Correlation	n/a	0.6794	0.6030	0.3006

Please note that it's only possible to calculate a correlation coefficient between two equally sized samples. Therefore, you can use only rows 2 through 9 of Lag 1 when calculating the first correlation coefficient, rows 3 through 10 of Lag 2 for the second, and rows 4 through 11 of the Lag 3 for the third. In real life, you would likely have enough historical data to always use rows 1 through 9.

You can see that the correlation coefficients of the first few lags are declining rather sharply. This is an indication that the time series has a trend (i.e., the values are consistently rising or falling). As you can see, the values of the first three autocorrelations in our example are declining.

The first correlation is the strongest; therefore, the neighboring cases are related significantly. Cases that are 2 and 3 lags apart are still correlated, but not as strongly as the closest cases. In other words, the behavior of neighboring lags is related proportionally to the distance they are apart from each other. If two consecutive cases are increasing, it is probable that the third one will increase as well. The series has a trend. A decreasing autocorrelation is an indicator of a trend, but it has nothing to do with the direction of the trend. Regardless of whether the trend is increasing or decreasing, autocorrelation is still strongest for the closest cases (Lag 1) and weakest for the more distant lags. A sharp increase in the correlation coefficient at regular intervals indicates a cyclical pattern in your data. For example, if you were looking at monthly sales for a toy store, it is likely that every 12th lag you would observe a strong increase in the correlation coefficient due the Christmas holiday sales.

In one of the recipes we show later in this chapter, you'll see how autocorrelation can be implemented in SQL. In addition, you'll see how SQL can be used to generate a crude graph of the autocorrelation results quickly.

Moving Averages

A *moving average* is used when some kind of smoothing is needed on a set of time-series data. To compute a moving average, you combine every value in the series with some number of preceding values and then compute the average of those values. The result is a series of averages giving a smoother representation of the same data, though some accuracy will be lost because of the smoothing.

 Moving averages only apply to time series data.

Moving averages are commonly used in the financial industry to smooth out daily oscillations in the market price of a stock or other security. Table 8-3 shows a moving average for a stock price over a 10-day period. The left-hand column shows the daily stock price, while the right-hand column shows a 5-day moving average of that price. During the first four days, no moving average is possible, because a 5-day moving average requires values from 5 different days. Thus, the average begins on Day 5.

Table 8-3. A 5-day moving average

Day	Stock price	5-day moving average
1	10	n/a
2	18	n/a
3	12	n/a
4	20	n/a
5	10	14.0
6	9	13.8
7	19	14.0
8	13	14.2
9	18	17.8
10	15	14.8
11	16	16.2
12	17	15.8
13	15	16.2
14	18	16.2
15	17	16.6

You can readily see that the 5-day moving average values in Table 8-3 smooth out most of the wild oscillations in the day-to-day price of the stock. The moving average also makes the very slight upward trend much more clear. Figure 8-1 shows a graph of this same data.

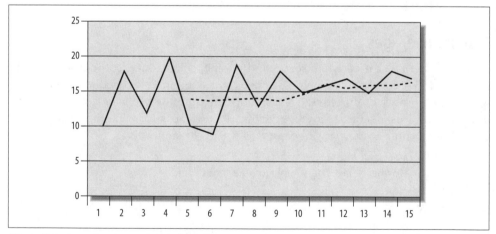

Figure 8-1. A stock price and its 5-day moving average

There are a number of different moving averages possible. A simple moving average, such as the one just shown in Table 8-3, represents the mean over a period for every case in the data set. All cases in the period are summed together, and the result is then divided by the number of cases in the period.

It is possible, however, to extend the concept of a moving average further. For example, a simple *exponential average* uses just two values: the current value and the one before it, but different weights are attached to each of them. A 90% exponential smoothing would take 10% of each value, 90% of each preceding value (from the previous period), and sum the two results together. The list of sums then becomes the exponential average. For example, with respect to Table 8-3, an exponential average for Day 2 could be computed as follows:

```
(Day 2 * 10%) + (Day 1 * 90%)
= (18 * 10%) + (10 * 90%)
= 1.8 + 9
= 10.8
```

Another interesting type of moving average is the *weighted average*, where the values from different periods have different weights assigned to them. These weighted values are then used to compute a moving average. Usually, the more distant a value is from the current value, the less it is weighted. For example, the following calculation yields a 5-day weighted average for Day 5 from Table 8-3.

```
(Period 5 * 35%) + (Period 4 * 25%) + (Period 3 * 20%)
+ (Period 2 * 15%) + (Period 1 * 5%)

= (10 * 35%) + (20 * 25%) + (12 * 20%) + (18 * 15%) + (10 * 5%)
= 3.5 + 5 + 2.4 + 2.7+ 0.5
= 14.1
```

As you can readily see, a weighted moving average would tend to favor more recent cases over the older ones.

8.2   The Light-Bulb Factory Example

The recipes in this chapter all make use of some sales and quality-assurance data from a hypothetical light bulb factory. This factory is building a quality-support system to store and analyze light-bulb usage data. Managers from every product line send small quantities of light bulbs several times a day to a testing lab. Equipment in the lab then tests the life of each bulb and stores the resulting data into a SQL database. In addition to the bulb-life data, our company also tracks sales data on a monthly basis. Our job is to build queries that support basic statistical analysis of both the bulb-life test data and the sales data.

Bulb-Life Data

Bulb-life test data is stored in the following table. Each bulb is given a unique ID number. Each time a bulb is tested, the test equipment records the bulb's lifetime in terms of hours.

```
CREATE TABLE BulbLife (
    BulbId INTEGER,
    Hours INTEGER,
    TestPit INTEGER
)
```

The test floor is divided into several test pits. In each test pit, a number of light bulbs can be tested at the same time. The table stores the number of hours each light bulb lasted in the testing environment before it burned out. Following is a sampling of data from two test pits:

BulbId	Hours	TestPit
1	1085	1
2	1109	1
3	1093	1
4	1043	1
5	1129	1
6	1099	1
7	1057	1
8	1114	1
9	1077	1
10	1086	1
1	1103	2
2	1079	2
3	1073	2
4	1086	2
5	1131	2
6	1087	2
7	1096	2
8	1167	2
9	1043	2
10	1074	2

Sales Data

The marketing department of our hypothetical light-bulb company tracks monthly sales. The sales numbers are stored in a table named BulbSales and are used to analyze the company's performance. The table is as follows:

```
CREATE TABLE BulbSales(
    Id INT IDENTITY,
    Year INT,
    Month INT,
    Sales FLOAT
)
```

The following records represent a sampling of the data from the BulbSales table:

Id	Year	Month	Sales
1	1995	1	9536.0
2	1995	2	9029.0
3	1995	3	8883.0
4	1995	4	10227.0
5	1995	5	9556.0
6	1995	6	9324.0
7	1995	7	10174.0
8	1995	8	9514.0
9	1995	9	9102.0
10	1995	10	9702.0

You can download a file from the book's web site that contains the complete set of sample sales data used for this chapter's examples. Figure 8-2 shows a graphical representation of this sales data. The company produces specialized light-bulb equipment and has three major customers. Historically, all three customers generally order three-months worth of supplies every three months and at approximately the same time. The sales record, therefore, shows a peak every three months. A six-month moving average can be used to smooth out this data and show the long-term trend. You see this moving average as the smoother line on the chart.

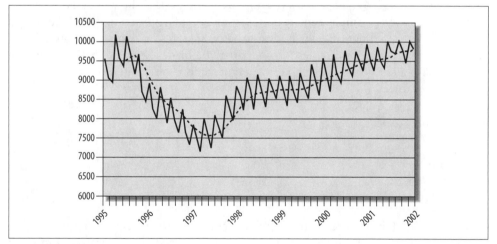

Figure 8-2. Monthly light-bulb sales

The chart in Figure 8-2 is only an example of the type of statistics that need to be produced from the sales and quality-assurance data. You'll see how to generate the moving average needed to create this chart in a recipe later in this chapter.

8.3   Calculating a Mean

Problem

You want to calculate the average life of light bulbs in a sample, where the sample consists of all bulbs tested in a particular test pit.

Solution

Computing a mean is fairly easy, because the standard SQL function AVG produces the desired result. For example:

```
SELECT AVG(Hours) Mean
FROM BulbLife
WHERE TestPit=1

Mean
-----------
1089
```

Discussion

Probably the easiest of all statistics to compute using SQL is the mean. The mean is just a simple average implemented by the standard SQL function AVG. The AVG function is a group function, which means that it operates on a group of rows. In the recipe solution, the group in question consisted of all rows for Test Pit #1. Using the GROUP BY clause, you can extend the query to report the mean bulb life for all test pits. For example:

```
SELECT TestPit, AVG(hours) Mean
FROM BulbLife
GROUP BY TestPit

TestPit     Mean
----------- -----------
1           1089
2           1093
```

Using the HAVING clause, you can implement measurement rules requiring that results only be reported for those test pits that have a specified minimum number of measurements available. For example, the following query limits the report to test pits where more than eight light bulbs have been tested:

```
SELECT TestPit, AVG(hours) Mean
FROM BulbLife
GROUP BY TestPit
HAVING COUNT(*) >= 8
```

8.4   Calculating a Mode

Problem

You want to calculate a modal average of the bulb-life results in your database. Recall from the discussion earlier in this chapter that the mode represents the most frequently occurring value in a sample.

Solution

SQL Server is not equipped with a mode function, so calculating the mode is a bit more difficult than calculating the mean. As the following solution shows, you can calculate the mode using a creative combination of COUNT and TOP:

```
SELECT TOP 1 COUNT(*) frequency, Hours mode
FROM BulbLife
WHERE TestPit=1
GROUP BY hours
ORDER BY COUNT(*) DESC

frequency    mode
-----------  -----------
2            1085
```

Discussion

Although it appears strange at first, how the query works becomes clear once you think about the basic definition for mode. A mode is the value that occurs most frequently in an observed sample. You can begin by writing a query to group values together:

```
SELECT Hours
FROM BulbLife
WHERE TestPit=1
GROUP BY hours

hours
-----------
1043
1057
1077
1085
1093
1099
1109
1114
1129
```

Next, add the COUNT function to the query to include a count of each distinct value with the query's results:

```
SELECT COUNT(*) frequency, Hours
FROM BulbLife
WHERE TestPit=1
GROUP BY Hours

frequency   Hours
----------- -----------
1           1043
1           1057
1           1077
2           1085
1           1093
1           1099
1           1109
1           1114
1           1129
```

Finally, use an ORDER BY clause to put the results in descending order by frequency, so that the most frequently occurring value is listed first. Then, use the TOP 1 syntax in your SELECT clause to limit the results to the first row. The hours value in that first row will be the mode.

What happens when you have more than one mode in the observed sample and you need to report all such values? In our hypothetical bulb-life data, the mode for Test Pit #1 is 1085, while the mode for Test Pit #2 is 1043. For both modes, the occurrence count is 2. If you want the mode for all light bulbs, regardless of test pit, then both values should be returned. The following query shows one way to deal with this:

```
SELECT COUNT(*) frequency, Hours mode FROM BulbLife
GROUP BY Hours
HAVING COUNT(*)>= ALL(
    SELECT COUNT(*)
    FROM BulbLife
    GROUP BY Hours)

frequency   mode
----------- -----------
2           1043
2           1085
```

The subquery that you see in this example returns a list of all occurrence counts for all distinct values in the BulbLife table. It follows, logically, that one of those counts will represent a maximum. The HAVING clause in the outer query specifies that the occurrence count be greater than or equal to all values returned by the subquery, which, in effect, restricts the results to only those rows with an occurrence count that equals the maximum occurrence count.

Be aware that mode is a weak statistic. The mode can be useful if you know the distribution and the nature of the sample, but it can easily be altered by adding a few cases with extreme values. For example, let's say that we get 2 additional bulbs with a duration of 1129 hours. The mode is then 1129, which is misleading information, since all other bulbs lasted for much shorter periods.

8.5   Calculating a Median

Problem

You want to calculate the median bulb life for all bulbs that have been tested. From the discussion earlier in this chapter, you should recognize that the median bulb life represents the case where the number of bulbs with shorter lives is equivalent to the number of bulbs with longer lives.

Solution

To calculate the median of the light-bulb test results, use the following query:

```
SELECT x.Hours median
FROM BulbLife x, BulbLife y
GROUP BY x.Hours
HAVING
   SUM(CASE WHEN y.Hours <= x.Hours
      THEN 1 ELSE 0 END)>=(COUNT(*)+1)/2 AND
   SUM(CASE WHEN y.Hours >= x.Hours
      THEN 1 ELSE 0 END)>=(COUNT(*)/2)+1

median
-----------
1086
```

Discussion

This query follows the definition of the median very closely and uses the solution published several years ago by David Rozenshtein, Anatoly Abramovich, and Eugene Birger. Their solution is still regarded as one of the classical solutions to the problem of finding the median value in a sample. To understand their solution, it helps to look at the query in two phases. First, you have a GROUP BY query that returns the number of bulbs for each distinct lifetime. The following is a modified version of the first part of the solution query that returns the occurrence count corresponding to each distinct bulb-life value:

```
SELECT COUNT(*) occurrences, x.Hours xhours
FROM BulbLife x, BulbLife y
GROUP BY x.Hours
```

occurrences	xhours
40	1043
20	1057
20	1073
20	1074
20	1077
20	1079
40	1085
20	1086
20	1087
20	1093
20	1096
20	1099
20	1103
20	1109
20	1114
20	1129
20	1131
20	1167

Because these results represent a self-join of the BulbLife table with itself, each group represents a number of detail rows equivalent to the number of rows in the sample. The two groups of 40 occurrences each exist because the data contains 2 cases with values of 1043 and 2 cases with values of 1085. The detail for the 1086 group is as follows:

xhours	yhours
1086	1043
1086	1043
1086	1057
1086	1073
1086	1074
1086	1077
1086	1079
1086	1085
1086	1085
1086	1086
1086	1087
1086	1093
1086	1096
1086	1099
1086	1103
1086	1109
1086	1114
1086	1129
1086	1131
1086	1167

The question now is whether the value 1086 represents the median. To determine that, follow these steps:

1. Count the cases where the y.hours value is less than or equal to the x.hours value.

2. Count the cases where the x.hours value is less than or equal to the y.hours value.

3. Compare the two results. If they are equal, then 1086 is the median value.

The HAVING clause in our solution query performs the counts for steps 1 and 2 using the following two invocations of the SUM function combined with a CASE statement:

```
SUM(CASE WHEN y.Hours <= x.Hours
    THEN 1 ELSE 0 END)
SUM(CASE WHEN y.Hours >= x.Hours
    THEN 1 ELSE 0 END)
```

In our example, the values for these 2 sums work out to 10 and 11, respectively. Plug these two values in for the two SUM expressions in the HAVING clause, and you have the following:

```
10 >= (COUNT(*)+1)/2 AND
11 >= (COUNT(*)/2)+1
```

At this point, the two COUNT expressions deserve some additional explanation. They have been carefully crafted to allow us to derive a median, even in cases where we have an even number of values in the sample. Let's step back for a moment, and assume that our sample contained 21 values, instead of the 20 that it does contain. If that were the case, the two COUNT expressions would evaluate as follows:

```
(COUNT(*)+1)/2        (COUNT(*)/2)+1
(21+1)/2              (21/2)+1
22/2                  10+1
11                    11
```

 In SQL Server, 21/2 represents an integer division and, hence, yields an integer value of 10 as the result.

Whenever you have an odd number of values in the sample, the two expressions will yield the same result. Given an even number, however, the first expression will yield a result that is one less than the other. Here is how the HAVING expression works out for the data in our example:

```
10 >= (20+1)/2 AND
11 >= (20/2)+1

10 >= 10 AND
11 >= 11
```

For the case where x.Hours = 1086, both expressions are true, so 1086 is returned as the median value. In actual fact, because we have an even number of values, there are 2 candidates for the median: 1086 and 1087. The value 1086 has 9 values below it and 10 above it. The value for 1087 has 10 values below it and 9 above it. Due to how we've written the COUNT expressions, our solution query arbitrarily returns the lower value as the median.

It's possible to use a slightly modified version of our solution query to return the financial median. Recall, from earlier in this chapter, that in the case of an even number of values, the financial median represents the mean of the two inner neighbors. With respect to our example, that would be the mean of 1086 and 1087, which works out to 1086.5. Use the following query to calculate the financial median:

```
SELECT
    CASE WHEN COUNT(*)%2=1
        THEN x.Hours
        ELSE (x.Hours+MIN(CASE WHEN y.Hours>x.Hours
                            THEN y.Hours
                    END))/2.0
    END median
FROM BulbLife x, BulbLife y
GROUP BY x.Hours
HAVING
    SUM(CASE WHEN y.Hours <= x.Hours
        THEN 1 ELSE 0 END)>=(count(*)+1)/2 AND
    SUM(CASE WHEN y.Hours >= x.Hours
        THEN 1 ELSE 0 END)>=(count(*)/2)+1
```

The basic query remains the same, the only difference being in the SELECT statement's column list. If there is an odd number of cases, the median is reported directly as the x.Hours value. However, if the number of cases is even, the smallest y.Hours value that is higher than the chosen x.Hours value is identified. This value is then added to the x.Hours value. The result is then divided by 2.0 to return the mean of those two values as the query's result.

The original query reported only the lesser of the two values that were in the middle of the sample. The added logic in the SELECT clause for the financial-median causes the mean of the two values to be calculated and reported. In our example, the result is the following:

```
median
-------------------
1086.5
```

After you run the query to obtain a financial median, you'll get a warning like this:

```
Warning: Null value eliminated from aggregate.
```

This is an important warning, because it's a sign that our query is working correctly. We did not want to write an ELSE clause for the CASE statement inside the MIN function. Because if we wrote such an ELSE clause and had it return a 0, the result of the MIN function would always be 0, and, consequently, the financial-median calculation would always be wrong for any sample with an even number of values.

8.6 Calculating Standard Deviation, Variance, and Standard Error

Problem

You want to calculate both the standard deviation and the variance of a sample. You also want to assess the standard error of the sample.

Solution

Use SQL Server's built-in STDEV, STDEVP, VAR, and VARP functions for calculating standard deviation and variance. For example, the following query will return the standard deviation and variance for the sample values from each of the test pits:

```
SELECT TestPit, VAR(Hours) variance, STDEV(Hours) st_deviation
FROM BulbLife
GROUP BY TestPit

TestPit variance  st_deviation
------- --------- ------------
1       672.99    25.94
2       1173.66   34.26
```

To get the standard error of the sample, simply use the following query, which implements the formula for standard error shown earlier in this chapter:

```
SELECT AVG(Hours) mean, STDEV(Hours)/SQRT(COUNT(*)) st_error
FROM BulbLife

mean        st_error
----------- ----------
1091        6.64
```

Discussion

Since SQL Server provides functions to calculate standard deviation and variance, it is wise to use them and not program your own. However, be careful when you use them. You need to know whether the data from which you calculate the statistics represents the whole population or just a sample. In our example, the table holds data for just a sample of the entire population of light bulbs. Therefore, we used the STDEV and VAR functions designed for use on samples. If your data includes the entire population, use STDEVP and VARP instead.

8.7   Building Confidence Intervals

Problem

You want to check to see whether the calculated sample statistics could be reasonably representative of the population's statistics. With respect to our example, assume that a light bulb's declared lifetime is 1100 hours. Based on a sample of lifetime tests, can you say with 95% probability that the quality of the production significantly differs from the declared measurement? To answer this question, you need to determine whether the confidence interval around the mean of the sample spans across the declared lifetime. If the declared lifetime is out of the confidence interval, then the sample mean does not represent the population accurately, and we can assume that our declared lifetime for the light bulbs is probably wrong. Either the quality has dropped and the bulbs are burning out more quickly, or quality has risen, causing the bulbs to last longer than we claim.

Solution

The solution is to execute a query that implements the calculations described earlier for computing a confidence interval. Recall that the confidence interval was plus or minus a certain amount. Thus, the following solution query computes two values:

```
SELECT
    AVG(Hours)-STDEV(Hours)/SQRT(COUNT(*))*MAX(p) in1,
    AVG(Hours)+STDEV(Hours)/SQRT(COUNT(*))*MAX(p) in2
FROM BulbLife, T_distribution
WHERE df=(
    SELECT
        CASE WHEN count(*)<=29
        THEN count(*)-1
        ELSE -1 END FROM BulbLife)

in1      in2
-------- --------
1077.11  1104.89
```

Based on the given sample, we cannot say that the quality of production has significantly changed, because the declared value of 1100 hours is within the computed confidence interval for the sample.

Discussion

The solution query calculates the mean of the sample and adds to it the standard error multiplied by the t-distribution coefficient from the T_distribution table. In our sample, the degree of freedom is the number of cases in the sample less 1. The CASE statement ensures that the appropriate index is used in the T_distribution table. If the number of values is 30 or more, the CASE statement returns a −1. In the

T_distribution table, the coefficient for an infinite number of degrees of freedom is identified with a −1 degree of freedom value. Expressions in the SELECT clause of the solution query calculate the standard deviation, expand it with the coefficient from the T_distribution table, and then calculate the interval around the mean.

This example is interesting, because it shows you how to refer to a table containing coefficients. You could retrieve the coefficient separately using another query, store it in a local variable, and then use it in a second query to compute the confidence interval, but that's less efficient than the technique shown here where all the work is done using just one query.

8.8   Calculating Correlation

Problem

You want to calculate the correlation between two samples. For example, you want to calculate how similar the light-bulb sales patterns are for two different years.

Solution

The query in the following example uses the formula for calculating correlation coefficients shown earlier in this chapter. It does this for the years 1997 and 1998.

```
SELECT
    (COUNT(*)*SUM(x.Sales*y.Sales)-SUM(x.Sales)*SUM(y.Sales))/(
    SQRT(COUNT(*)*SUM(SQUARE(x.Sales))-SQUARE(SUM(x.Sales)))*
    SQRT(COUNT(*)*SUM(SQUARE(y.Sales))-SQUARE(SUM(y.Sales))))
    correlation
FROM BulbSales x JOIN BulbSales y ON x.month=y.month
WHERE x.Year=1997 AND y.Year=1998

correlation
----------------------------------------------------
0.79
```

The correlation calculated is 0.79, which means that the sales patterns between the two years are highly correlated or, in other words, very similar.

Discussion

The solution query implements the formula shown earlier in the chapter for calculating a correlation coefficient. The solution query shown here is an example of how you implement a complex formula directly in SQL. To aid you in making such translations from mathematical formulas to Transact-SQL expressions, Table 8-4 shows a number of mathematical symbols together with their corresponding Transact-SQL functions.

Table 8-4. Mathematical symbols related to Transact-SQL functions

Symbol	Formula	Description
$\lvert a \rvert$	ABS(a)	Absolute value of a
e^{a}	EXP(a)	Exponential value of a
a^{2}	SQUARE(a)	Square of a
a^{n}	POWER(a,n)	nth power of a
n	COUNT(*)	Sample size
$\sqrt{a}$	SQRT(a)	Square root of a
Σa	SUM(a)	Sum of all cases in a sample
$\bar{a}$ or μ	AVG(a)	Average of all cases in a sample—the mean
s	STDDEV(x)	Standard deviation of a sample
σ	STDDEVP(x)	Standard deviation of a population
s^{2}	VAR(x)	Variance of a sample
σ^{2}	VARP(X)	Variance of a population

To write the query shown in this recipe, take the formula for correlation coefficient shown earlier in this chapter, and use the Table 8-4 to translate the mathematical symbols in that formula into SQL functions for your query.

8.9   Exploring Patterns with Autocorrelation

Problem

You want to find trend or seasonal patterns in your data. For example, you wish to correlate light-bulb sales data over a number of months. To save yourself some work, you'd like to automatically correlate a number of samples.

Solution

Use the autocorrelation technique described earlier in this chapter, and print a graphical representation of the results. You need to calculate up to 15 correlations of the light-bulb sales data. 15 is a somewhat arbitrary number. In our experience, we rarely find a gain by going beyond that number of correlations. For the first correlation, you want to compare each month's sales data with that from the immediately preceding month. For the second correlation, you want to compare each month's sales data with that from two months prior. You want this pattern to repeat 15 times, with the lag increasing each time, so that the final correlation compares each month's sales data with that from 15 months prior. You then wish to plot the results in the form of a graph.

Because you want to compute 15 separate correlations, you need to do more than just join the BulbSales table with itself. You actually want 15 such joins, with the lag between months increasing each time. You can accomplish this by joining the BulbSales table with itself, and then joining those results with the Pivot table. See the Pivot table recipe in Chapter 1 for an explanation of the Pivot table.

After you create the necessary Pivot table, you can use the query shown in the following example to generate and graph the 15 correlations that you wish to see:

```
SELECT
    p.i lag, STUFF( STUFF(SPACE(40),
        CAST(ROUND((COUNT(*)*SUM(x.Sales*y.Sales)-
            SUM(x.Sales)*SUM(y.Sales))/
            (SQRT(COUNT(*)*SUM(SQUARE(x.Sales)))-SQUARE(SUM(x.Sales)))*
            SQRT(COUNT(*)*SUM(SQUARE(y.Sales)))-SQUARE(SUM(y.Sales))))*
            20,0)+20 AS INT),1,'*'),20,1,'|') autocorrelation
FROM BulbSales x, BulbSales y, Pivot p
WHERE x.Id=y.Id-p.i AND p.i BETWEEN 1 AND 15
GROUP BY p.i
ORDER BY p.i
```

```
lag          autocorrelation
-----------  ----------------------------------------
1                             |                 *
2                             |                *
3                             |                   *
4                             |             *
5                             |            *
6                             |                *
7                             |        *
8                             |       *
9                             |          *
10                            |     *
11                            |    *
12                            |       *
13                            |    *
14                            | *
15                            |     *
```

You can see from this graph that, as the lag increases, the correlation drops towards 0. This clearly indicates a trend. The more distant any two cases are, the less correlated they are. Conversely, the closer any two cases are, the greater their correlation.

You can make another observation regarding the 3rd, 6th, 9th, 12th, and 15th lags. Each of those lags shows an increased correlation, which indicates that you have some sort of seasonal pattern that is repeated every three periods. This is true. If you look at the sample data, you will see that sales results increase significantly every three months.

Discussion

This code demonstrates how you can extend a correlation, or any other kind of formula, so that it is calculated several times on the same data. In our solution, the first 15 correlation coefficients are calculated from the sample. Each coefficient represents the correlation between the sample and the sample lagged by one or more steps. We use the Pivot table to generate all the lagged data sets. Let's look at a simplified version of the query that doesn't contain the plotting code:

```
SELECT
    p.i lag,
    (COUNT(*)*SUM(x.Sales*y.Sales)-SUM(x.Sales)*SUM(y.Sales))/
        (SQRT(COUNT(*)*SUM(SQUARE(x.Sales))-SQUARE(SUM(x.Sales)))*
        SQRT(COUNT(*)*SUM(SQUARE(y.Sales))-SQUARE(SUM(y.Sales))))
        autocorrelation
FROM BulbSales x, BulbSales y, Pivot p
WHERE x.Id=y.Id-p.i AND p.i BETWEEN 1 AND 15
GROUP BY p.i
ORDER BY p.i
```

When you execute this query, the first few lines of the result should look like this:

```
lag           autocorrelation
----------- -------------------
1             0.727
2             0.703
3             0.936
4             0.650
5             ...
```

The code in the SELECT clause that calculates the correlations is the same as that used in the earlier recipe for calculating a single correlation. The difference here is that we define the matching months differently. Since our research spans a period greater than one year, we cannot match months anymore. Instead, we have to use the period index. Hence, the WHERE clause specifies the condition, x.id=y.id-p.i. For pivot value 1, each x value will be matched with the preceding y value. For pivot value 2, each x value will be matched by the y value from two periods in the past. This pattern continues for all 15 lags.

For every calculation, the data must be lagged. We use the Pivot table to generate 15 groups, where the group index is also used as a lag coefficient in the WHERE clause. The result is a list of correlation coefficients, each calculated for a combination of the sample data and correspondingly lagged sampled data.

Now that you understand the use of the Pivot table to generate the 15 lags that we desire, you can return your attention to our original query. To make use of autocorrelation, we need to print the data in a graphical format. We do that by printing an asterisk (*) in the autocorrelation column of the output. The greater the correlation value, the further to the right the asterisk will appear. The following query highlights the Transact-SQL expression that we use to plot the results. To simplify things, we use the pseudovariable correlation coefficient (CORR) to represent that part of the code that calculates the correlation values.

```
SELECT
    p.i lag, STUFF( STUFF(SPACE(40),
        CAST(ROUND(CORR*20,0)+20 AS INT),1,'*'),20,1,'|')
        autocorrelation
FROM BulbSales x, BulbSales y, Pivot p
WHERE x.Id=y.Id-p.i AND p.i BETWEEN 1 AND 15
GROUP BY p.i
ORDER BY p.i
```

You have to look at this expression from the inside out. The CORR is multiplied by 20, and any decimal digits are rounded off. This translates our correlation coefficient values from the range −1 to 1 into the range −20 to 20. We add 20 to this result to shift those values into the range 0 to 40. For example, −0.8 is translated into 4, and 0.7 is translated into 34. Since all the values are positive, we can place each asterisk into its correct relative position simply by preceding it with the number of spaces indicated by our result.

The SPACE function in our expression generates a string containing 40 spaces. The STUFF function is then used to insert an asterisk into this string of blanks. After that, the outermost STUFF function inserts a vertical bar (|) character to indicate the middle of the range. This allows us to see easily when a correlation coefficient is positive or negative. Any asterisks to the left of the vertical bar represent negative coefficients. If the coefficient came out as zero, it would be overwritten by the vertical bar.

8.10   Using a Simple Moving Average

Problem

You want to develop a moving-average tool for your analysis. For example, you want to smooth out monthly deviations in light-bulb sales using a six-month moving average. This will allow you to get a good handle on the long-term trend.

Solution

Calculating a moving average turns out to be a fairly easy task in SQL. With respect to the example we are using in this chapter, the query shown in the following example returns a six-month moving average of light-bulb sales:

```
SELECT x.Id, AVG(y.Sales) moving_average
FROM BulbSales x, BulbSales y
WHERE x.Id>=6 AND x.Id BETWEEN y.Id AND y.Id+5
GROUP BY x.Id
ORDER BY x.Id
```

```
id          moving_average
----------- ----------------
6           9425.83
7           9532.17
8           9613.00
9           9649.50
10          9562.00
11          9409.33
12          9250.67
13          9034.83
14          8812.83
15          8609.83
16          8447.83
17          8386.33
18          ...
```

The query shown in this example was used to generate the chart shown earlier in this chapter in Figure 8-2. Please refer to that chart to see the graphical representation of the query results that you see here.

Discussion

In our solution, the moving average is calculated through the use of a self-join. This self-join allows us to join each sales record with itself and the sales records from the preceding six periods. For example:

```
SELECT x.Id xid, y.Id yid, y.Sales
FROM BulbSales x, BulbSales y
WHERE x.Id>=6 AND x.Id BETWEEN y.Id AND y.Id+5
ORDER BY x.Id
```

```
xid         yid         Sales
----------- ----------- ------------------------------------------------------
6           1           9536.0
6           2           9029.0
6           3           8883.0
6           4           10227.0
6           5           9556.0
6           6           9324.0
7           2           9029.0
7           3           8883.0
7           4           10227.0
7           5           9556.0
7           6           9324.0
7           7           10174.0
8           3           8883.0
8           4           10227.0
8           5           9556.0
8           6           9324.0
8           7           10174.0
8           8           9514.0
```

To compute a 6-month moving average, we need at least 6 months worth of data. Thus, the WHERE clause specifies x.Id>=6. Period 6 represents the first period for which we can access 6 months of data. We cannot compute a 6-month moving average for periods 1 through 5.

The WHERE clause further specifies x.Id BETWEEN y.Id AND y.Id+5. This actually represents the join condition and results in each x row being joined with the corresponding y row, as well as the five prior y rows. You can see that for x.Id=6, the query returns sales data from periods 1 through 6. For x.Id=7, the query returns sales data from periods 2 through 7. For x.Id=8, the window shifts again to periods 3 through 8.

To compute the moving average, the Id value from the first table is used as a reference—the results are grouped by the x.Id column. Each grouping represents six rows from the second table (aliased as y), and the moving average is computed by applying the AVG function to the y.Sales column.

8.11   Extending Moving Averages

Problem

You want to calculate an extended moving average such as is used in the financial industry. In particular, you want to calculate exponential and weighted moving average. Let's say that by looking at a chart of light-bulb sales, you find that they closely mimic the company's stock-price data from the stock exchange. As a possible investor, you want to calculate some of the same moving averages that financial analysts are using.

Solution

To calculate a 90% exponential moving average, you begin with the same basic moving-average framework shown in the previous recipe. The difference is how you calculate the average. Recall that a 90% exponential moving average gives 90% of the importance to the previous value and only 10% of the importance to the current value. You can use a CASE statement in your query to attach the proper importance to the proper occurrence. The following example shows our solution query:

```
SELECT x.Id,
    SUM(CASE WHEN y.Id=x.Id
            THEN 0.9*y.Sales
            ELSE 0.1*x.Sales END) exponential_average
FROM BulbSales x, BulbSales y
WHERE x.Id>=2 AND x.Id BETWEEN y.Id AND y.Id+1
GROUP BY x.Id
ORDER BY x.Id
```

```
id          exponential_average
----------- --------------------
2           9029.0
3           8883.0
4           10227.0
5           9556.0
6           9324.0
7           10174.0
8           9514.0
9           9102.0
10          ...
```

The framework for calculating an exponential moving average remains the same as for calculating a simple moving average; the only difference is in the part of the query that actually calculates the average. In our solution, the CASE statement checks which y row is currently available. If it is the latest one, the code places a 90% weight on it. Only a 10% weight is given to the preceding value. The SUM function then sums the two adjusted values, and the result is returned as the exponential weighted average for the period.

As an example of how to extend this concept, think about calculating a six-month weighted moving average where each period has an increasing weight as you move towards the current point. The query in the following example shows one solution to this problem. As you can see, the framework again remains the same. The average calculation has just been extended to include more cases.

```
SELECT x.Id,
    SUM(CASE WHEN x.Id-y.Id=0 THEN 0.28*y.Sales
             WHEN x.Id-y.Id=1 THEN 0.23*y.Sales
             WHEN x.Id-y.Id=2 THEN 0.20*y.Sales
             WHEN x.Id-y.Id=3 THEN 0.14*y.Sales
             WHEN x.Id-y.Id=4 THEN 0.10*y.Sales
             WHEN x.Id-y.Id=5 THEN 0.05*y.Sales
        END)weighted_average
FROM BulbSales x, BulbSales y
WHERE x.Id>=6 AND x.Id BETWEEN y.Id AND y.Id+6
GROUP BY x.Id
ORDER BY x.Id

Id          weighted_average
----------- -----------------
6           9477.31
7           9675.97
8           9673.43
9           9543.89
10          9547.38
11          9286.62
12          9006.14
13          8883.86
14          8642.43
15          ...
```

The CASE statement in this example checks to see how far the current y row is from the x row used as a reference and adjusts the value accordingly using a predefined coefficient. You can easily extend the calculation to include ranges, or even dynamic coefficient calculations, depending on your needs. You just need to be careful that the sum of the coefficients is 1. Your weights need to add up to 100%, otherwise your results might look a bit strange.

Discussion

There is a small difference between the two averages shown in this recipe. When calculating an exponential moving average, you assign a proportion of the weight, expressed as a percentage, to each value used in computing the average. Exponential moving averages are calculated using two cases—the current case and its predecessor. When calculating a weighted moving average, you assign weight in terms of multiples to a value in the average. There is no limit to the number of cases that you can use in a weighted moving-average calculation. Exponential moving averages are an often-used special case of weighted moving averages.

Appendix:
The T-Distribution Table

The t-distribution is a probability distribution with a symmetrical, bell-shaped curve (similar to the standard normal curve), the shape of which is affected by a parameter known as the "degrees of freedom." We used t-distributions in Chapter 8 of this book to compute confidence intervals. In that usage, the degrees of freedom controlled how far out you had to go (in terms of standard deviations) on the t-distribution curve from the mean to encompass a given percentage of values. The higher the degrees of freedom, the larger the interval on the curve.

Table A-1 gives t-distribution values for various probabilities, with each row representing 1 additional degree of freedom. Those values in the column for 0.05 (95%) were used in Chapter 8.

Table A-1. The t-distribution table referenced in Chapter 8

DF	Probabilities						
	0.2	0.1	0.05	0.02	0.01	0.002	0.001
1	3.078	6.314	12.706	31.82	63.66	318.3	637
2	1.886	2.92	4.303	6.965	9.925	22.33	31.6
3	1.638	2.353	3.182	4.541	5.841	10.21	12.92
4	1.533	2.132	2.776	3.747	4.604	7.173	8.61
5	1.476	2.015	2.571	3.365	4.032	5.893	6.869
6	1.44	1.943	2.447	3.143	3.707	5.208	5.959
7	1.415	1.895	2.365	2.998	3.499	4.785	5.408
8	1.397	1.86	2.306	2.896	3.355	4.501	5.041
9	1.383	1.833	2.262	2.821	3.25	4.297	4.781
10	1.372	1.812	2.228	2.764	3.169	4.144	4.587
11	1.363	1.796	2.201	2.718	3.106	4.025	4.437
12	1.356	1.782	2.179	2.681	3.055	3.93	4.318
13	1.35	1.771	2.16	2.65	3.012	3.852	4.221
14	1.345	1.761	2.145	2.624	2.977	3.787	4.14

Table A-1. The t-distribution table referenced in Chapter 8 (continued)

DF	Probabilities						
	0.2	0.1	0.05	0.02	0.01	0.002	0.001
15	1.341	1.753	2.131	2.602	2.947	3.733	4.073
16	1.337	1.746	2.12	2.583	2.921	3.686	4.015
17	1.333	1.74	2.11	2.567	2.898	3.646	3.965
18	1.33	1.734	2.101	2.552	2.878	3.61	3.922
19	1.328	1.729	2.093	2.539	2.861	3.579	3.883
20	1.325	1.725	2.086	2.528	2.845	3.552	3.85
21	1.323	1.721	2.08	2.518	2.831	3.527	3.819
22	1.321	1.717	2.074	2.508	2.819	3.505	3.792
23	1.319	1.714	2.069	2.5	2.807	3.485	3.768
24	1.318	1.711	2.064	2.492	2.797	3.467	3.745
25	1.316	1.708	2.06	2.485	2.787	3.45	3.725
26	1.315	1.706	2.056	2.479	2.779	3.435	3.707
27	1.314	1.703	2.052	2.473	2.771	3.421	3.69
28	1.313	1.701	2.048	2.467	2.763	3.408	3.674
29	1.311	1.699	2.045	2.462	2.756	3.396	3.659
30	1.31	1.697	2.042	2.457	2.75	3.385	3.646
32	1.309	1.694	2.037	2.449	2.738	3.365	3.622
34	1.307	1.691	2.032	2.441	2.728	3.348	3.601
36	1.306	1.688	2.028	2.434	2.719	3.333	3.582
38	1.304	1.686	2.024	2.429	2.712	3.319	3.566
40	1.303	1.684	2.021	2.423	2.704	3.307	3.551
42	1.302	1.682	2.018	2.418	2.698	3.296	3.538
44	1.301	1.68	2.015	2.414	2.692	3.286	3.526
46	1.3	1.679	2.013	2.41	2.687	3.277	3.515
48	1.299	1.677	2.011	2.407	2.682	3.269	3.505
50	1.299	1.676	2.009	2.403	2.678	3.261	3.496
55	1.297	1.673	2.004	2.396	2.668	3.245	3.476
60	1.296	1.671	2	2.39	2.66	3.232	3.46
65	1.295	1.669	1.997	2.385	2.654	3.22	3.447
70	1.294	1.667	1.994	2.381	2.648	3.211	3.435
80	1.292	1.664	1.99	2.374	2.639	3.195	3.416
100	1.29	1.66	1.984	2.364	2.626	3.174	3.39
150	1.287	1.655	1.976	2.351	2.609	3.145	3.357
200	1.286	1.653	1.972	2.345	2.601	3.131	3.34

Index

We'd like to hear your suggestions for improving our indexes. Send email to *index@oreilly.com*.

BuildProjectPathsRecursive stored
    procedure, 105
Bulk Copy Program (BCP), 189
bulk importing, 190
BULK INSERT statement, 189, 198

C

calendar information
    durations, 147
    periods, 145
calendars
    Pivot table and, 4
    printing, 124
Cartesian products, Pivot tables, 2
CASE function, 22
CASE statement
    SUM function and, 257
case, statistics, 237
CAST function, 114
children, hierarchies, 80
    locating immediate, 96
    subprojects, 83
classes
    aggregated, summarizing, 27
    sets, summarizing, 24
classification system, dynamic
    (recipe), 40–44
columns, nonaggregated, 28
comparisons recipe, 16–18
complements, sets, 11
    recipes
        different universe, 38
        finding, 34
        missing, 36
        size, 33
components of sets, 6–8
confidence intervals, statistics, 242
    building, recipe, 260
    calculations, 243
    degrees of freedom, 243
    t-distribution table, 242
contains operation, 9
continuous periods, recipe, 138–145
CONVERT clause, granularity, 120
CONVERT function, 114
correlation coefficient, statistics, 244
correlation, statistics
    calculating, recipe, 261
COUNT function, 253
counting duplicates, 195, 231
cross-sectional data, statistics, 236

cumulative aggregates, lists, 61
cumulative aggregation queries, lists, 46
CURRENT_TIMESTAMP function, 113,
    115, 158
CURRENT_USER function, 158
cursors
    global, 98
    procedures, 98

D

Data Manipulation Language (DML), 152
data normalization (see normalized data)
data structures, 45
    linear, 45–50
    multidimensional, 49
Data Transformation Services (DTS), 189
databases
    master/detail framework, 194
    normalized data and, 191
    periods, 117
    tables, audit logs and, 153
datatypes
    granularity, 113
    temporal data, 111, 113
        DATETIME, 111, 113
        SMALLDATETIME, 113
        TIMESTAMP, 113
date and time input, 114
date notation, 114
DATEDIFF function, 117
DATENAME function, 116
DATEPART function, 136
DATETIME datatype, 111, 113
    durations, 117
    instants, 115
degrees of freedom, statistics, 243
DELETE statement
    lists, 46
    log triggers, 159
    row-level logs, 152
    sets and, 5
deleting records, audit log, 172
@Depth variable, vertexes, 105
descriptor, audit log records, 154
differences, sets, 11
    NOT EXISTS statement, 15
    recipe, 13–15
    SELECT statement, 15
    subqueries, 14
dissertations, importing example, 197

About the Authors

Aleš Špetič is an independent consultant living in Slovenia. He holds a degree in computer science from the University of Ljubljana and an MBA degree from California State University, Hayward. He spent a few years in the financial industry, leading teams developing specialized software for investment banking in Slovenia and Austria. He designed and led the development of one of the first online brokerage and trading systems in Europe in 1997. He enjoys books, cooking, and working on SQL projects.

Jonathan Gennick is a writer and editor with extensive database and programming experience. He has written or contributed to a number of database-related books, including *Oracle SQL*Loader: The Definitive Guide* and *Oracle SQL*Plus: The Definitive Guide*. Jonathan is a member of MENSA, and he holds a BA in Information and Computer Science from Andrews University in Berrien Springs, Michigan.

Colophon

Our look is the result of reader comments, our own experimentation, and feedback from distribution channels. Distinctive covers complement our distinctive approach to technical topics, breathing personality and life into potentially dry subjects.

The animal on the cover of *Transact-SQL Cookbook* is a tree swift. Swifts are small, swallow-like birds related to hummingbirds. They are found all over the world, especially in the tropics. There are many different species of swifts that are specific to certain regions.

Swifts range from 3.5 to 9 inches in length. Their powerful, streamlined bodies have long wings; small, weak legs; and small feet. Swifts perch on vertical surfaces, but, due to their weak legs, once they perch, they have a difficult time returning to flight. Because of this, swifts do nearly everything on the wing, including feeding, drinking, bathing, courting, and sometimes mating. Their strong wings also make them rapid fliers.

Jeffrey Holcomb was the production editor and proofreader for *Transact-SQL Cookbook*. Tatiana Apandi Diaz was the copyeditor. Linley Dolby, Leanne Soylemez, and Claire Cloutier provided quality control. Phil Dangler, Leanne Soylemez, and David Chu provided production assistance. Johnna VanHoose Dinse wrote the index.

Ellie Volckhausen designed the cover of this book, based on a series design by Edie Freedman. The cover image is a 19th-century engraving from the Dover Pictorial Archive. Emma Colby produced the cover layout with QuarkXPress 4.1 using Adobe's ITC Garamond font.

David Futato designed the interior layout. Neil Walls converted the files from Microsoft Word to FrameMaker 5.5.6 using tools created by Mike Sierra. The text font is Linotype Birka; the heading font is Adobe Myriad Condensed; and the code font is LucasFont's TheSans Mono Condensed. The illustrations that appear in the book were produced by Robert Romano and Jessamyn Read using Macromedia Free-Hand 9 and Adobe Photoshop 6. The tip and warning icons were drawn by Christopher Bing. This colophon was written by Linley Dolby.

How to stay in touch with O'Reilly

1. Visit Our Award-Winning Web Site

http://www.oreilly.com/

★ "Top 100 Sites on the Web" —PC Magazine
★ CIO Magazine's Web Business 50 Awards

Our web site contains a library of comprehensive product information (including book excerpts and tables of contents), downloadable software, background articles, interviews with technology leaders, links to relevant sites, book cover art, and more. File us in your bookmarks or favorites!

2. Join Our Email Mailing Lists

Sign up to get email announcements of new books and conferences, special offers, and O'Reilly Network technology newsletters at:
elists.oreilly.com.
It's easy to customize your free elists subscription so you'll get exactly the O'Reilly news you want.

3. Get Examples from Our Books

To find example files for a book, go to:
http://www.oreilly.com/catalog
select the book, and follow the "Examples" link.

4. Contact Us via Email

order@oreilly.com
For answers to problems regarding your order or our products. To place a book order online visit:
http://www.oreilly.com/order_new/

catalog@oreilly.com
To request a copy of our latest catalog.

booktech@oreilly.com
For book content technical questions or corrections.

proposals@oreilly.com
To submit new book proposals to our editors and product managers.

international@oreilly.com
For information about our international distributors or translation queries. For a list of our distributors outside of North America check out:
http://international.oreilly.com/distributors.html

5. Work with Us

Check out our web site for current employment opportunites:
http://jobs.oreilly.com/

6. Register your book

Register your book at:
http://register.oreilly.com

O'Reilly & Associates, Inc.
1005 Gravenstein Hwy North
Sebastopol, CA 95472 USA
TEL 707-827-7000 or 800-998-9938
(6am to 5pm PST)
FAX 707-829-0104

O'REILLY®

TO ORDER: *800-998-9938* • *order@oreilly.com* • *www.oreilly.com*
ONLINE EDITIONS OF MOST O'REILLY TITLES ARE AVAILABLE BY SUBSCRIPTION AT *safari.oreilly.com*
ALSO AVAILABLE AT MOST RETAIL AND ONLINE BOOKSTORES

International Distributors

http://international.oreilly.com/distributors.html • international@oreilly.com

UK, EUROPE, MIDDLE EAST, AND AFRICA (EXCEPT FRANCE, GERMANY, AUSTRIA, SWITZERLAND, LUXEMBOURG, AND LIECHTENSTEIN)

INQUIRIES
O'Reilly UK Limited
4 Castle Street
Farnham
Surrey, GU9 7HS
United Kingdom
Telephone: 44-1252-711776
Fax: 44-1252-734211
Email: information@oreilly.co.uk

ORDERS
Wiley Distribution Services Ltd.
1 Oldlands Way
Bognor Regis
West Sussex PO22 9SA
United Kingdom
Telephone: 44-1243-843294
UK Freephone: 0800-243207
Fax: 44-1243-843302 (Europe/EU orders)
or 44-1243-843274 (Middle East/Africa)
Email: cs-books@wiley.co.uk

FRANCE

INQUIRIES & ORDERS
Éditions O'Reilly
18 rue Séguier
75006 Paris, France
Tel: 33-1-40-51-71-89
Fax: 33-1-40-51-72-26
Email: france@oreilly.fr

GERMANY, SWITZERLAND, AUSTRIA, LUXEMBOURG, AND LIECHTENSTEIN

INQUIRIES & ORDERS
O'Reilly Verlag
Balthasarstr. 81
D-50670 Köln, Germany
Telephone: 49-221-973160-91
Fax: 49-221-973160-8
Email: anfragen@oreilly.de (inquiries)
Email: order@oreilly.de (orders)

CANADA
(FRENCH LANGUAGE BOOKS)
Les Éditions Flammarion ltée
375, Avenue Laurier Ouest
Montréal, QC H2V 2K3 Canada
Tel: 1-514-277-8807
Fax: 1-514-278-2085
Email: info@flammarion.qc.ca

HONG KONG
City Discount Subscription Service, Ltd.
Unit A, 6th Floor, Yan's Tower
27 Wong Chuk Hang Road
Aberdeen, Hong Kong
Tel: 852-2580-3539
Fax: 852-2580-6463
Email: citydis@ppn.com.hk

KOREA
Hanbit Media, Inc.
Chungmu Bldg. 210
Yonnam-dong 568-33
Mapo-gu
Seoul, Korea
Tel: 822-325-0397
Fax: 822-325-9697
Email: hant93@chollian.dacom.co.kr

PHILIPPINES
Global Publishing
G/F Benavides Garden
1186 Benavides Street
Manila, Philippines
Tel: 632-254-8949/632-252-2582
Fax: 632-734-5060/632-252-2733
Email: globalp@pacific.net.ph

TAIWAN
O'Reilly Taiwan
1st Floor, No. 21, Lane 295
Section 1, Fu-Shing South Road
Taipei, 106 Taiwan
Tel: 886-2-27099669
Fax: 886-2-27038802
Email: mori@oreilly.com

INDIA
Shroff Publishers & Distributors PVT. LTD.
C-103, MIDC, TTC Pawane
Navi Mumbai 400 701
India
Tel: (91-22) 763 4290, 763 4293
Fax: (91-22) 768 3337
Email: spdorders@shroffpublishers.com

CHINA
O'Reilly Beijing
SIGMA Building, Suite B809
No. 49 Zhichun Road
Haidian District
Beijing, China PR 100080
Tel: 86-10-8809-7475
Fax: 86-10-8809-7463
Email: beijing@oreilly.com

JAPAN
O'Reilly Japan, Inc.
Yotsuya Y's Building
7 Banch 6, Honshio-cho
Shinjuku-ku
Tokyo 160-0003 Japan
Tel: 81-3-3356-5227
Fax: 81-3-3356-5261
Email: japan@oreilly.com

SINGAPORE, INDONESIA, MALAYSIA, AND THAILAND
TransQuest Publishers Pte Ltd
30 Old Toh Tuck Road #05-02
Sembawang Kimtrans Logistics Centre
Singapore 597654
Tel: 65-4623112
Fax: 65-4625761
Email: wendiw@transquest.com.sg

AUSTRALIA
Woodslane Pty., Ltd.
7/5 Vuko Place
Warriewood NSW 2102
Australia
Tel: 61-2-9970-5111
Fax: 61-2-9970-5002
Email: info@woodslane.com.au

NEW ZEALAND
Woodslane New Zealand, Ltd.
21 Cooks Street (P.O. Box 575)
Waganui, New Zealand
Tel: 64-6-347-6543
Fax: 64-6-345-4840
Email: info@woodslane.com.au

ARGENTINA
Distribuidora Cuspide
Suipacha 764
1008 Buenos Aires
Argentina
Phone: 54-11-4322-8868
Fax: 54-11-4322-3456
Email: libros@cuspide.com

ALL OTHER COUNTRIES
O'Reilly & Associates, Inc.
1005 Gravenstein Hwy North
Sebastopol, CA 95472 USA
Tel: 707-827-7000
Fax: 707-829-0104
Email: order@oreilly.com

O'REILLY®

TO ORDER: **800-998-9938** • **order@oreilly.com** • **www.oreilly.com**
ONLINE EDITIONS OF MOST O'REILLY TITLES ARE AVAILABLE BY SUBSCRIPTION AT **safari.oreilly.com**
ALSO AVAILABLE AT MOST RETAIL AND ONLINE BOOKSTORES